MW01629223

# BUGAKU MASKS

Japanese Arts Library

General Editor

John Rosenfield

With the cooperation and under the editorial supervision of:

The Agency for Cultural Affairs of the Japanese Government
Tokyo National Museum
Kyoto National Museum
Nara National Museum

KODANSHA INTERNATIONAL LTD. AND SHIBUNDO
Tokyo, New York, and San Francisco

# Bugaku Masks

Kyōtarō Nishikawa

translated and adapted by

Monica Bethe

Distributed in the United States by Kodansha International/USA Ltd., through Harper & Row Publishers, Inc., 10 East 53rd Street, New York, New York 10022; in Europe by Boxerbooks Inc., Limmatstrasse 111, 8031 Zurich; and in Japan by Kodansha International Ltd., 2–12–21 Otowa, Bunkyo-ku, Tokyo 112.

*Bugaku Masks* was originally published in Japanese by the Shibundo publishing company, Tokyo, 1971, under the title *Bugaku-men,* as volume 62 in the series *Nihon no bijutsu*. The English edition was prepared at Kodansha International, Tokyo, by Saburo Nobuki, Takako Suzuki, and Michael Brase.

Published by Kodansha International Ltd., 2–12–21 Otowa, Bunkyo-ku, Tokyo 112 and Kodansha International/USA Ltd., 10 East 53rd Street, New York, New York 10022 and 44 Montgomery Street, San Francisco, California 94104. 

Bethe, Monica.
Bugaku masks.

(Japanese arts library; v. 5)
Bibliography: p.
Includes index
1. Masks—Japan. 2. Bugaku. I. Nishikawa, Kyōtarō.
II. Title. III. Series.
GT1747.B4313 731′.75′0952 77-75971
ISBN 0-87011-312-7

*First edition, 1978*

JBC 1371–786025–2361

# CONTENTS

## Japanese Art Periods

| | | |
|---|---|---|
| Prehistoric | | –537 |
| Asuka | | 538–644 |
| *Nara | | 645–781 |
| Hakuhō | 645–710 | |
| Tempyō | 711–81 | |
| *Heian | | 782–1184 |
| Jōgan | 782–897 | |
| Fujiwara | 898–1184 | |
| *Kamakura | | 1185–1332 |
| *Nambokuchō | | 1333–91 |
| *Muromachi | | 1392–1572 |
| *Momoyama | | 1573–99 |
| *Edo | | 1600–1867 |

Note: This table has been provided by the Agency for Cultural Affairs of the Japanese Government. Periods marked with an asterisk are described in the Glossary.

# ILLUSTRATIONS

A Note to the Reader

Japanese names are given in the customary Japanese order, surname preceding given name. The names of temples and subordinate buildings can be discerned by their suffixes: *-ji, -tera, -dera* referring to temples (Tōdai-ji; Taima-dera); *-in* usually to a subtemple attached to a temple (Shōryō-in at Hōryū-ji); *-dō* to a building with a special function (Miei-dō); *-bō* and *-an* to larger and smaller monastic residences, respectively (Gokuraku-bō; Ryūgin-an).

# INTRODUCTION

## THE BUGAKU DANCE

> Prince Genji danced the "Waves of the Blue Sea." . . . There was a wonderful moment when the rays of the setting sun fell upon him and the music grew suddenly louder. Never had the onlookers seen feet tread so delicately nor head so exquisitely poised; and in the song which follows the first movement of the dance his voice was sweet as that of Kalavinka whose music is Buddha's Law. So moving and beautiful was this dance that at the end of it the Emperor's eyes were wet, and all the princes and great gentlemen wept aloud. When the song was over and, straightening his long dancer's sleeves, he stood waiting for the music to begin again and at last the more lively tune of the second movement struck up—then indeed, with his flushed and eager face, he merited more than ever his name of Genji the Shining One.*

The official Japanese court dances, Bugaku, enjoy one of the longest histories of the performing arts in Japan—from about A.D. 500 to the present. Some of the dancers are masked, and anyone who has seen a performance will not forget the striking vitality of these expertly sculpted and vividly painted masks. During its heyday in the Heian period (782–1184), Bugaku was so integrated into court life that hardly a festival or ceremony would pass without some dance. The dances were performed not only by the official court musicians and dancers of the Bureau of Music, but also by the young princes and lords. Today performances are restricted to a few shrines and the Imperial Palace, where an official troupe of musicians and dancers is maintained.

The Gagaku orchestra accompanying the Bugaku dances, located at the back of the stage, consists of percussion and wind instruments. The *san-no-tsuzumi* drum or the *kakko* hourglass drum lead the orchestra with complex rolls and sharp syncopated beats; while the large *dadaiko* drums (pls. 15, 17), standing at the back of the stage to right and left, or the smaller *taiko* drum (pl. 102, left), produce the periodic reverbera-

*Murasaki Shikibu, *The Tale of Genji*, trans. Arthur Waley (London: George Allen and Unwin, 1935), p. 129.

ting boom that marks the end of each phrase. Yet the characteristic sound of the Gagaku orchestra is determined by the wind instruments. The clear tones of the *yokobue* (flute) blend with the strident *hichiriki* (a double-reed bamboo instrument) to produce the melody, which is filled out and given body by the harmonic chords of the *shō,* a mouth organ made of bamboo drones set in a lacquered base. Each chord begins softly with single tones. As one harmonic is added to another, the volume swells until the *shō* player has expelled all his breath. As he inhales, he swells the tone further before beginning a diminuendo that dies down at the end of the phase. The rhythmic inhaling and exhaling of the *shō* seems to draw the whole orchestra into one pulsating rhythm.

One by one the dancers mount the steps to the raised square stage bounded by a wooden railing. Each wears a flowing costume with broad sleeves and a train trailing the ground. A shoulder-length brocaded hood frames the mask. Thick white cloth shoes highlight the feet. When a dancer reaches center stage he does a few solo steps and then takes his place in one of the four corners of the stage. Once all the dancers have assembled, and after a short orchestral interlude, they begin to move in unison, slowly at first, then faster, each restricted to a small portion of the stage.

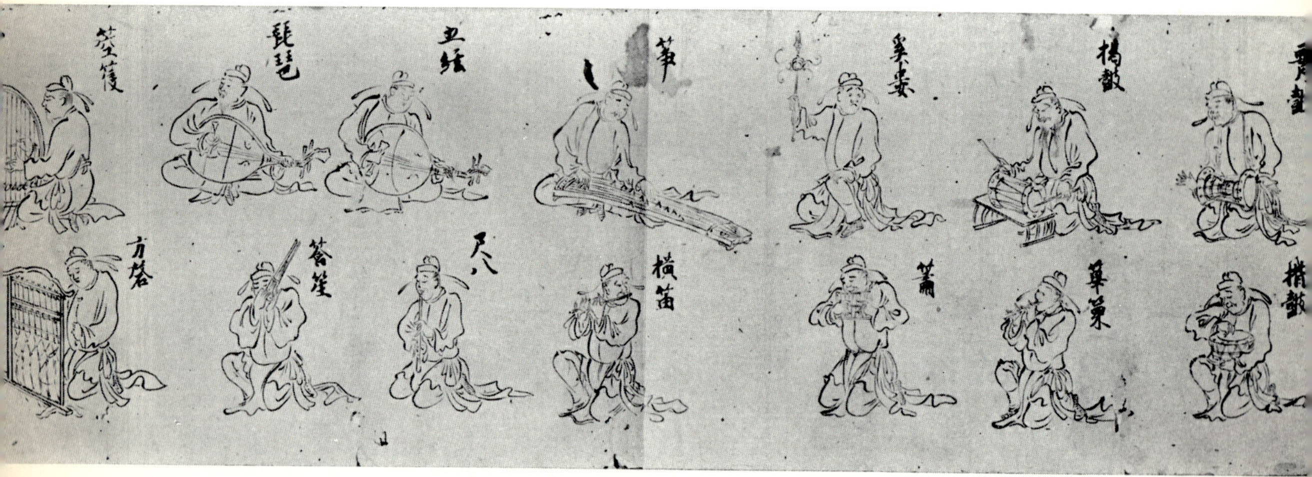

1. Gagaku instruments. Detail from the *Shinzei kogakuzu* (Shinzei's Illustrations of Ancient Music). Monochrome ink handscroll. Twelfth century. Yōmei Bunko, Kyoto.
The instruments played today in the ensemble accompanying the Bugaku dances are shown here, except for the *taiko* and *dadaiko*. In the upper row are the *san-no-tsuzumi* (right-hand corner) and the *kakko* (second from the right). Nowadays the *san-no-tsuzumi* is not played with the hands, but beat with a stick. On the bottom row, second from the left, is the *shō,* fourth from the left the *yokobue,* and second from the right the *hichiriki.* Other instruments used today in the full Gagaku orchestra *(kangen)* include the *biwa* (lute ; upper row, second from the left) and the *koto* (zither; upper row, fourth from the left). All the other instruments were discarded when Gagaku and Bugaku were revised and amalgamated in the ninth century.

Synchronized precisely, they appear to be breathing in time with the music. As their feet swing out with the boom of the large *dadaiko* and their arms spread wide and close again, the rich brocade and silk costumes flow back and forth. A roll of the head brings the mask to life.

A single program presents a series of pairs of related dances. One pair *(tsugaimai)* consists of a "statement" dance of the Left and a "answer" dance of the Right.* For the first of the pair, the dancers enter from the left, moving in a swinging, somewhat syncopated rhythm. For the second, the dancers enter from the right, placing sharp emphasis on the beat. The program usually begins with graceful, restrained dances performed in unison by four or six people. These are followed by dances of greater variety of movement and dramatic interest, and then by "military" dances. A pair of quick-tempoed dances performed by a single dancer moving across the entire stage brings the program to a close. This progression of slow, moderate, fast—or of simple, complex, climactic—is known as *jo-ha-kyū*. It applies to the construction of a single dance, which gradually gathers momentum and repeats the patterns at a faster and faster pace, and on a smaller scale, to every motion, which begin slowly and then increase in speed. Later forms of dance and drama, such as Nō and Kabuki, borrowed the fundamental theory of *jo-ha-kyū*.

Most of the dances have little story element. Whatever scraps of story remain are mentioned in the discussion of the individual dances, but because these are often varied and contradictory, they should not be taken as plot summary, but as a guide to the mood of the dance. Since the choreography is composed of a limited number of formalized and repetitious patterns, the manner in which the movements are executed becomes all the more important. Grace or vigor do much to set the atmosphere; the costumes and masks do more.

A different mask is used for each dance, and the mask bears the same name as the dance. The body of this book is devoted to discussing each of the known types of masks through representative examples and historical background. Care is taken to mention dated masks and stylistic considerations indicating chronology. While the most important examples of each type of mask are mentioned in the body of the text, all the old masks still extant are listed by type in Appendix 3. Appendix 2 gives the dated masks in chronological order.

Even a casual glance at the illustrations in this book reveals the wide variety of Bugaku masks. While some are dynamic and have devices like rolling eyes, dangling chins, and jiggling cheeks, others express a refined serenity. The large noses and bulging eyes of some suggest their distant origins, while the flat, smooth features of others obviously reflect Japanese facial characteristics. The oldest masks preserved date from the middle to late Heian period (eleventh and twelfth centuries), when the masks were being refined and stylized. Since the dances had been introduced

* *Mai* in such words as *tsugaimai* means "dance." See Glossary.

into Japan as early as the sixth century, it is unclear why no masks, with one possible exception, remain from the Nara period (645–781).

Masks are at once theatrical tools and art objects. As a minor branch of Japanese sculpture, they employ the same techniques of carving, priming, and painting as are used in making Buddhist images, and they bear similar inscriptions. Chapters four and five are devoted to questions of technique and to inscriptions.

The difference between a mask and a statue is obvious: one is ensconced permanently in a protected place; the other is continuously handled and used. The result is that masks suffer from wear and tear leading to damage that must be repaired and to the the necessity of replacement through copying. Since the size and the expression of the copied masks were determined by prototypes and earlier styles, and since techniques were faithfully maintained, dating masks has posed a problem that most art historians have avoided. Mr. Nishikawa has brought to these questions a thorough training in technical and stylistic analysis, particularly enriched by his careful study of portrait sculpture. While the scope of this book prohibits discussion of minute stylistic considerations, the material presented here is based on authoritative research. This is the only book in either English or Japanese devoted solely to the Bugaku mask.

As translator I have, on the whole, followed Mr. Nishikawa's format, reorganizing and expanding only for clarity and where necessary to fill in background for the Western reader. I am greatly indebted to Mr. Nishikawa for his perusal of the translation and frequent clarifications. I would also like to thank Louise Court for her suggestions.

Monica Bethe

# BUGAKU MASKS

# 1

# HISTORICAL BACKGROUND

Japanese masks used in performance have a history of 1,300 years, documented by numerous surviving specimens and critical studies. The rich variety of Japanese masks include Gigaku, Bugaku, Gyōdō, Nō, Kyōgen, and folk masks. All of these, except Gigaku masks, are still used in performances today, each an eloquent relic of the age in which the dance form flourished.

Gigaku masks (pls. 2–5) are large and constructed to cover the upper part of the head as well as the face. Their realistically modeled faces have continental, un-Japanese features, while their relaxed, free expressions reflect the artistic trends of the Nara period (645–781), when the temple dramas of Gigaku enjoyed great popularity. Some may be imports from China.

Although Bugaku dances filtered into Japan from Korea and China concurrently with Gigaku, extant Bugaku masks date mostly from the late Heian and Kamakura periods (eleventh to thirteenth centuries) and reflect the grace and refinement of the Heian court. Smaller than Gigaku masks, they vary greatly in size, but rarely cover more of the head than the face. Some of them, such as Ni-no-mai (pls. 53–57) and early versions of Kotokuraku (pl. 39), resemble Gigaku masks in expression and size, but others, such as Ayakiri (pl. 30), Saisōrō (pls. 51–52), and Shintoriso (pl. 14), seem to approach the subtlety and shallow dimensions of Nō masks (pls. 8–11). A peculiarity of some Bugaku masks is their elaborate construction, with separate noses, chins, eyes, or cheeks so attached that they sway and roll with the movement of the dance. Their remarkably exaggerated expressions are boldly formalized and standardized; the wrinkles and swelling flesh often appear to be designed as an abstract pattern. This formalization is perfectly suited to the rhythmically based symbolic form of the Bugaku dance, but it is diametrically opposed to the dramatic style and strongly naturalistic masks of Gigaku.

Gyōdō masks (pls. 6–7) represent Buddhist deities and cover the entire head in such a way that the costumed dancer looks like a statue come to life. They are used in memorial services and temple processions, particularly in enactments of *raigō* (the descent of Amida [Amitābha] to save mankind), a central concept of the Jōdo sect popular in the late Heian period.

Nō masks (pls. 8–11) have a distinctly Japanese, restrained beauty mirroring the taste of the Muromachi (1392–1572) and Edo (1600–1867) periods. Slightly smaller than the human face, their subtle expressions aim at understatement and implication. The comic Kyōgen masks date from the same period.

In this array, Bugaku masks stand between the Gigaku masks of foreign origin and the purely Japanese Nō masks. Not so large or realistic as the earlier Gigaku masks, they are also not as small or as restrained as the later Nō masks.

## Early History

The Bugaku of the Heian court, which has been preserved more or less unchanged to the present day, developed out of a variety of dances imported from the Asian continent during the Asuka (538–644) and Nara (645–781) periods. The first dances came with missions from the three ancient states of Korea: Silla, Paekche, and Koryŏ. Due to the Confucian precept that musical harmony fostered political harmony and thus was indispensable to court functions, music and dance were among the early cultural imports to Japan. In 453, according to the *Nihon shoki,* a Nara-period chronicle of the early history of Japan, the king of Silla sent eighty tributary ships and eighty musicians to Japan to perform at the funeral ceremonies for Emperor Ingyō. This gift was probably the beginning of *shiragigaku* ("dance from Silla"). The nineteenth book of the *Nihon shoki* further reports that in 554, during the reign of Emperor Kimmei, four court musicians were sent from the Korean state of Paekche. And according to the seventeenth-century treatise on Bugaku, the *Gakkaroku* (The Records of a Musician), the reign of Empress Suiko (r. 592–628) saw the importation of dances from Koryŏ.

Once imported, the dances were learned by the Japanese and incorporated into their festivals and court functions. Each type of dance was known by the name of its country of origin (read in Japanese): *shiragigaku* from Silla, *kudaragaku* from Paekche, and *komagaku* from Koryŏ.

Other dances came from the T'ang court in China *(tōgaku)* and even from as far away as India and Southeast Asia *(rin'yūgaku).* Though at first these dances came mostly through Korea, by the seventh century the Japanese missions to the T'ang court imported directly from China. Despite a sincere effort by the Japanese to emulate the T'ang government in forming their own, they most likely brought back the music and dance used for entertainment rather than the ritual Confucian music. The pieces still in the Bugaku repertory mirror the cosmopolitan atmosphere of the T'ang capital, with its busy comings and goings of many peoples along the Silk Road from as far west as Persia. A number of the dances feature drunken "barbarians" with long, hooked noses; others treat with awe the strange customs of the barbarians, such as eating snakes. The extensive nature of the Japanese importations during the Nara period is evidenced by the treasures, including many Gagaku instruments, in the Shōsō-in in Nara, and by the variety of faces depicted in Bugaku and Gigaku masks.

## Gigaku

Among the performing arts brought to Japan, Gigaku deserves special mention for its popularity in temple functions during the Nara period and for its magnificent masks. Some of the masks were preserved by the foremost Nara temples: Tōdai-ji (in the Shōsō-in) and Hōryū-ji, whose collection was removed to the Imperial Museum (present Tokyo National Museum) in the late nineteenth century.

At least two stories account for the introduction of Gigaku into Japan. According to the *Nihon shoki* it developed out of dances the Korean dancer Mimaji (in Japanese, Mimashi) brought back from the South Chinese kingdom of Wu. Another account claims that a descendant of the King of Wu came to Japan as an ambassador bringing *kure-no-uta-mai,* later known as Gigaku, and a complete set of musical instruments along with Buddhist texts and images. Judging, however, from what is known of the contents of the performance and from the expressions of the remaining masks, it is quite likely that Gigaku originated not in Wu, but somewhere outside of China, perhaps in West or Southeast Asia. Some scholars even find similarities between Gigaku masks and ancient Greek masks.

At its peak in the Nara period (645–781) Gigaku formed a major part of temple ceremonies, but it lost popularity in the Heian period (782–1184). Performances became very infrequent by the Kamakura period (1185–1332), and the last recorded performance was in the Genroku era (1688–1704). Very little is known of its contents; today only a rough reconstruction is possible from old records and from the bold, realistic masks (pls. 2–5). Gigaku seems to have consisted of dramatic masked dances performed to the accompaniment of simple music played by an orchestra composed of flute, drums, and gong. That the performances were not entirely solemn is suggested by one typical plot in which a barbarian man who falls in love with a princess is dragged around the stage by a rope tied to his sexual organ. Although this story would seem inappropriate for performance in front of a Buddhist altar, it does suggest that the plays were wide-ranging, explicit, and popular in appeal.

## The Flourishing of All Styles of Dance

By the eighth century a large variety of dances from all over Asia were flourishing side by side as court entertainment and as part of the religious ceremonies in the various temples around the capital. When the Taihō Code was promulgated in 701, establishing a new system of government and official grades, it included a bureau of music with official dance instructors of the court—twelve teachers of *tōgaku* and an equivalent number for *shiragigaku, kudaragaku,* and *komagaku.* In addition, each temple had come to specialize in its own particular style of dance. At such grand celebrations as the consecration ceremony for the image of the Great Buddha at Tōdai-ji in 752, famous dancers and musicians gathered for gala performances in which one style of dance followed another.

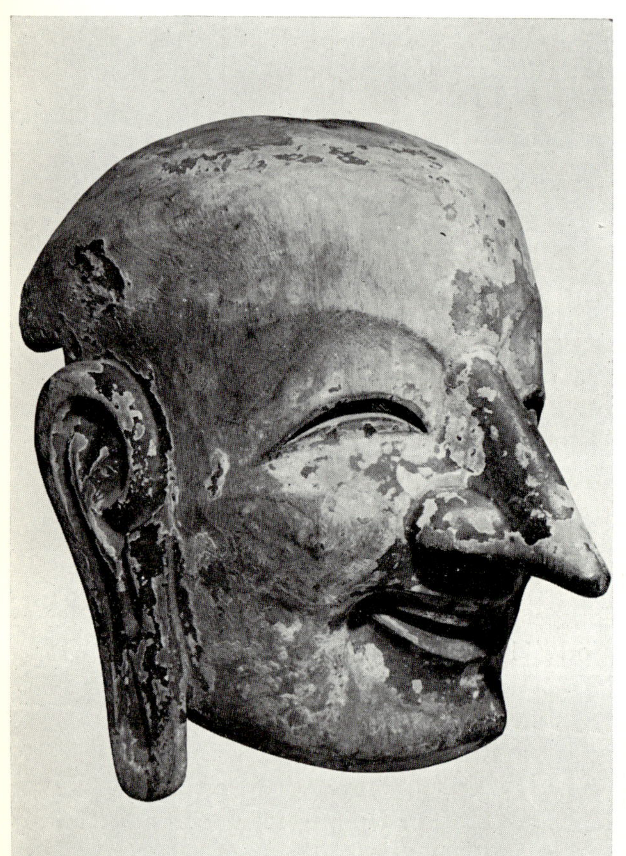

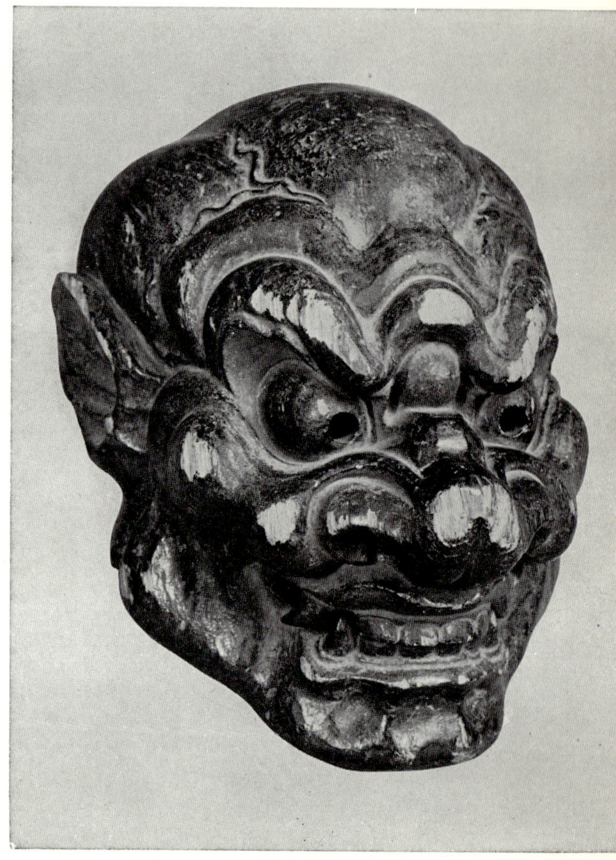

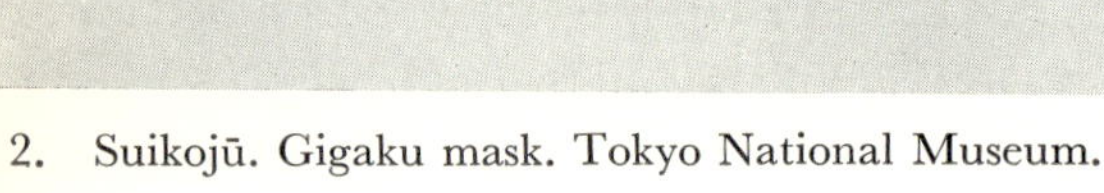

2. Suikojū. Gigaku mask. Tokyo National Museum.

3. Konron. Gigaku mask. Tōdai-ji.

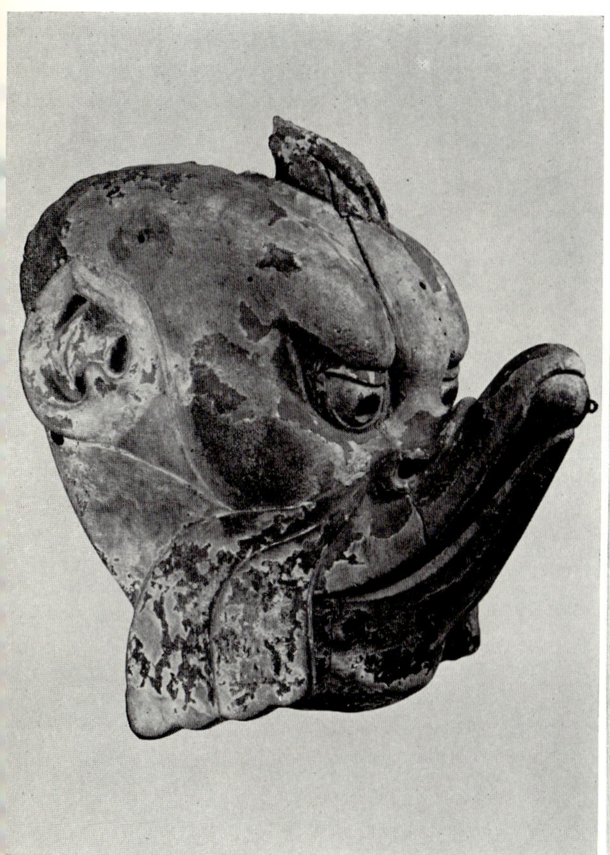

4. Karura. Gigaku mask. Tokyo National Museum.

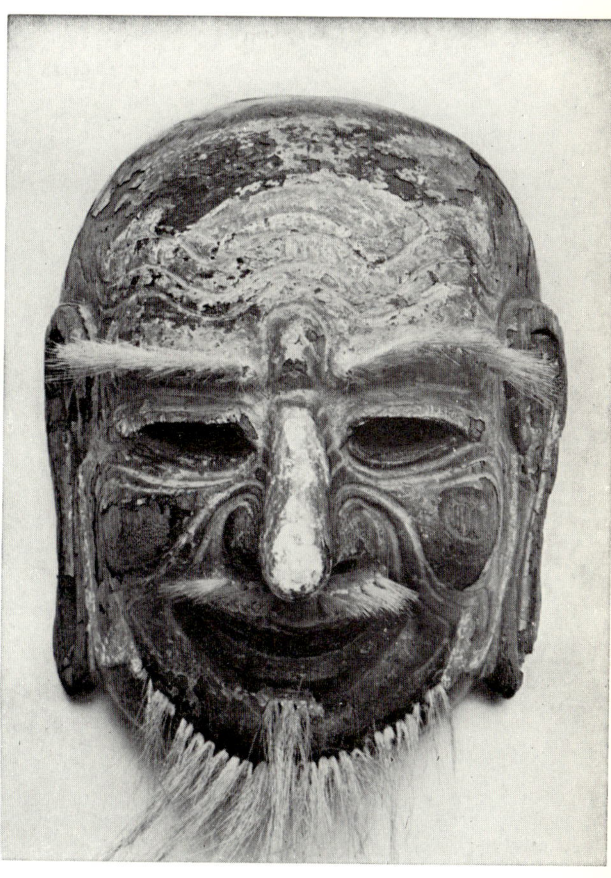

5. Taikofu. Gigaku mask. Tōdai-ji, Nara.

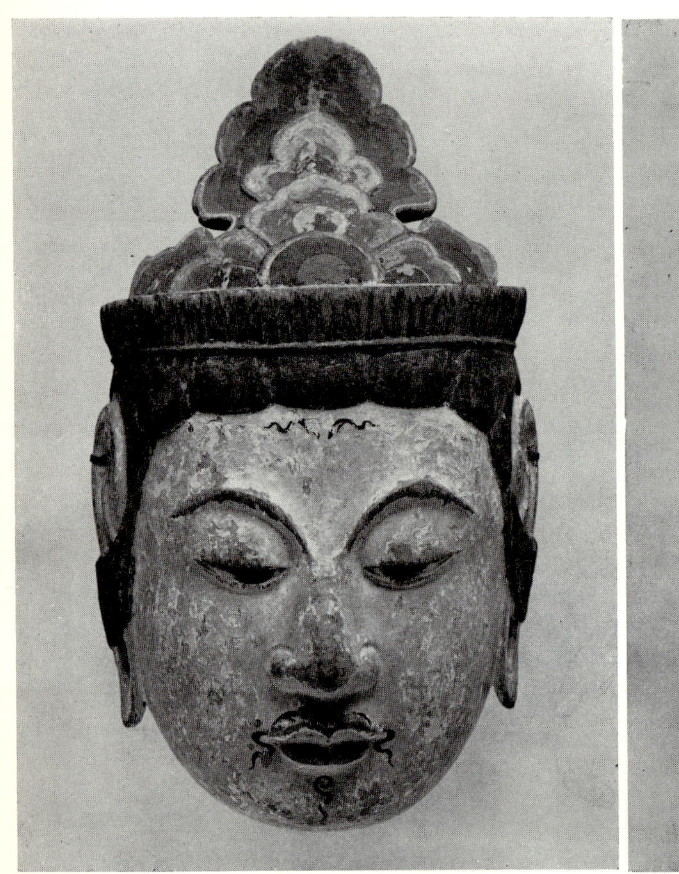

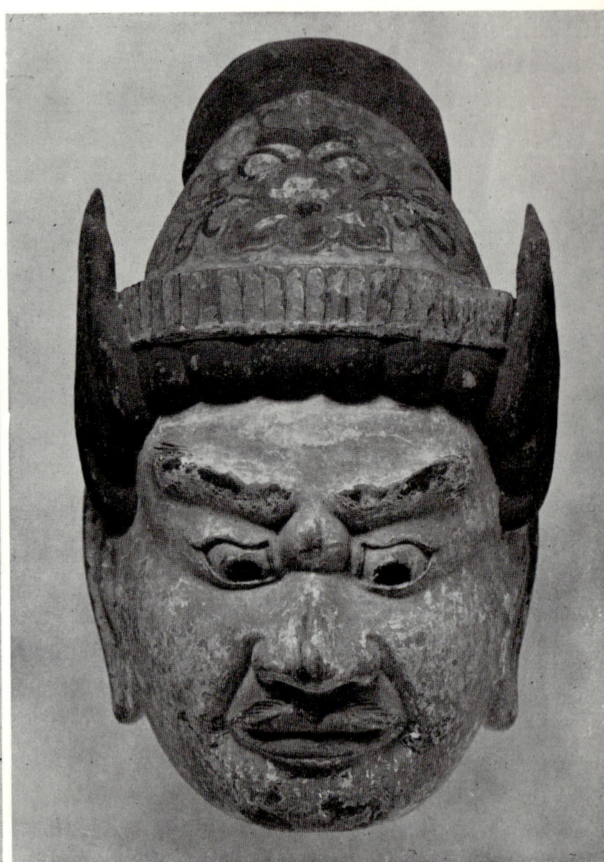

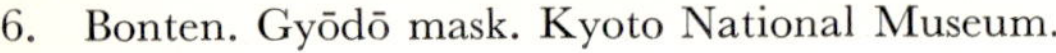

6. Bonten. Gyōdō mask. Kyoto National Museum.

7. Tamonten. Gyōdō mask. Kyoto National Museum.

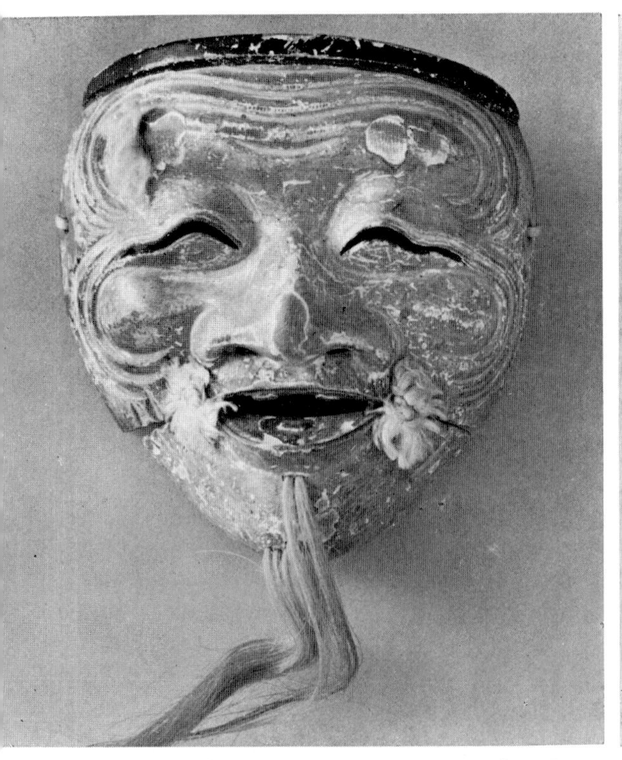

8. Okina. Nō mask. Private collection, Japan.

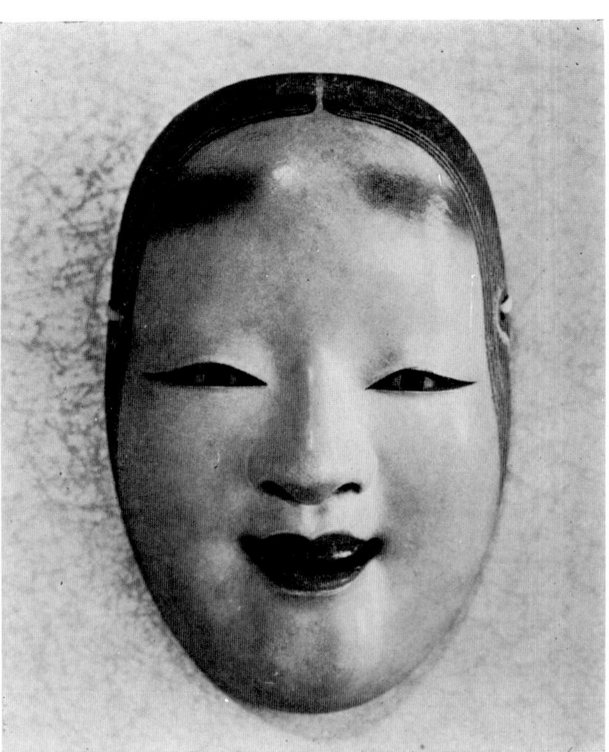

9. Ko-omote. Nō mask. Private collection, Japan.

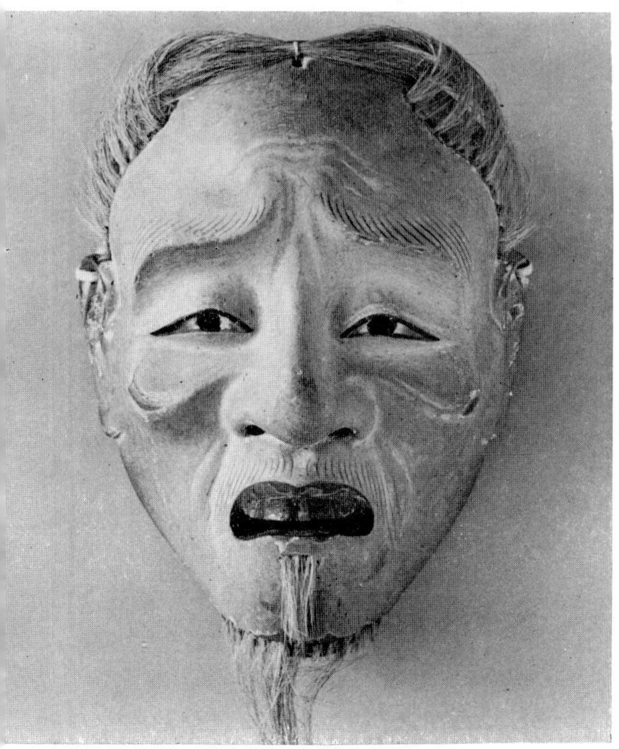

10. Koushijō. Nō mask. Private collection, Japan.

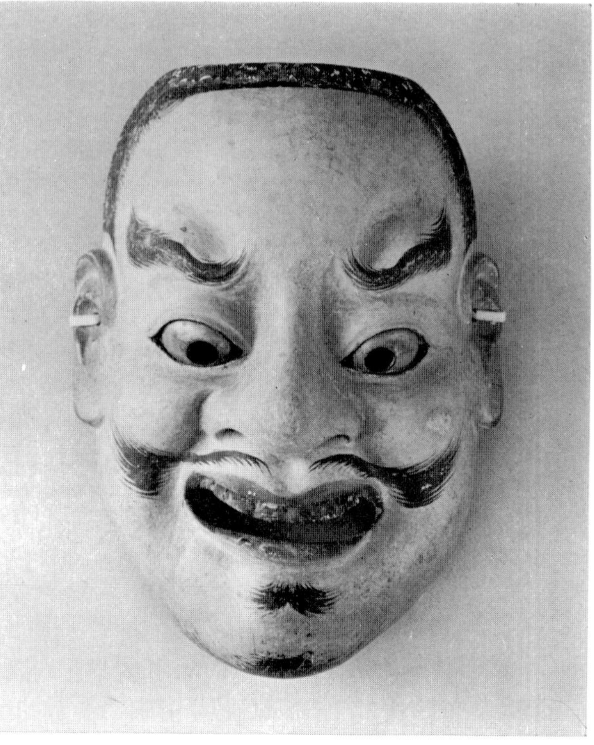

11. Tenjin. Nō mask. Private collection, Japan.

## The Birth of Bugaku

The ninth century saw a movement toward amalgamation and reform of the various styles of dance into one form—Bugaku or "dance music." Emperor Saga (r. 809–23) began the reforms that involved transposing the differing musical systems to make them fit either the *ritsu* or the *ryō* musical scale systems learned from China (see Glossary). In consequence those instruments tuned to the abandoned modes were discarded. By a similar process of culling and reforming, the Bureau of Music collected and rearranged the foreign dances into a definitive form suitable for the new Heian court, adding several native dances—*kume-no-mai, tatebuse-no-mai, tsukushi-no-mai, murakata-no-mai.* Under Emperor Nimmyō (r. 833–50), himself a musician and a composer, the government took responsibility for training the dancers and musicians. A standard form was set for the stage, costumes, and number of musicians and dancers. Creativity and excellence marked the period. The most famous Bugaku dancers—Owari Hamanushi, Ōto no Kiyokami, Wanibe no Ōtamaro, Tokoyo no Oto-uo—and the dance choreographers Inugami no Korenari and Ōto no Manawa were all active at the beginning of the Heian period, when Bugaku was being rearranged and standardized.

As part of the reorganization, the entire repertory was divided along new lines. Pieces were grouped by content: "literary" pieces *(bun-no-mai),* or quiet dances *(hiramai),* "military" dances *(bu-no-mai),* and quick, exciting dances *(hashirimai).* Records began to refer to pieces by name rather than by country of origin. Indeed, the gradual loss of awareness of the origin of the pieces led to a simplified categorization into *tōgaku* or *sa-no-mai* ("dances of the Left") for pieces from China, India, and Southeast Asia, and *komagaku* or *u-no-mai* ("dances of the Right") for pieces from the three Korean kingdoms. This system is still used today.

## Dances of the Left and Right

The assignation of the names Left and Right to Bugaku may have grown out of the role Bugaku played in the Heian court. The entire Heian government was divided into Left and Right on the T'ang model: ministries of Left and Right were housed appropriately to the left and right of the Imperial Palace, and every courtier, every guard, every dancer had his designation as Left or Right. As a part of military training, the militia of the Left and the Right staged games of skill such as horse races, wrestling matches, and archery contests. Sometimes they held meetings where all the swordsmen from the provinces gathered. At these festivals a performance of Bugaku often became the victory prize. With a loud shout the winners would announce whether it was to be *Ryō-ō* of the Left or *Nasori* of the Right. In case the teams tied, both dances would be performed. Such contests seem to have started at the beginning of the Heian period.



In Bugaku, Left and Right each has its own characteristic dance movements, musical instruments, and color. The Left group, belonging to the fifth rank in court, wore red, while the dancers of the Right, of the sixth rank, wore green. Even today, the Imperial Palace Gagaku troupe maintains separate training groups and teachers for Left and Right. In performance the two usually alternate according to a set rule of paired dances *(tsugaimai)*. The dancer of the Left will enter along the left bridge leading to the stage, while the large drum to the left at the back of the stage, ornamented with a golden sun and dragon, sounds the beat. The dancer of the Right will answer with a similar dance, entering from the right to the accompaniment of the large drum at the right of the back of the stage, topped by a silver moon and decorated with a phoenix.

### Bugaku at its Height

By the Heian period Bugaku had reached the status of official dance for a wide variety of public events in both the government and the religious establishments. Occasions on which Bugaku was performed at court included feasts, audiences held by a prince or emperor, festivals, and such annual ceremonies as the wrestling matches. It was also performed at temple and shrine gatherings for rites of purification and appeasement. Enjoying ever increasing popularity, Bugaku began to replace Gigaku. References to performances in the chronicles and diaries of the time are countless.

Bugaku formed an integral part of the nobleman's education. Stories such as that about a performance of *Nasori* by the nine-year-old son of a minister of the Left, as well as that about a young prince moving an audience to tears with his performance of *Ryō-ō,* affirm that Bugaku was not the preserve of professionals alone, but had deeply permeated the lives of the nobility.

### Dispersion to the Countryside

In the Kamakura period (1185–1332), regular performances of Bugaku in the Imperial Palace decreased. With the shift of the real power of the government to the military ruler *(shōgun)* in Kamakura, the Heian court gradually lost both influence and income, and the formerly lavish scale of its ceremonies was reduced. Naturally Bugaku suffered along with numerous other Heian pastimes.

Perhaps a fear for the decline of this art spurred the Nara dancer Koma Chikazane to compile what is now the oldest written treatise on Bugaku. In 1233 he wrote the *Kyōkunshō* (Books of Instruction), in which he detailed not only the secret traditions of the Koma family of dancers, but also facts and legends about Bugaku, Gagaku, and Gigaku. Correlated with illustrations of the dances found in the twelfth-century *Shinzei kogakuzu* (Shinzei's Illustrations of Ancient Music), the *Kyōkunshō,* as the only technical description of Bugaku by a near contemporary of the Heian period, provides a major key to reconstructing the arts of that time.

With the decline of the court, the dancers gathered around it scattered to temples and shrines in Nara and Kyoto, as well as to Shitennō-ji in Osaka. The dispersal of Bugaku throughout the provinces is evidenced by the wide distribution of Bugaku masks from the Kamakura period onward in temples and shrines all the way from northern Honshu to southern Kyushu. As Bugaku diffused, it was modified to suit the needs of the outlying areas. Other performing arts influenced and modified the orthodox form of Bugaku. Bugaku in turn stimulated and affected the existing performing arts in the countryside; it may well have prepared the ground for the eventual popularity of Nō plays in the provinces.

The unsettled years of the Nambokuchō and Muromachi periods, from the fourteenth to the sixteenth centuries, saw Bugaku at its lowest ebb of popularity. Other dramatic arts such as Nō and *kōwakamai* appealed more to the military aristocracy. At the court in Kyoto, Bugaku essential to certain ceremonies was performed by the guild of musicians attached to the Iwashimizu Hachiman Shrine in Kyoto. In the countryside, altered forms of Bugaku continued to be part of the yearly festivals of some temples and shrines.

## The Revival of Bugaku

With peace reestablished, the Tokugawa military government, or shogunate, set about consolidating various traditional forms of official entertainment, including Bugaku, Nō, and the tea ceremony. The first Tokugawa shogun, Ieyasu, sought out the orthodox Bugaku tradition still surviving at certain shrines and temples around Kyoto, Nara, and Osaka. Building stages both in the Imperial Palace in Kyoto and in Edo Castle, he put Bugaku once again under official protection.

In 1690 Abe Suenao wrote the *Gakkaroku* (The Records of a Musician), in which he collected all available material on Gagaku and Bugaku into fifty well-diagramed and carefully annotated volumes. Typical of the care given to detail in the Edo period, the *Gakkaroku* was written with an eye to the accurate preservation of tradition, and serves dancers today as an authoritative text on costuming, instrument making, tonal systems, and masks.

The Bugaku we see today at public performances in the Imperial Palace, and in temples and shrines, continues the form revived by the Edo shogunate.

## Bugaku Masks

Not all Bugaku dances require masks, but early records show that at one time masks were used in some thirty-two of the over one hundred Bugaku dances. Today we can identify with certainty only twenty-four dances requiring masks. Some of the Bugaku pieces ceased to be performed and some remain only as music, having discarded the dance at some point. For some pieces it is unclear which mask was used, while for others all examples of the masks have disappeared. Unlike Nō, in which a single mask can be used for a variety of roles, each masked Bugaku dance has its own distinct type of mask. The known varieties will be discussed in detail in the next chapter. At this point a few general stylistic points should be noted.

The history of Japanese masks runs parallel to the history of sculpture, though on a minor scale, and reflects the artistic styles and techniques of sculpture of the periods in which the masks were made. Certain peculiarities of masks, in contrast to sculpture, make dating difficult. Since the carver worked within the strict limitations set by a prototype, he had little freedom to vary the style, size, or expression of a mask. Indeed, in copying older masks, the carver faithfully preserved styles no longer current in sculpture. In the Edo period this type of archaism became extremely sophisticated, including conscious antiquing. In addition, much dating of sculpture is based on the lines and folds of drapery, nonexistent elements in a mask representing only the face. In sculpture, ears often provide a clue to the era, for their carving is easily influenced by prevailing fashions; however, many masks have no ears. As theatrical tools, moreover, masks are often cracked or bruised in handling, and subsequent repair and repainting obscure the original form. On the other hand, damaged surfaces and exposed wood often supply valuable clues to carving techniques and priming methods. In general, although clear-cut formulae for dating masks have not been established, there are certain criteria, which will become clear in the discussion of individual masks.

The history of extant Bugaku masks begins around the year 1000, when Bugaku performances reached the height of popularity and great numbers of masks must have been made. Although masks certainly had been imported in the Nara period from Korea and China along with the dances and instruments, no examples of Nara-period Bugaku masks survive. The lone possible exception is the recently disclosed Ryō-ō mask (pl. 114) made of dry lacquer, a technique common only to the Tempyō period (711–81). The mask formerly belonged to the Nara temple Ryōsen-ji and now is in the Fujita Art Museum in Osaka.

The oldest Bugaku masks at Hōryū-ji in Nara must have been made around the beginning of the eleventh century (pls. 24, 38–39). They are particularly notable examples of the formative period when Bugaku masks still retained a similarity to Gigaku masks in their large scale. Compare the calm, expansive expression and deep dimensions of the Kotokuraku mask from Hōryū-ji (pl. 39) with those of the Gigaku Suikojū mask (pl. 2). Typically, the early Bugaku mask covers a large portion of the face, extending back over the ears, and is thicker than the more sophisticated masks of later periods. The carver seems to have had only a broad conception of the character type as compared to later, more idiosyncratic Kotokuraku masks.

The other Kotokuraku at Hōryū-ji (pl. 35), as well as the Sessen at the same temple (pl. 95), was probably made during the first half of the eleventh century. Compared with masks believed to have been made earlier, these two are lighter, thinner, and more unified in conception; yet their expressiveness still has something of the older masks, and they still cover a large portion of the face. The heavy eyelids and the sharp, graceful lips retain the style of carving found in single-block Buddhist statues of the same period.

The oldest surviving examples of inscribed masks are dated 1042 (pls. 16, 21, 23, 25, 27–28, 42, 45, 150–51). They show a conspicuous advance in refinement; the individual types have become more easily distinguishable. The carving technique is quite free, indicating a form probably modeled on earlier, now lost masks, but not yet standardized. The fine sculpting around the large openings of the slanted, almond-shaped eyes and around the nose shows sharp, clean chisel work. Between the eyebrows, vertical wrinkles have been formalized as an oval, grooved, protruding medallion. All the masks are painted with a kaolin priming applied directly to the wood surface. This treatment abbreviates one step in a technique for finishing sculpture used since the Tempyō period on Buddhist images, in which layers of lacquer were followed by a layer of kaolin and then a final application of colored pigments.

Produced over a century later, the seven Kotokuraku masks dated 1160 (pls. 31–32, 36, 152–53) are carved with facile surety, though they are also painted with the simplified method of applying a kaolin priming directly on the wood, leaving off the complex lacquer ground commonly found on first-class masks of this period. Traces of older sculptural techniques linger in the undulant line of the eyes and the curve of the mouth. By this date carvers seems to be working with a clear, set form in mind, which freed them to play with subtle nuances and smooth over the natural contours of the face, lending the mask a cohesive harmony.

All the masks belonging to the height of mask production, such as the Batō (pl. 97) and the Genjōraku (pl. 103) dated 1144 at Hōryū-ji, as well as the Chikyū of the same date in a private collection, are scrupulously painted on both front and back with a hard lacquer priming of *sabi urushi,* a mixture of wheat flour, lacquer, and *tonoko.* They show great refinement and clearly indicate a conscious effort to systematize the type. The body of the mask has become very thin. The carving is uniform; the modeling is composed of graceful lines and smooth curves; the ridges of the hair, the wrinkles on the face, and the forehead "medallions" have become abstract and refined.

Equally superb are the seven masks dated 1173 at Itsukushima Shrine (pls. 58–59, 67, 73, 96, 106). Typical of these, the Ni-no-mai masks are filled with movement and vitality; yet grace, rather than power, characterize their carving (pls. 58–59). The subtle elegance of the four Ayakiri masks dated 1161 in Sumiyoshi Shrine is further evidence of the perfection Bugaku masks had reached (pl. 30).

Toward the end of the twelfth century some of the sculptors who carved masks began to sign their names on the back of their work. Thus we know that first-rank Buddhist sculptors *(busshi)* such as Jōkei, Inshō, and Inken also produced outstanding masks. Kasuga Shrine owns a Sanju (pl. 61) by Jōkei and also a Chikyū (pl. 13), a

Korobase (pl. 40), four Shintoriso (pl. 14), and an Ōnintei (pl. 46) by Inshō, all dated 1184 or 1185. At Tōdai-ji the two Sanju by Inken, originally at Saishō Shitennō-in, are dated 1207 (pls. 62, 69). Chapter five discusses the sculptors and their works in greater detail.

In general, the masks of the Kamakura period show a decline in quality. The eleven masks dated 1178 at Atsuta Shrine (pls. 43, 53–54, 99, 105, 116) and the thirteen dated 1211 at Masumida Shrine (pls. 41, 55–56), though still orthodox types, are less precisely and elegantly carved: they are thicker and shallower. This decline might well reflect the relative distance of Owari Province (modern Aichi Prefecture) from the capital. Most other masks of this period show a gradual alteration of the type: see, for example, the four masks dated 1228 at Konda Hachiman Shrine (pls. 68, 74) and the three dated 1259 originally at Tōdai-ji (pls. 113, 117). The Ryō-ō at Himuro Shrine (pl. 109), the five masks at Tsurugaoka Hachiman Shrine in Kamakura (pls. 70, 77, 93, 112), the Ryō-ō (pl. 110) and Nasori (pl. 156) at Shitennō-ji in Osaka, and the Ryō-ō and Nasori at Kanzeon-ji in Fukuoka have all deviated from the Heian-period types.

With few exceptions, the Kamakura- and Muromachi-period masks preserved in the countryside are considerably cruder than those found in the cultural centers. Many of these provincial masks are made of unorthodox materials and carved in a carefree manner; often the extreme deviation from the set form makes it difficult to identify the type. In part their artistic decline stems from cross influences with other performing arts such as Gyōdō, Nō, and Kyōgen. The problems posed by provincial Bugaku masks provide a fruitful field of study as yet scarcely explored.

In the Edo period, when Bugaku was again put under government protection, mask carving was brought back almost to the level of the Heian period. The old masks treasured at various temples and shrines around Kyoto and Nara were scrupulously copied. The techniques of painting and carving used in the Heian period were thoroughly studied and revived. Often the Edo masks were hollowed as thinly and painted as meticulously as their Heian models, with the result that it is sometimes difficult to determine to which period a given mask belongs.

# 2

# TYPES OF MASKS

The spectrum of Bugaku masks ranges from life-size, quiet, human faces to beastial faces constructed with mechanical devices. Broadly speaking, the lifelike masks are used for slow- and medium-tempoed dances *(hiramai)*. Their gentle sobriety often radiates joy. Larger, bold-featured masks are worn for the more energetic "military" dances *(bu-no-mai)*; while the exciting, quick-paced dances ending a program *(hashiri-mai)* use masks of exaggerated ferocity that often represent inhuman faces.

In the following discussion, the individual masks have been grouped in a manner suggesting the order of use in a program of Bugaku dances. The first group of masks, used for the slow, peaceful *hiramai* dances of the Right, includes Shintoriso, Ōnintei, Taishōtoku, Chikyū, and Korobase. Certain sculptural features characterize the entire group: 1) among the smallest of the Bugaku masks, they range in height from 18 to 23 cm., or just slightly larger than life-size; 2) the hairline is painted as a simple strip of black lacquer extending across the top of the forehead and down to where the ears would be; 3) the almond-shaped eyes slant sharply; 4) many have a medallionlike bump in the middle of the forehead; 5) all have a simplicity of form and sculpturing, particularly in the lower half of the face; 6) each of the masks listed above is represented among the masks ascribed or attributed to the date 1042 and housed originally at Tōdai-ji, Nara.

A subdivision of this group of masks includes those for all the other *hiramai* dances, of both Left and Right. Excepting *Ayakiri,* these dances are more humorous or dramatic than the rest of the group, and their masks reflect their content. While still retaining the realism of the main body of the group, Saisōrō and Kotokuraku have movable features, and the two Ni-no-mai masks are distorted by laughter and sickness.

The second group of masks are those for military dances *(bu-no-mai),* performed in military costume with sword and halberd. Representing stern, mature faces lined with dignity and reserve, the masks Shinnō, Sanju, and Kitoku are larger, more serious, and stronger in expression than the masks used in *hiramai* dances.

The third group includes masks for which the dances have been lost and masks for which there are no surviving examples. Some of these masks, such as Sessen, have strong sculptural similarities to masks mentioned above, while others, such as Bosatsu and Shishi, seem to have more in common with performances outside the Bugaku tradition.

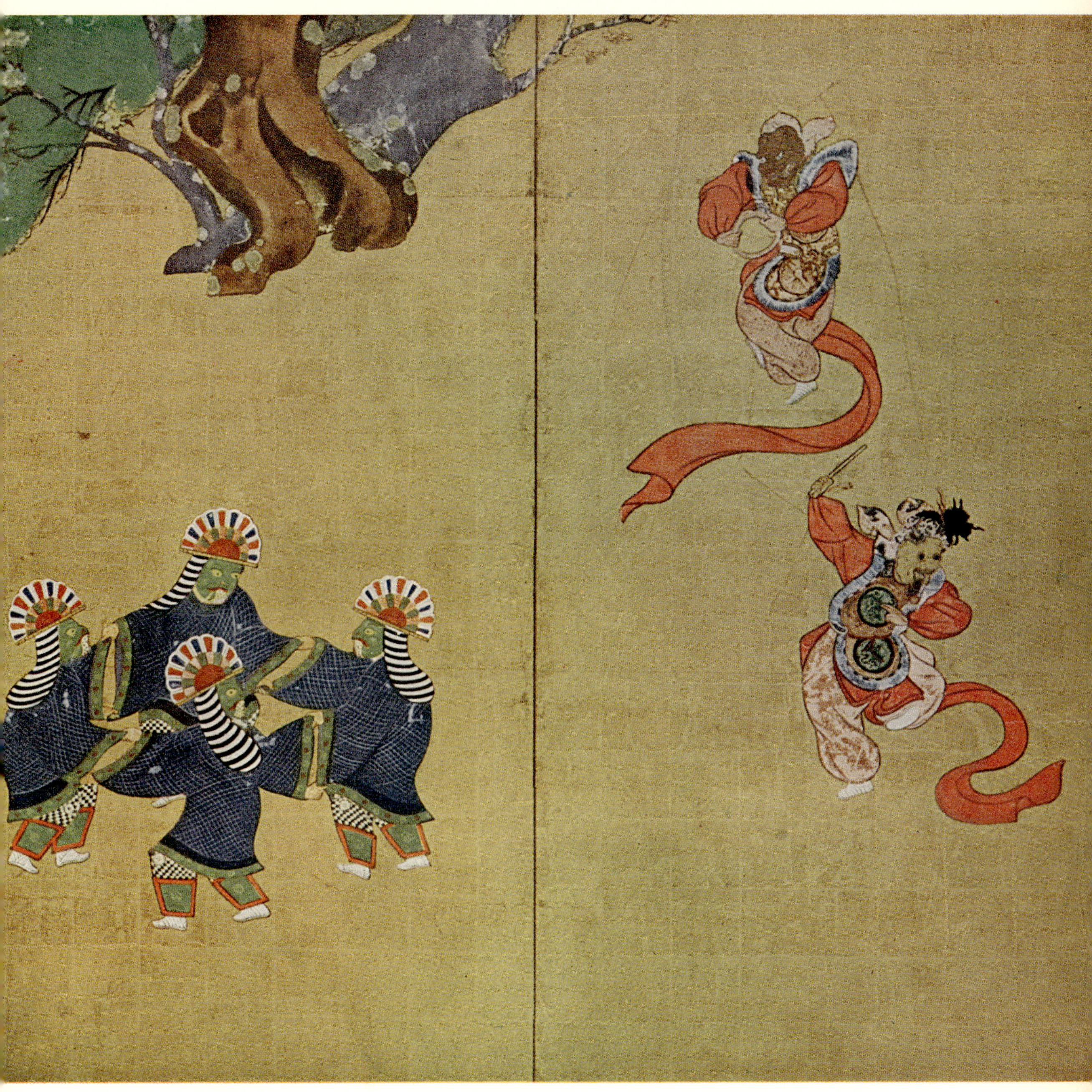

12. *Bugaku Screens,* by Tawaraya Sōtatsu. Left screen of a pair of two-fold screens. Colors and gold-leaf on paper. H. 169, w. 155 cm. (each screen). First half of seventeenth century. Daigo-ji, Kyoto.
The brilliantly painted figures against a gold-leaf background that dot this pair of screens recapture the color and variety found in Bugaku costumes. Although not the only screens of their type, these stand out for the dynamic grace inherent in the placement of the figures. The dances portrayed here are *Genjōraku* (top right), *Ryō-ō* (bottom right), and *Korobase* (left).

Following the sequence of *jo-ha-kyū* (slow, moderate, fast) the fourth group consists of the rich, powerful, exaggerated masks of the vigorous *hashirimai* dances. Batō, Genjōraku, Ryō-ō, and Nasori are large in scale and overexpressive to the point of grotesqueness. They make use of mechanical devices such as movable eyes, dangling chins, and rope hair, which in their shaking and clacking serve to accentuate the sharp rhythms of the dance.

## Masks for Quiet Dances

### *Shintoriso*

The clownlike, oval Shintoriso mask is painted in natural skin color. Small squinting eyes, whose downward sweep is echoed in the curve of the eyebrows, are filled with mirth. A slender pointed mustache with corkscrew tips embellishes the smiling mouth, and two red lacquer circles decorated with seven black spots highlight the cheeks.

The ten surviving examples of Shintoriso provide a good survey of the development of carving style from the earliest dated masks (1042) to the height of Bugaku mask carving at the end of the twelfth century. Though conspicuously damaged, the mask at Tamukeyama Shrine seems to be an authentic early example (pl. 21). With its wide-open eyes, depth of structure, and simplicity of features, it strongly resembles the Chikyū mask in plate 25, which, inscribed with the date 1042, belongs to the same shrine and was made by the same carver. The great likelihood that this Shintoriso was carved in 1042 makes it by far the oldest example of the type.

The five masks at Hōryū-ji dating from the twelfth century (pl. 22) still retain freedom in carving as compared to the four masks at Kasuga Shrine inscribed by Inshō in 1185 (pl. 14). The latter are fine works, representative of the sophistication that Bugaku masks reached. Essentially identical in form with those at Hōryū-ji, they are more symmetrical and have somewhat more prominent foreheads.

The light-hearted *Shintoriso* dance is performed by four or six dancers wearing large hats and carrying either fly swatters made with long animal hair or *gosambachi,* which resemble short polo sticks. The dance must have been performed as early as the Nara period since the name *Toriso* appears in the *Saidai-ji shizaichō* (Register of Saidai-ji Treasures) written in 780. Its partner dance is *Ōtai Hajinraku,* which uses no mask.

### *Chikyū*

A smile brightens the florid face of the cheerful, large-nosed Chikyū mask. The outer corners of the drooping eyes echo the delicate curve of the thin eyebrows and the curl of the smiling lips. A protruding medallion stands between the brows.

Close to forty examples of Chikyū masks remain today. The oldest is kept at Hōryū-ji (pl. 24). Its thick sculpting and iconographic features, which do not conform to the standard type, suggest an early date. The broad smile that characterizes all later Chikyū masks is only barely hinted by the somewhat slack lips of the Hōryū-ji mask.

13 (overleaf). Chikyū, by Inshō. Japanese cypress, cloth and *sabi urushi* priming, and kaolin base with colors. H. 21.3, w. 16, dpt. 12.7 cm. 1185. Kasuga Shrine, Nara.
Said to celebrate the eternal existence of Heaven and Earth, *Chikyū* is danced in unison by four or six men wearing happily smiling masks. Of all the extant Chikyū masks, this is the most highly refined, with deft carving of the broadly arched eyebrows, squinting eyes, and thick nostrils.

14 (overleaf). Shintoriso, by Inshō. Hardwood (unidentified), cloth and *sabi urushi* priming, and kaolin base with colors. H. 21.2, w. 16.5, dpt. 10.7 cm. 1185. Kasuga Shrine, Nara.
Six people perform the spritely dance called *Shintoriso*. Curved eyes and eyebrows, finely twirled mustache, and smiling lips lend a comic appearance to the mask, the spots of red on the cheeks resembling the make-up of a pierrot.

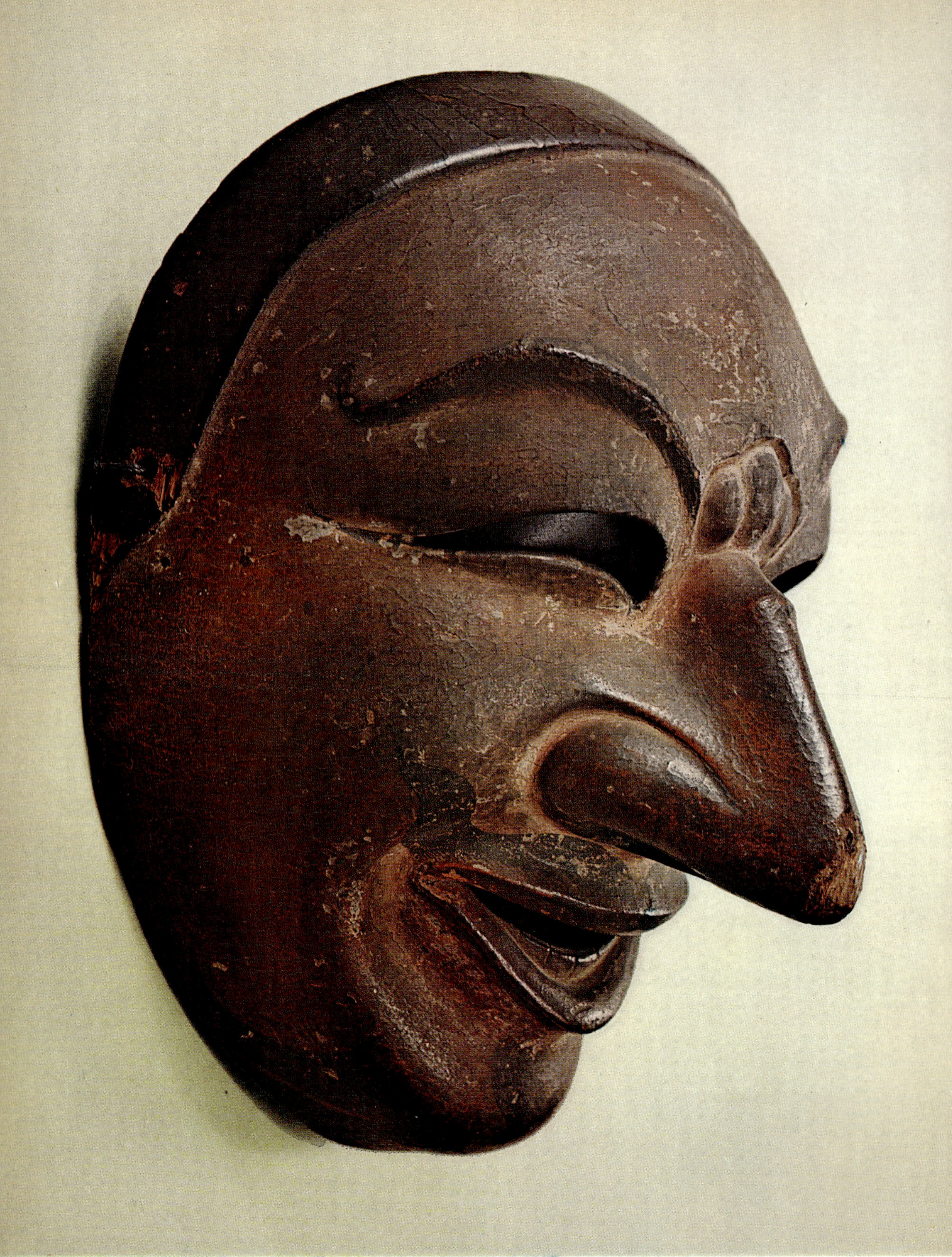

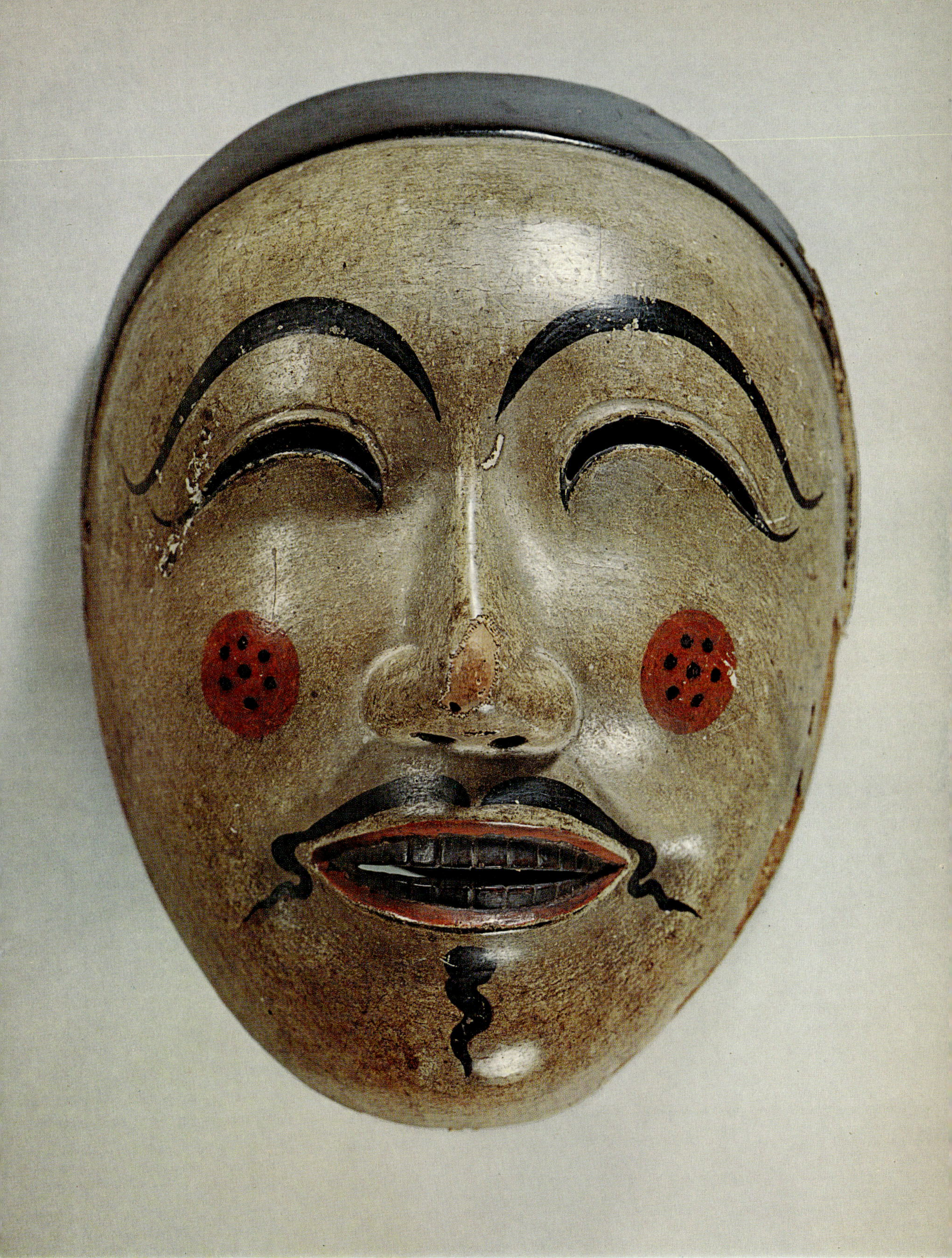

Five excellent masks dated 1042, originally from Tōdai-ji (four now at Tamukeyama Shrine, pls. 20, 150–51, and one in a private collection in Tokyo, pl. 23), have a quality indicative of their early date, prior to the standardization of types. In a manner typical of masks dated 1042, the eye openings of these masks are particularly large. Another Chikyū mask dated 1144 and originally from Hōryū-ji is now in a private collection in Tokyo.

The best example of a highly refined Chikyū of the established form is the mask at Kasuga Shrine dated 1185 (pl. 13). The elegant curve of the eyebrows, the droll slant of the eyes, the smiling lips and contracted nostrils are executed with a perfectly controlled technique that still manages to preserve the freshness of conception of the earlier masks. Five of the seven masks at Hōryū-ji (of which four have been repainted; pl. 26) are considered to be of a later date.

*Chikyū* is danced in unison by four or six men wearing brightly colored helmets fashioned with a bird on top (pl. 15). The piece is said to be congratulatory,

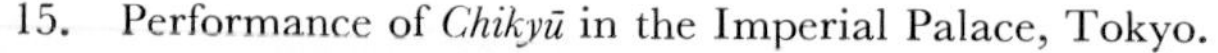

15. Performance of *Chikyū* in the Imperial Palace, Tokyo.

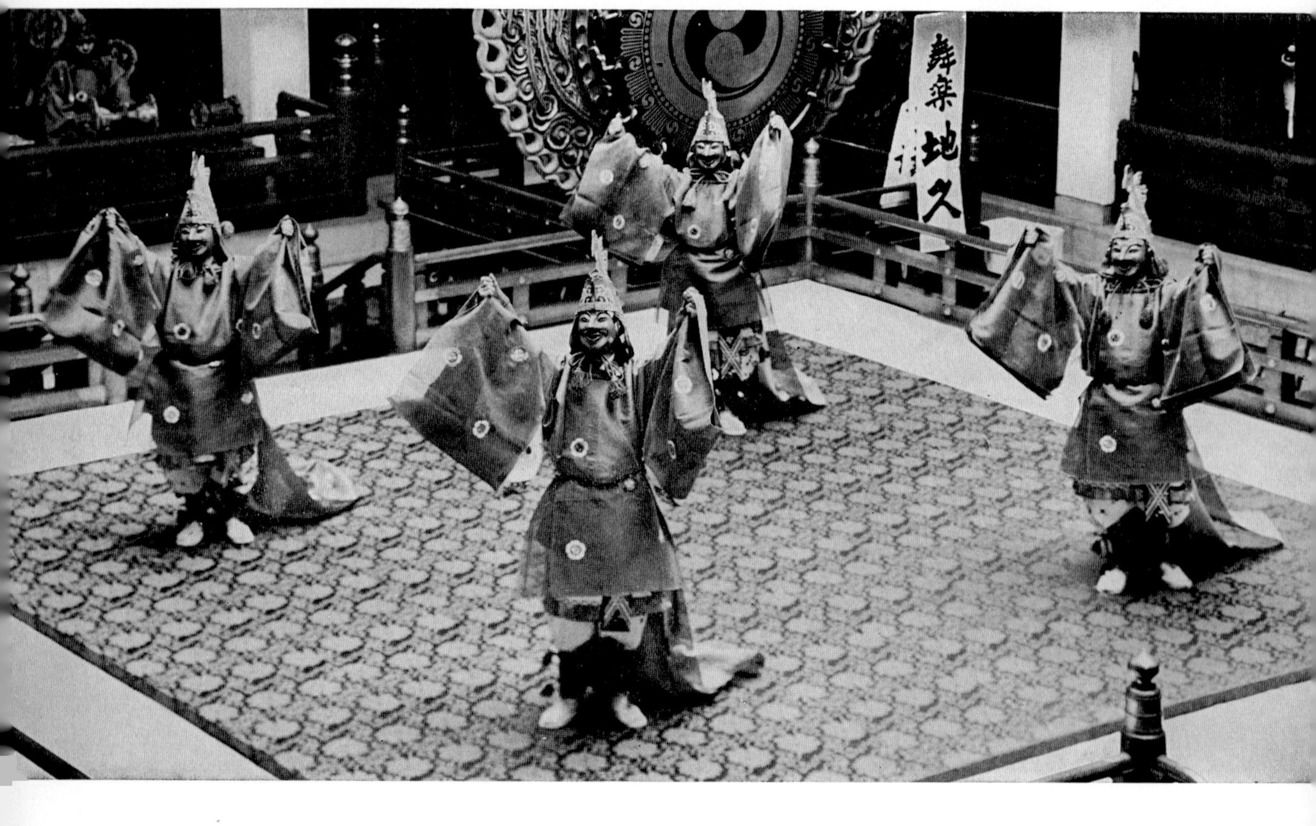

celebrating the eternity of heaven and earth. Often it appears as a partner dance to *Manzairaku,* a congratulatory piece of the Left not requiring a mask. The history of *Chikyū* in Japan began in the mid-Heian period, though its earlier form can be traced back to the Korean kingdom of Koryŏ.

*Taishōtoku and Shinshōtoku*

The mask of Taishōtoku has no great charm, with its large nose, bulging crossed eyes, and furrowed cheeks. Between the sharply arched eyebrows stand two or three creases or wenlike bulges. These protuberances, which look like a medallion decorating the forehead, appear on a number of Bugaku masks, but there is no reliable explanation as to their source.

A total of thirty-two Taishōtoku and Shinshōtoku masks are known. Four are in Hōryū-ji, two in the Ise Shrine Repository (one, pl. 27, dated 1042), one at Tamukeyama Shrine (pl. 28), one at Chōgo Sonshi-ji in Nara, and five in Konda Hachiman Shrine in Osaka (of which three are dated 1343, pl. 29, and one 1498). The mask in the repository of Ise Shrine has a restored nose, but it is an early piece of fine craftsmanship.

The thirteenth-century treatise on Bugaku, the *Kyōkunshō,* describes Taishōtoku as being flesh-colored with white eyebrows, and Shinshōtoku as red with black eyebrows: the distinction between the two masks seems to lie in their coloring alone. All the abovementioned masks are now classed as Taishōtoku. If, however, they are distinguished on the basis of color alone, then the dark-red mask at Ise Shrine, the four at Hōryū-ji, which are in dark-red or vermilion lacquer, and the bare wood mask at Tamukeyama Shrine, which shows vestiges of red in the hollows, should probably be labeled Shinshōtoku.

*Ōnintei*

The firmly closed mouth of the Ōnintei mask gives it a look of serious dignity. The eyes, wide at the center and narrowing sharply at the outer corners, curve strongly upward. The parallel angles of the eyebrows and mustache further accentuate the severity of the mask. Like Taishōtoku and Chikyū, Ōnintei has a medallionlike protuberance between the eyebrows, which suggests that the three pieces share the same ancestry.

The seventeen known Ōnintei masks include four at Tōdai-ji (pl. 45) and one at Tamukeyama Shrine (pl. 16), all dated 1042. This ranks them among the oldest inscribed Bugaku masks. The two Ōnintei at Hōryū-ji, judging from the quality of the workmanship, date from the latter half of the twelfth century, and the mask at Kasuga Shrine (pl. 46), dated 1185, has an inscription by the carver Inshō. Unique for its well-rounded cheeks and rather young face is the mask at Sumiyoshi Shrine in Osaka. In addition, there is one Ōnintei mask at Masumida Shrine in Aichi Prefecture dated 1308.

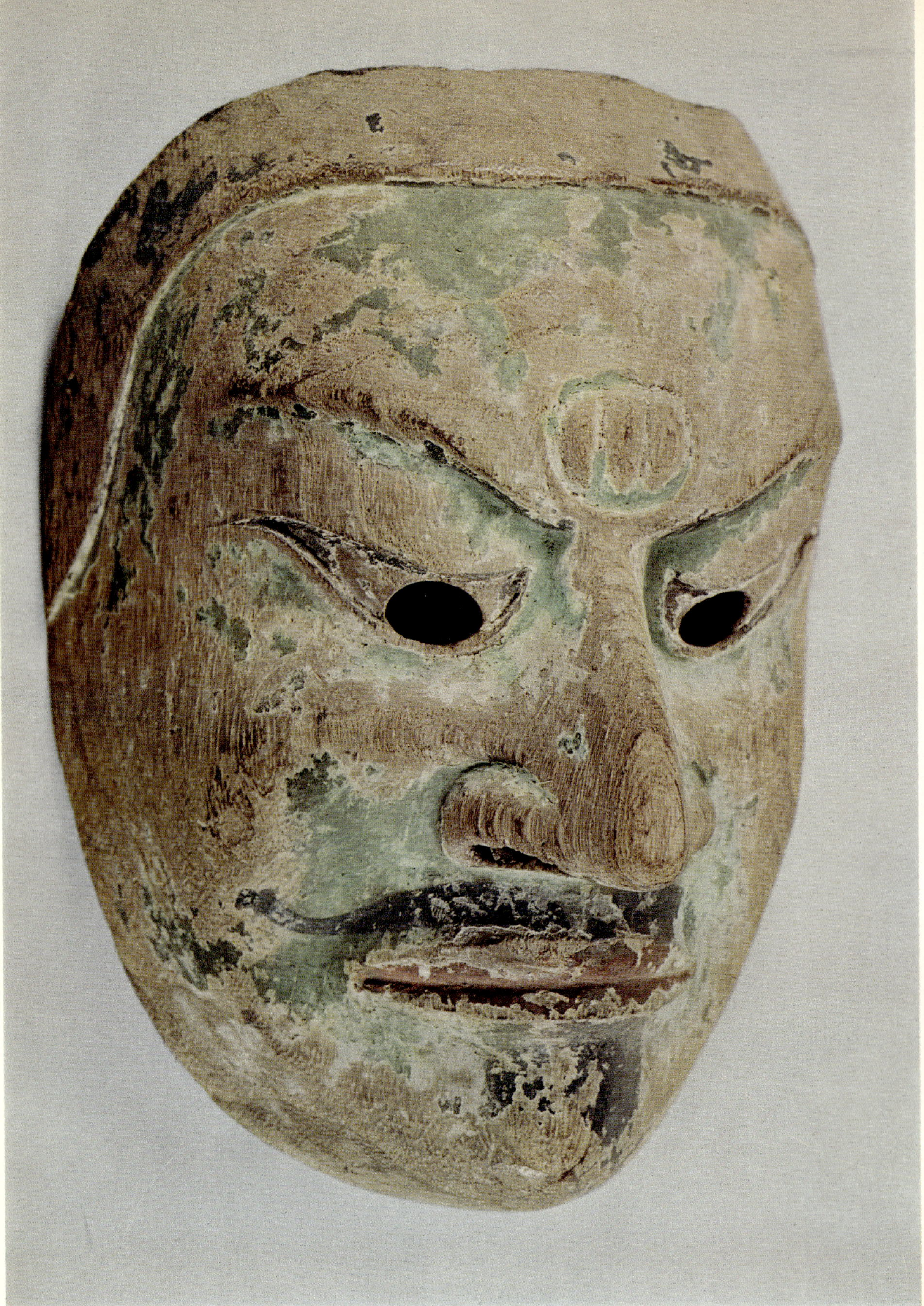

16. Ōnintei. Paulownia with kaolin base and colors. H. 21.2, w. 15.3, dpt. 16.8 cm. 1042. Tamukeyama Shrine, Nara.

Tradition places the beginning of the dance *Ōnintei* in 313 with a performance by the Paekche scholar Wani at the coronation of the Emperor Nintoku. It became customary to perform it as a part of the coming-to-manhood ceremony for the crown prince. In this mask, the rhythmic sweep of the upward slanting eyes shows the same sense of line found in other masks dated 1042.

The *Kyōkunshō* indicates the color of Ōnintei as being either green or tan. Although the masks at Tōdai-ji have recently been repainted, the original blue-green coloring is still visible on the mask at Tamukeyama Shrine (pl. 16). All the other remaining masks are tan or flesh-colored.

At the time of Emperor Nintoku's enthronement (dated by the *Nihon shoki* to A.D. 313), the scholar Wani (Japanese reading) from the Korean kingdom of Paekche is said to have danced *Ōnintei* in the palace to celebrate the event. Later it became the custom to perform it in the Eastern Shrine of the Imperial Palace as a part of the ceremony of attaining adulthood.

*Korobase*

The mask Korobase is said to be patterned after a crowned crane, and the golden bell hanging from the beak of the green birdlike face to symbolize the cry of the bird. An alternate name for this dance is *Tsurumai* (Crane Dance). With movements that indeed recall the gracefulness of cranes, the four dancers join hands and sweep around in a circle. They wear simple blue robes decorated with fish caught in a gauze net (pls. 12, lower left, and 44). *Korobase* is probably related to the Gigaku piece *Karura,* which represented the mythical Garuda bird of Hindu legend and used a similar birdlike mask (pl. 4) in a fast-moving dance.

The oldest examples of Korobase masks are the four dated 1042 originally in Tōdai-ji. They are now dispersed: one is at Tamukeyama Shrine (pl. 42), two are in the Fujita Art Museum in Osaka, and one is in a private collection in Kanagawa Prefecture. Since they are made from soft, light paulownia wood, the damage over the years has been great, although it has not obscured their fine workmanship. Like Chikyū and Ōnintei, these masks have medallions on their foreheads.

Five masks in Aichi Prefecture, four at Atsuta Shrine (dated 1178; pl. 43) and one at Masumida Shrine (dated 1211; pl. 41), are characterized by remarkably large beaks, petallike fleshy beards adorning their cheeks, and deep furrows grooving their foreheads in a manner reminiscent of the mask Emi-men, which is discussed later. Their round eyes and tapered beaks express a droll humor.

By contrast, the mask at Kasuga Shrine (pl. 40), thought to have been made in 1185, is rather flat and linear in conception, with shallow carving. The beak is neither very long nor very tapered. Between the eyes concentric rings form an oblong wen. This mask seems to have become a model for later versions, for there are nineteen later masks in essentially the same style: seven at Kasuga Shrine, four at Hōryū-ji (including one dated 1452), four at Tōshōgū Shrine in Nikko (dated 1656), four much later works at Shitennō-ji, and four at Itsukushima Shrine.

Most of the more recent Korobase masks have fur tacked on as eyebrows, and the mask at Kasuga Shrine (pl. 40) has nail holes around the eyebrows suggesting that it, too, originally had fur there. In this feature Korobase resembles the Sanju mask at Tōdai-ji discussed later (pl. 69).

*Ayakiri*

The thirteenth-century treatise on Bugaku, the *Kyōkunshō,* describes *Ayakiri* as a dance of female characters performed in unison by four people wearing white masks. The name, which can be interpreted as "beautiful woman," implies the feminine character of the dance, and it is the only female piece in the Bugaku repertory, with the exception of the vulgar dance of Hare-men in the piece *Ni-no-mai.*

Few examples remain of Ayakiri. A set of four at Sumiyoshi Shrine in Osaka (pl. 30) are notable for their gentle grace. Painted in creamy flesh color, with broadly arched eyebrows, serene eyes, and bowed lips accentuated in vivid red, these Ayakiri embody a radiant, softly rounded woman's visage. Their treatment closely resembles the physiognomy of later images of Bosatsu (Bodhisattva) from the Heian period and of Gyōdō masks (pl. 6). The inscriptions on the back of the masks give the name, Ayakiri, the year, 1161, and the notation "set of four."

In comparison with the masks at Sumiyoshi Shrine, the three Ayakiri at Hōryū-ji seem remarkably thick-skinned. Areas around the eyes and mouth have been recently

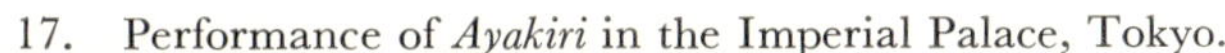

17. Performance of *Ayakiri* in the Imperial Palace, Tokyo.

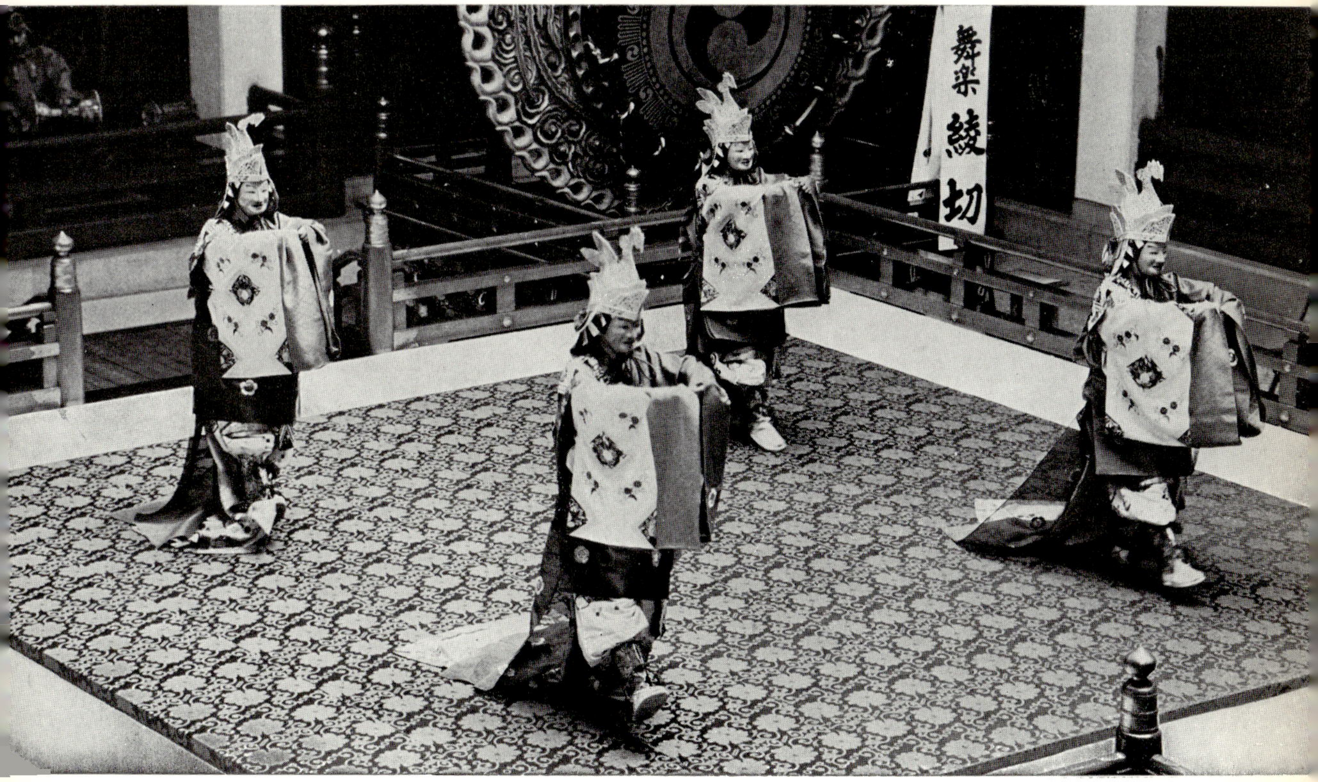

recarved and covered with coarse repainting, serving only to increase their lack of refinement. Nevertheless, they have value as three of the few extant examples of Ayakiri. They probably date from the end of the Kamakura period or even later. Four additional masks that are even more recent belong to Shitennō-ji in Osaka.

Early records of performance of *Ayakiri* date back to 928, when it was performed as one of eighteen dances at a banquet preceding a *sumō* wrestling match. Subsequently, however, there seems to have been a period when it was not performed. The four Ayakiri masks found today at Itsukushima Shrine in Hiroshima Prefecture are not of young women, but of old men, indicating that in its revived form the dance changed radically. Plate 17 shows *Ayakiri* performed recently in the Imperial Palace with youthful masks.

*Kotokuraku*

In contrast to all the pieces discussed so far, which have no story and are danced in unison, *Kotokuraku* has a cast of varied personae who enact a short episode. Four young barbarians sit on the stage. The master of the house brings them wine cups, which are generously filled from a flask of wine passed around by a bearer. Exhilarated by the wine, the four young men begin to dance in a ring, their noses swinging back and forth clownishly (pl. 18). Only one dancer's nose does not swing; he has not had sufficient drink because the bearer, watching for his chance, has stolen his wine. Dead drunk, the bearer follows the circle of dancing barbarians and then retreats, staggering off the stage. Parallels to this amusing, good-humored display of drunkness can be found in the Bugaku piece *Konju* and in the Gigaku piece *Suiko*.

*Kotokuraku* requires three kinds of masks: Kotokuraku (Barbarian Youth), Kempai (Host), and Heishitori (Wine Bearer). The set of six Kotokuraku masks housed at Tamukeyama Shrine (five masks; pl. 31) and at Himuro Shrine (one) are all of

18. *Kotokuraku*. Detail from the *Shinzei kogakuzu* (Shinzei's Illustrations of Ancient Music). Monochrome ink handscroll. Twelfth century. Tokyo University of Fine Arts.

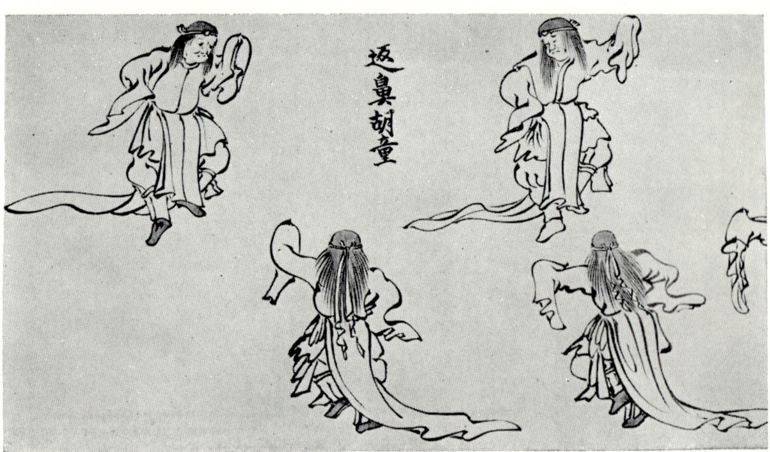

essentially the same style. Their flushed faces are gloriously drunk. Their teeth sparkle and their smiling eyes are narrow slits in red-brown faces. A string attaches their separately carved drooping noses to the bridges in such a way that the nose sways to and fro with the movement of the dance. The delicate treatment of the curling lips and the soft modeling of the cheeks make these masks sculpturally close to Chikyū. All of these masks are dated 1160, and the inscriptions indicate that there were originally nine masks in all. With such a large number of performers, this drunken frolic must have been quite a spectacle.

As the accompanying Kempai (Host) mask at Tamukeyama Shrine bears the same date, it must also be included in the group of nine (pl. 32). The swollen face sticks out its tongue and casts down its eyes, but its nose does not move. Unfortunately this mask has been extensively repaired around the nose and right cheek. Since in modern performances the host *(kempai)* wears a cloth mask *(zōmen),* it may be that this mask with a fixed nose was actually meant to be the one barbarian youth whose nose is not activated by drunkenness, but this is only speculation.

The delightful Heishitori (Wine Bearer) mask at Tamukeyama Shrine (pl. 34) is a later product than the masks discussed above, probably dating from the early Kamakura period. Its general form resembles the Emi-men of *Ni-no-mai.* Its dumpling nose, thick lips, grinning mouth with large round teeth, and uncouth expression suit the role of a crafty servant who manages to steal the wine he is passing around. The wine flask *(heishi)* in plate 33, which the wine bearer passes around, is an outstanding example of early Kamakura lacquer ware.

The thirteenth-century treatise on Bugaku, the *Kyōkunshō,* specifies the use of Emi-men (pl. 59) for the "wine bearer," presumably referring to this role in *Kotokuraku.* It goes on to mention that "in a performance at the Byōdō-in, at that time still the detached

19. Kotokuraku (left) and Kempai (right). Detail from the *Bugaku kōhon* (Bugaku Sketches). Monochrome ink handscroll. Edo-period copy of lost Muromachi-period original. Tokyo National Museum.

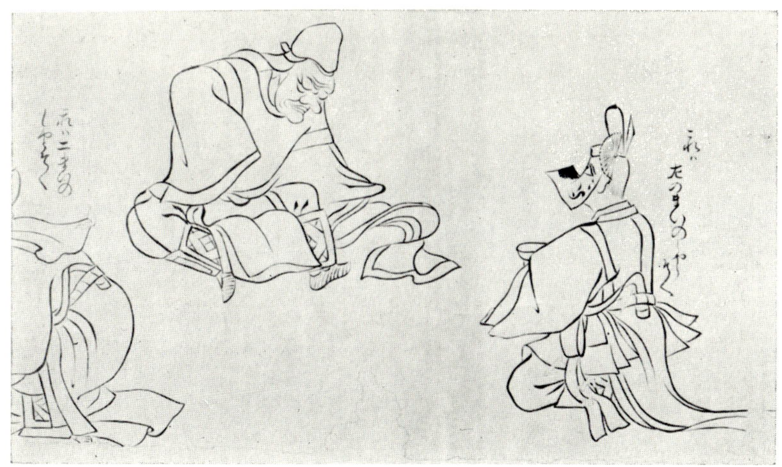

villa of Fujiwara no Michinaga, in 1089, the audience was greatly surprised at the use of a Ni-no-mai mask for the host [*kempai*]. In fact, masks for both the wine bearer [*heishitori*] and the host, distinct from, but very similar to, the masks of Ni-no-mai, are kept at Yamashina-dera [Kōfuku-ji]." Although the masks at Kōfuku-ji no longer exist, the Kempai and Heishitori originally at Tōdai-ji (pls. 32, 34) can certainly be said to resemble the Ni-no-mai masks.

In present-day performances only four barbarian youths appear. As the wine bearer and host are considered to be native Japanese, they do not wear wooden masks, and their costumes likewise are typical of nonmasked dances. The hat, in particular, with its side whiskers, is impossible to wear with any but a paper mask. Normally the wine bearer goes completely unmasked while the host, as indicated in plate 19, wears a paper mask.

The nine Kotokuraku masks at Hōryū-ji fall into four groups on the basis of their style. The first group consists of two masks that appear to have been made in the mid-Heian period or even earlier and as such are almost the oldest Bugaku masks still extant (pls. 38–39). The temple formerly identified them as Gigaku masks; and their large size and sedate appearance would make that plausible. Like Ōnintei and Chikyū, they have two or three grooves in the middle of their foreheads. The nose of one is an integral part of the mask, but the other one had an attached nose that has been lost. Their lively sculpturing, large scale, and composed expression mark them as early masks predating the refinement of Bugaku masks.

The mask in plate 35, composing the second group, is thought to have been made by the same sculptor who made the Sessen in plate 95. A long nose twisting to the right distinguishes this excellent Kotokuraku, whose craftsmanship makes it the finest of the nine Hōryū-ji masks. It must date from no later than the eleventh century.

The third group, from the late Heian period, consists of four masks that chronologically follow the masks dated 1160 at Tamukeyama Shrine. All of them have separately carved noses. Rich in expression, all the masks have differing eyes; their mouths, one greatly distorted, one tightly shut with pursed lips, and another wide open, are also distinctive in style. The last group consists of two recent copies based on these four masks.

Additional Kotokuraku masks include ten at Shitennō-ji in Osaka (five of which are dated 1637), six at Kasuga Shrine in Nara, and four at Itsukushima Shrine in Hiroshima Prefecture. These Edo-period masks can still be seen in use in the spring and autumn Bugaku performances.

### *Ama*

*Ama* is danced in slow, graceful movements by two men dressed in the ceremonial attire of the ancient court, with lacquer hats having flaps and side bristles; the dancers wear square paper or cloth masks *(zōmen)* and carry scepters (pl. 47). The piece is said to have been introduced by the monk Buttetsu in 736 and may have originated in an ancient Indian ground-breaking ceremony, but it was recomposed by Ōto no Kiyokami during the reign of Emperor Nimmyō (r. 833–50). *Ama* is inextricably joined to its partner dance, *Ni-no-mai,* which begins a baudy imitation of *Ama* before the *Ama* dancers have even left the stage (pl. 20).

The mask for *Ama* is made out of a rectangular piece of cloth or paper on which abstract features are painted in black *sumi* ink: triangles for the eyes, straight lines for the eyebrows, *tomoe* (three entwining *yin-yang* symbols) for the cheeks, a vine-shaped curl for the nose, and a large triangle for the beard (pl. 49). A hemp cloth mask dating from the Nara period kept in the Shōsō-in in Nara seems to have provided the model for this extremely formalized mask.

The ease of remaking these masks and the perishability of the material, whether paper or cloth, make it understandable that no Heian-period examples survive. One Ama mask dated 1693 and another dated 1695, however, are still preserved, respectively, at Risshaku-ji and at Honzanjion-ji in Yamagata Prefecture. The author has not seen the actual masks, but they appear to be closer to the cloth mask of the Shōsō-in than to the abstract mask pictured in plate 49. Still, such sources as the screens by Tosa Tōō depicting Bugaku (pl. 20) and the twelfth-century *Shinzei kogakuzu* portray the Ama mask with a schematic design essentially similar to that shown in plate 49.

The paper mask in plate 48, very similar to Ama, is used in the dance of the Right called *Soriko,* which is often performed to bless the brewing of sake.

20. *Ama* and *Ni-no-mai.* Detail from *Bugaku Screens,* by Tosa Tōō. A six-fold screen. Colors and gold-leaf on paper. Mid-Edo period. Private collection, Japan.

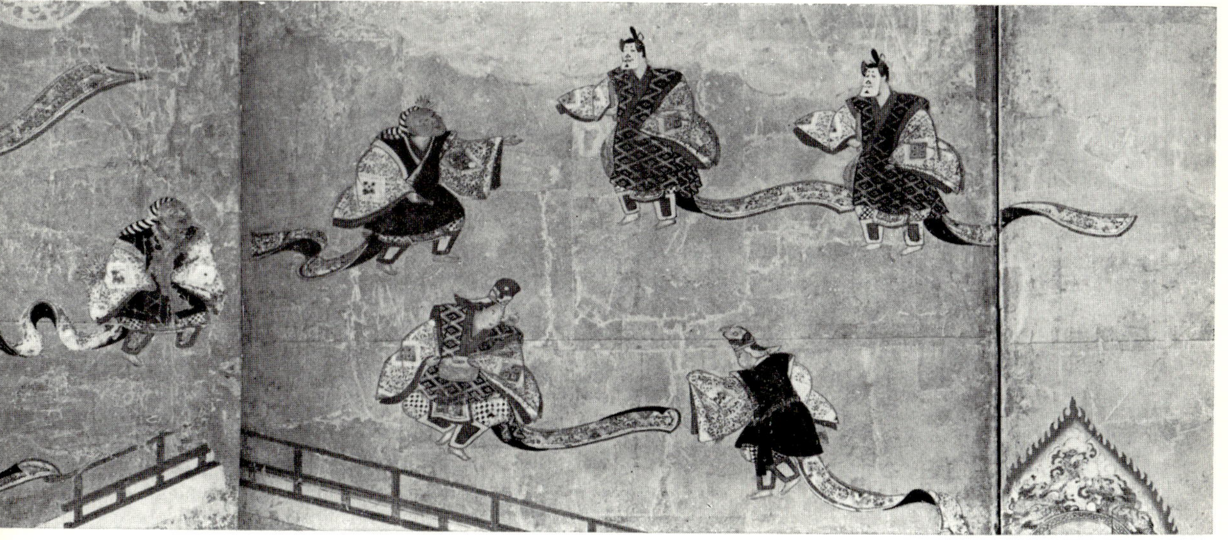

*Ni-no-mai (Emi-men and Hare-men)*

As the dance of *Ama* comes to an end, the dancers of *Ni-no-mai* enter the stage wearing masks of an ugly old man and of a leprous woman. They beg for the scepter of the *Ama* dancers with crude, comical gestures, and when they are rebuffed, they proceed to mock the movements of *Ama* in a rough imitation. The phrase "to dance *Ni-no-mai*" has come to mean to imitate another in a blundering fashion, while the role of Ni-no-mai is roughly equivalent to a Japanese pierrot. It is the only Bugaku dance meant to inspire baudy laughter in the audience.

The thirteenth-century commentary on Bugaku, the *Kyōkunshō,* attributes the piece to the dance master Ōto no Kiyokami, who was active during the reign of Emperor Nimmyō (r. 833–50), but other sources trace its origin to India. Although the actual background of *Ni-no-mai* is unclear, it may well have come from northwest India, where many masks depicting victims of leprosy very similar to Hare-men (the female Ni-no-mai) can still be found. One Japanese tradition claims that *Ni-no-mai* is patterned after the drunken dance of the Hindu divinity Śiva; another attributes it to the drunken dance of the Earth God at the cosmic ground breaking in Japan. In either case, bold and lewd gestures would be in order. Both in the expressions of the masks and in the comic movements of the dance, *Ni-no-mai* resembles Gigaku pieces.

The masks of the old man, Emi-men (pl. 53), and of the old woman, Hare-men (pl. 54), are large and fleshy. Like Gigaku masks, they have ears and completely cover the upper part of the head. Emi-men (Smiling Face) has a wide-open mouth disclosing both rows of teeth. Rippling waves of wrinkles embellish the entire face. In contrast to the laughing Emi-men, Hare-men (Swollen Face) wears a pained expression, her cheeks and eyes grossly swollen, her tongue hanging out of her mouth. These grotesque features of excessive laughter and extreme agony lend a comic appearance to the Ni-no-mai masks. Most Emi-men and Hare-men are similar in type to these two, which are from Atsuta Shrine in Nagoya and inscribed with the year 1178.

The two masks at Itsukushima Shrine made by Gyōmyō are rather special. Unsurpassed in technique, they appear to be alive. The laughing Emi-men (pl. 59) seems to have opened his mouth as if to speak. His wrinkles are not so deep, and here and there long strands of hair stuck perpendicularly into the mask remain around the eyebrows and beard. The gaping mouth of Hare-men (pl. 58) is quite painfully distorted. On their backs the inscriptions (pl. 166) have a dedication dated 1173 from the Taira family, the chief patrons of the shrine, by which we know that these are the oldest examples of Ni-no-mai still extant; it is very likely that they bear close resemblance to the Ni-no-mai masks first brought to Japan.

In a variation performance, when only one dancer performs *Ama,* a single person wearing Emi-men dances the *Ni-no-mai.*

*Saisōrō*

An old man, so decrepit that he can scarcely support his own body, creeps slowly on stage dressed in a light-purple robe. As he mounts the steps to the stage leaning on his stick, the following poem is recited:

At thirty his passion flowers.
At forty his vitality flags.
At fifty he begins the decline into old age.
At sixty he can still walk.
At seventy he needs a stick to stand.
At eighty even sitting makes him dizzy.
At ninety he becomes seriously ill.
At one hundred he can no longer doubt death.

*Saisōrō* is a death dance (pl. 50): the dancer, who has to be an old man, is expected to die within a year of the performance. Due to this superstition, this unique old man's dance is not generally performed today and can be reconstructed only vaguely. Whether the intent of the dance was comic, heroic, or congratulatory is unclear, but it was probably intended to make the audience reflect upon the impermanence of human life. In this, *Saisōrō* is thought to have been similar to the Gigaku performance of *Taikofu* (see pl. 5 for mask). *Saisōrō* is the preserve of the Ō family of Bugaku dancers.

The eyes and the chin of Saisōrō are carved out of separate pieces of wood and inserted in such a way that they can move up and down. The flat, lenselike eyes *(dōgan)* are attached by means of strings threaded through holes in the mask. This is a simpler technique than that used for the movable eyes of other masks. The detached chin *(kiriago)* appears to have been severed from the main mask by a saw inserted at a slight diagonal from the corners of the mouth, then reattached with strings strung through small holes in the mask and the chin (pls. 158–59). A similar device can be found in the Nō mask Okina (pl. 8) and in some Korean and Southeast Asian masks, but among Bugaku masks it is peculiar to Saisōrō; all other Bugaku masks with separate chins have rounded chins dangling from long cords.

The famous Saisōrō mask dated 1249 at Itsukushima Shrine in Hiroshima Prefecture is an excellent specimen (pl. 51). Numerous wrinkles line the forehead and cheeks of its white face, and hair was implanted for the eyebrows, beard, and mustache. Its open mouth shows widely spread teeth. Most other Saisōrō of this type date from the Edo period: typical are the two at Kasuga Shrine in Nara. The mask at Tōshōgū Shrine in Nikko (dated 1656) and that at Shitennō-ji in Osaka are similar.

A somewhat different style is represented by the mask at Tamukeyama Shrine (pl. 52). Although said to postdate the mask at Itsukushima Shrine, the carving is quite orthodox and the whole of the mask hollowed out quite thinly with a light touch, which suggests a date toward the end of the Heian period. This would make the Tamukeyama Shrine mask the oldest Saisōrō mask. Except for the wrinkles around the inserted eyes, the face is smooth. Drawn as a simple line, the hair extends farther down toward the ears than the line marking the hair (or perhaps hat) on the Saisōrō at Itsukushima Shrine. Regrettably the chin is lost, the joint warped, and the hair implanted for eyebrows and mustache has fallen out.

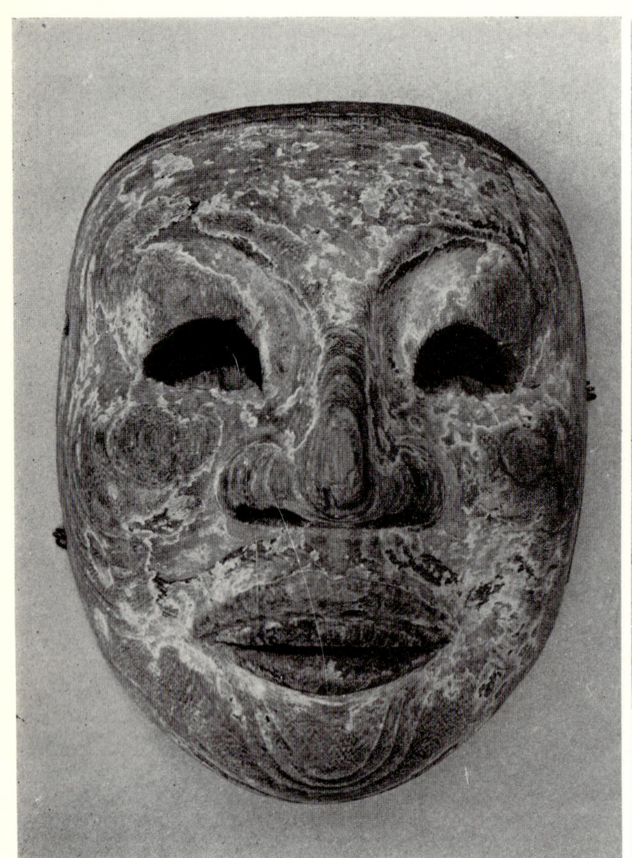

21. Shintoriso. C. 1042. Tamukeyama Shrine, Nara.

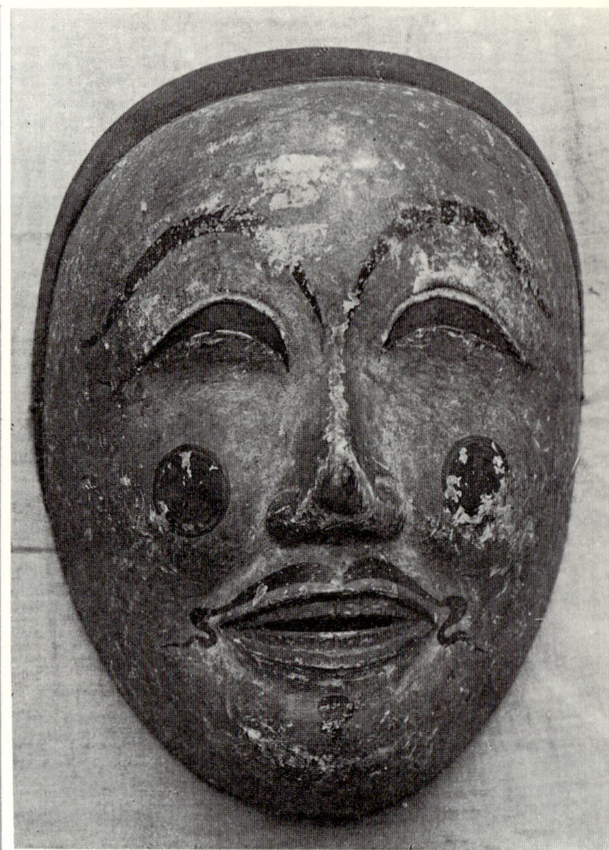

22. Shintoriso. Hōryū-ji, Nara Prefecture.

23. Chikyū. 1042. Private collection, Tokyo.

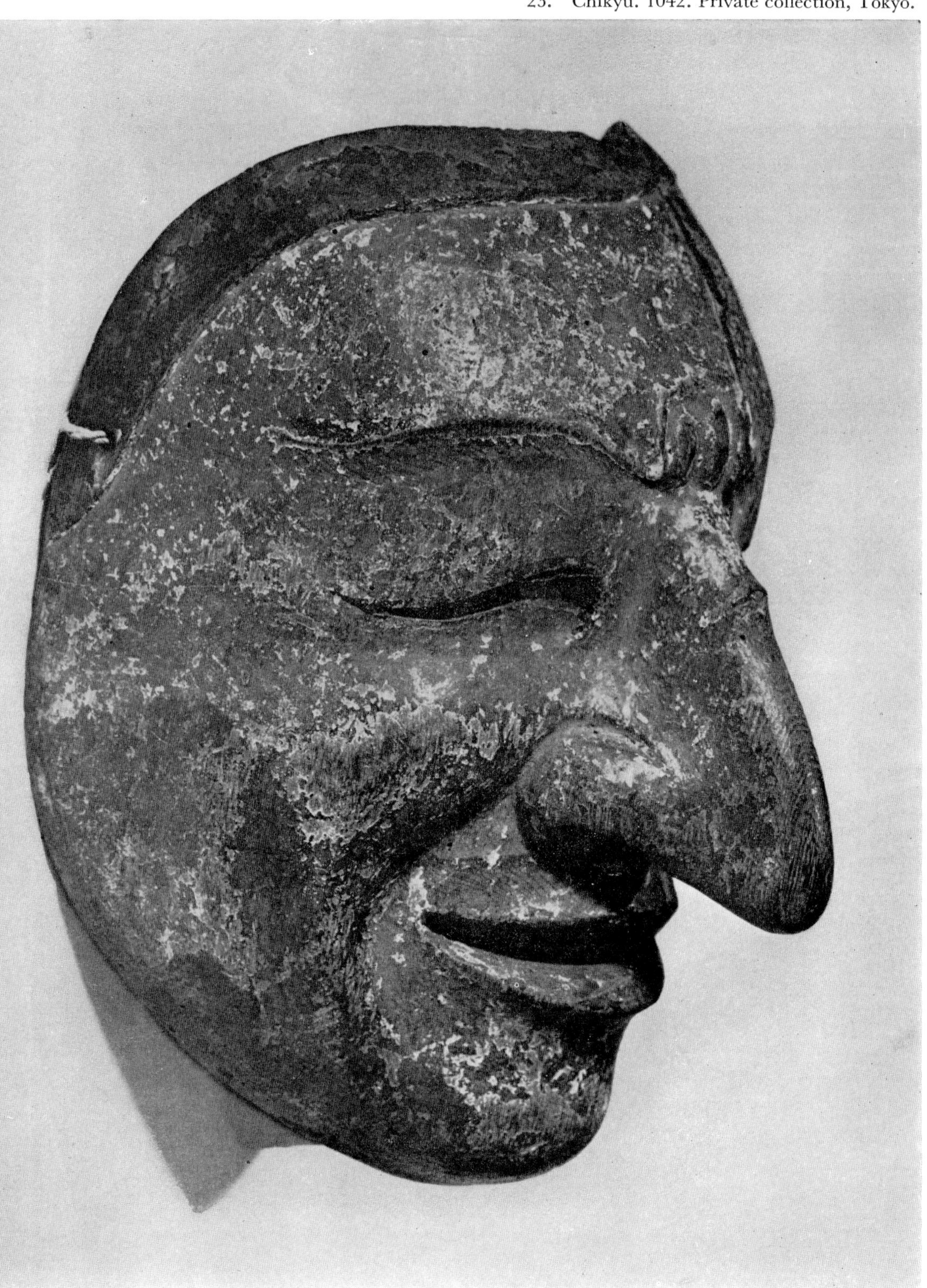

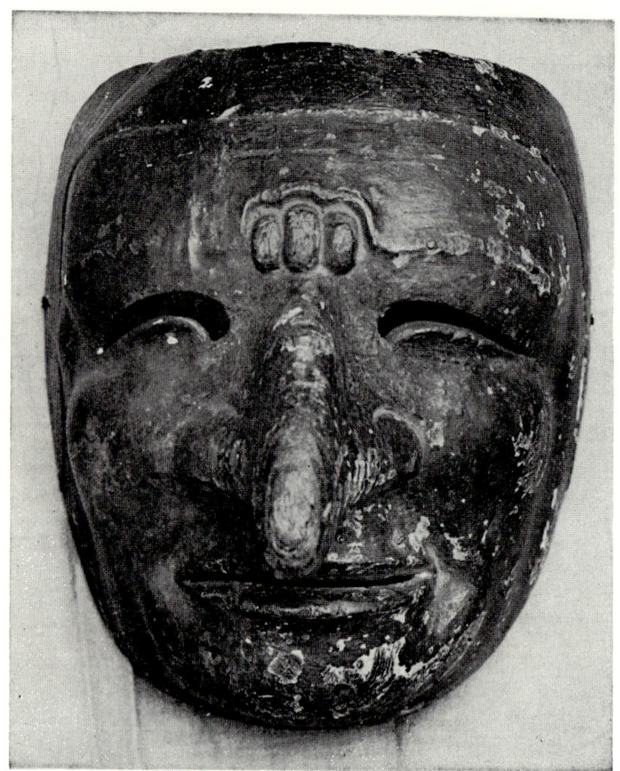

24. Chikyū. Hōryū-ji, Nara Prefecture.

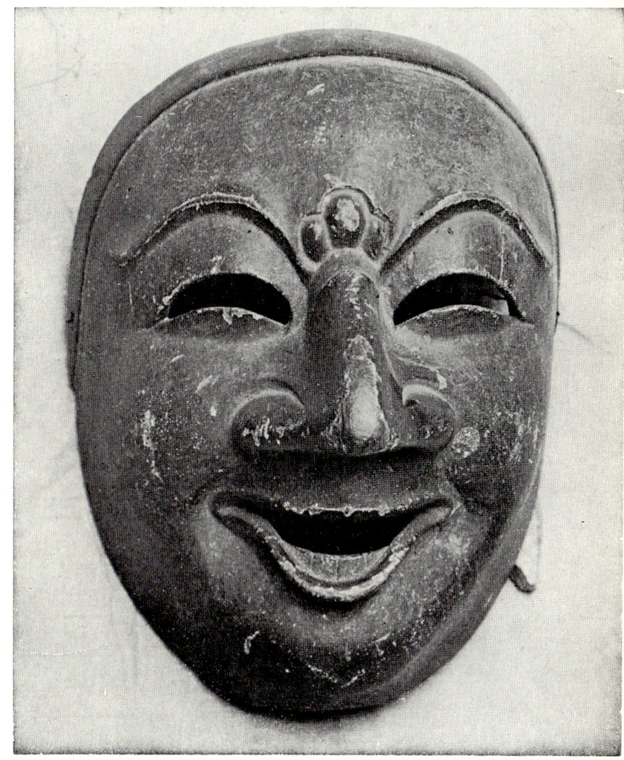

26. Chikyū. Hōryū-ji, Nara Prefecture.

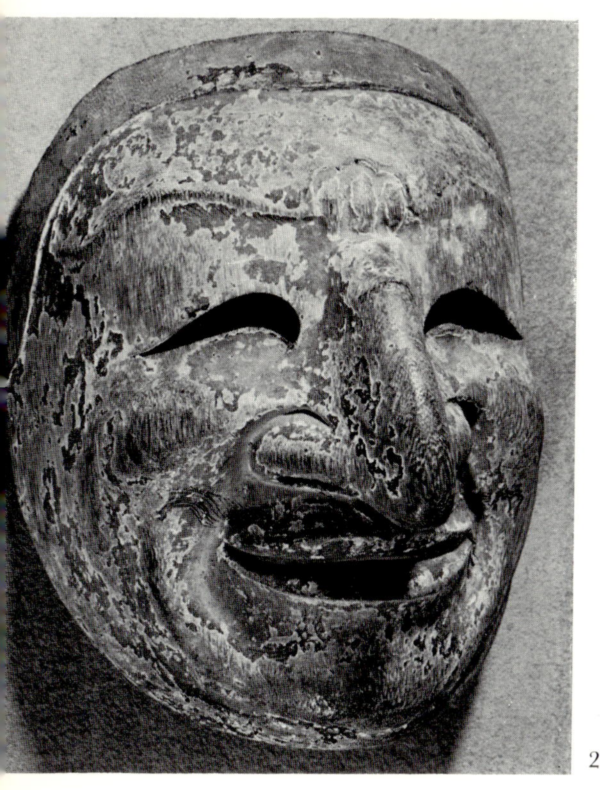

25. Chikyū. 1042. Tamukeyama Shrine, Nara.

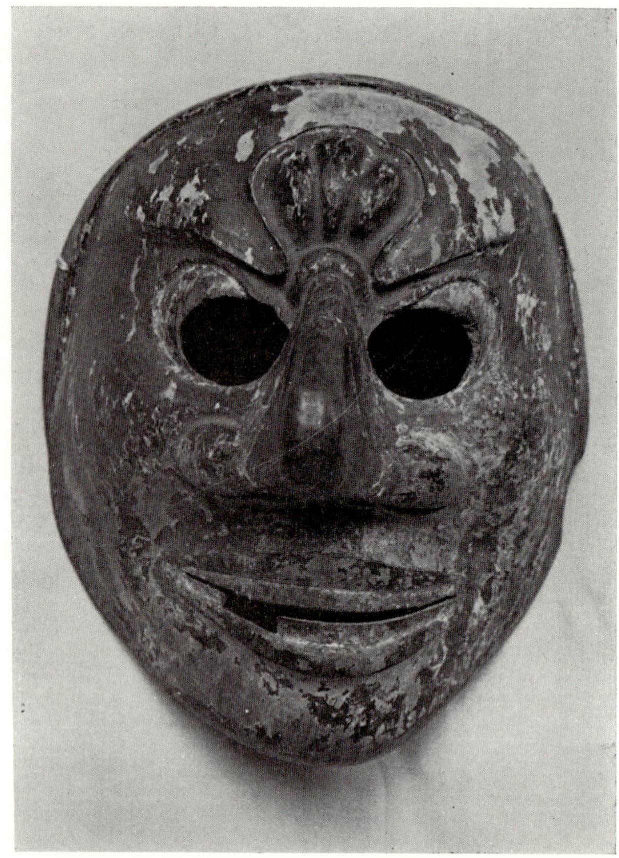

27. Taishōtoku. 1042. Ise Shrine Repository, Mie Prefecture.

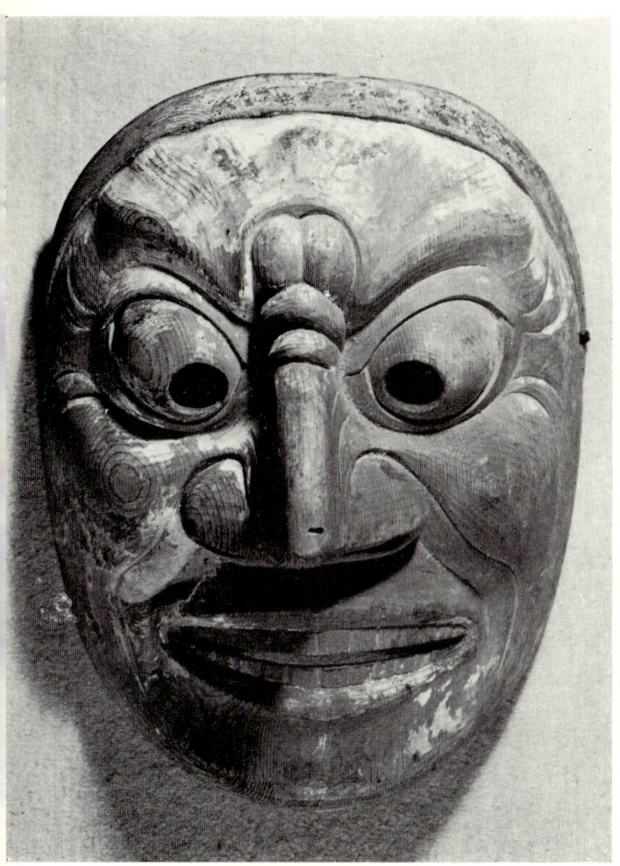

28. Taishōtoku. Tamukeyama Shrine, Nara.

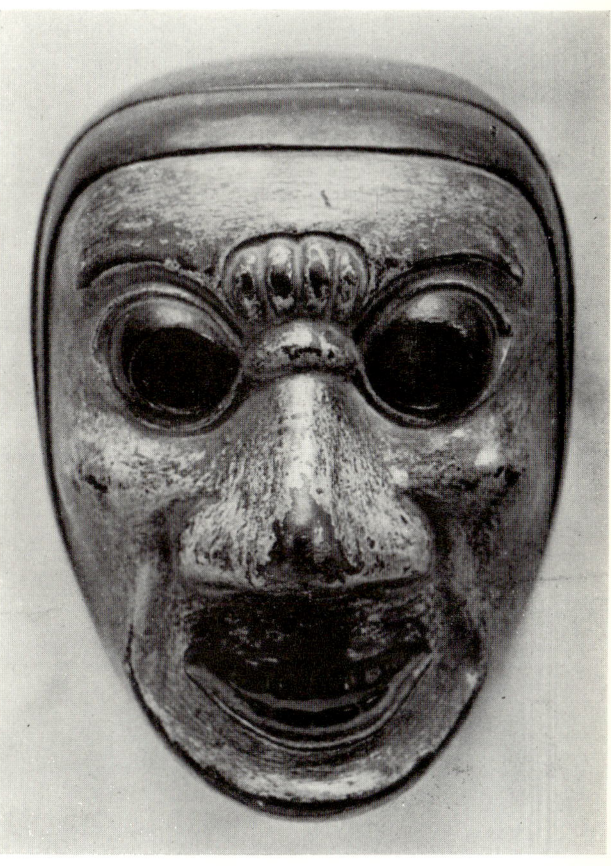

29. Taishōtoku. 1343. Konda Hachiman Shrine, Osaka Prefecture.

30. Ayakiri. Japanese cypress, *sabi urushi* priming (cloth reinforcement on back), and kaolin base with colors. H. 20.6, w. 15.7, dpt. 8 cm. 1161. Sumiyoshi Shrine, Osaka.

The only "female dance" in Bugaku, *Ayakiri* is performed by four people in unison. Perhaps because this dance died out in the middle ages (1185–1572), examples of the mask are rare. Fortunately, Sumiyoshi Shrine has preserved a set of four. The gentle beauty of the mask shown here, with its clear eyes and small mouth, resembles Buddhist statues of the same period.

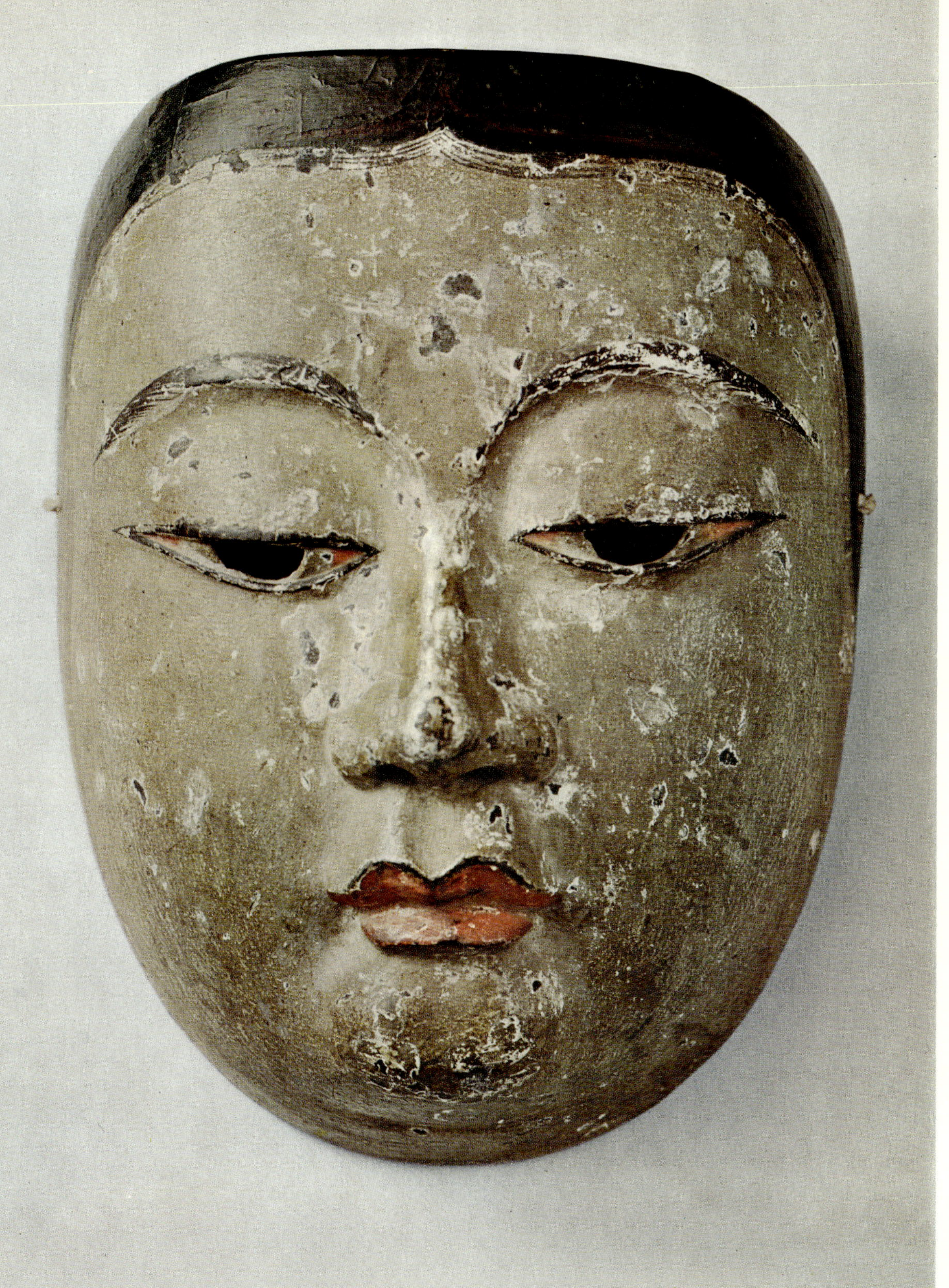

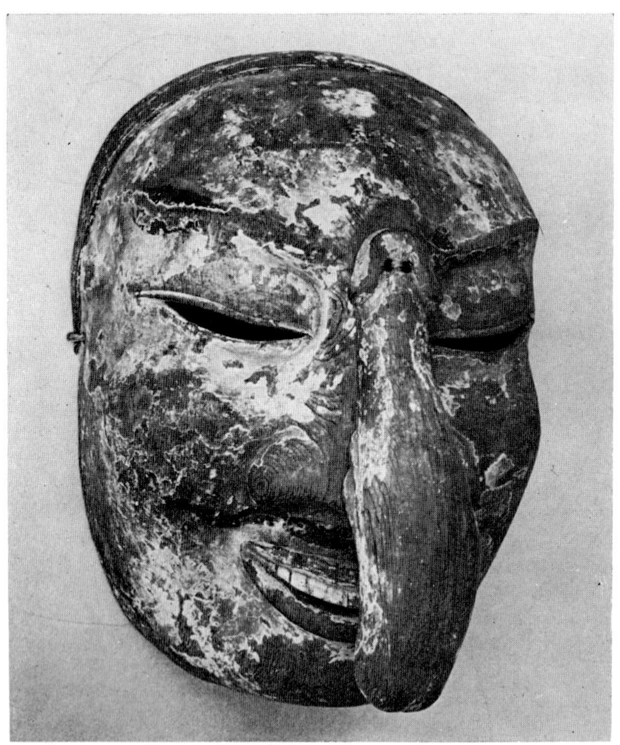

31. Kotokuraku. 1160. Tamukeyama Shrine, Nara.

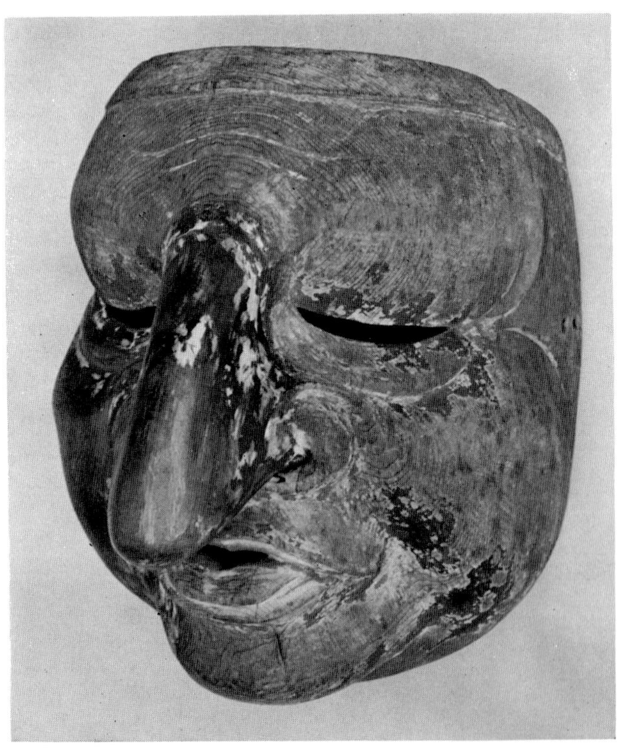

32. Kotokuraku Kempai. 1160. Tamukeyama Shrine. Nara.

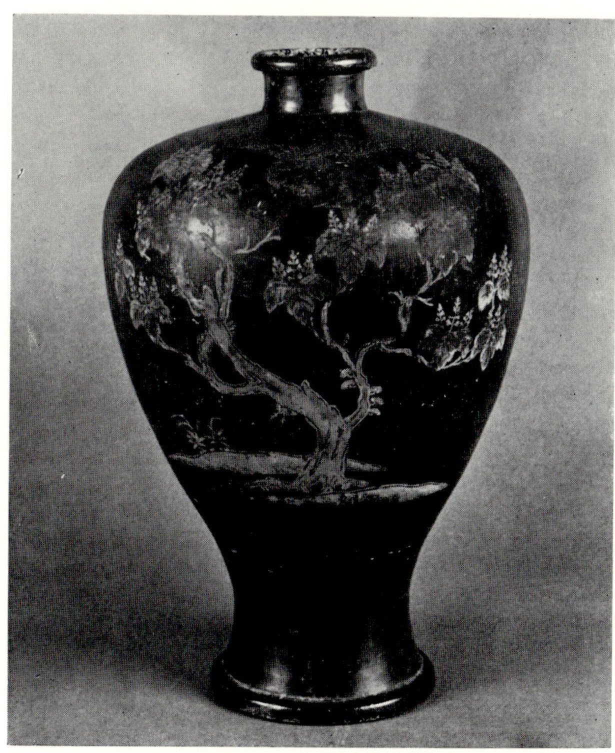

33. Wine jug used in *Kotokuraku*. Kamakura period. Tamukeyama Shrine, Nara.

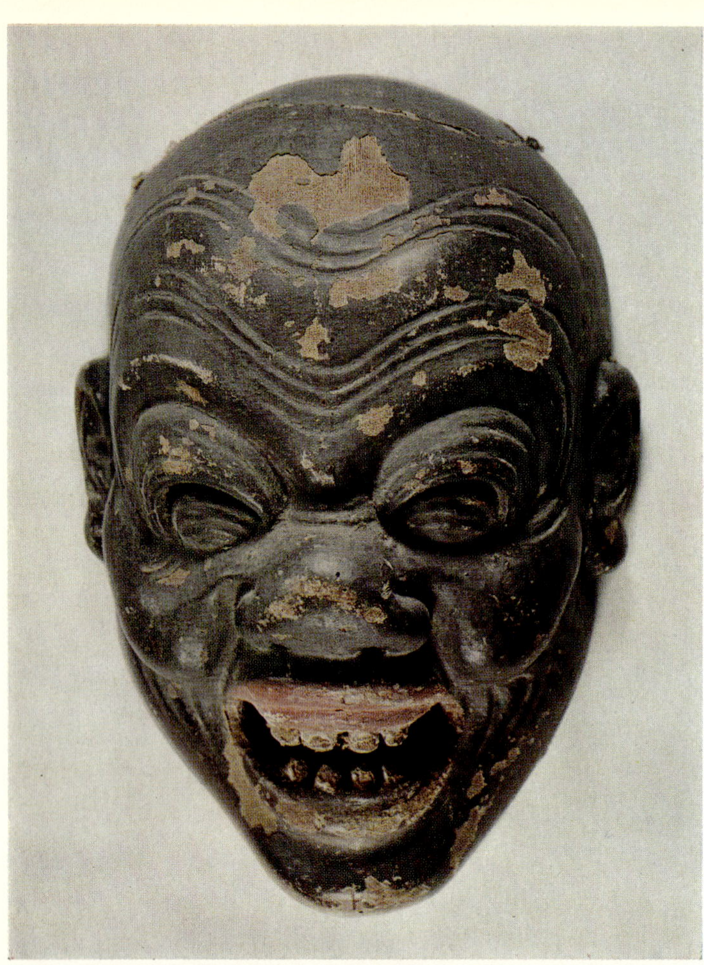

34. Heishitori. Japanese cypress, cloth and *sabi urushi* priming, and kaolin base with colors. H. 31.5, w. 24.1, dpt. 16.7 cm. Early thirteenth century. Tamukeyama Shrine, Nara.
Carrying a full jug of wine, the wine bearer *(heishitori)* serves each of the young barbarians sitting on the stage, not hesitating to steal some of the wine for himself. A drunken luster shines in his smiling face with its widely spread teeth and pudgy nose.

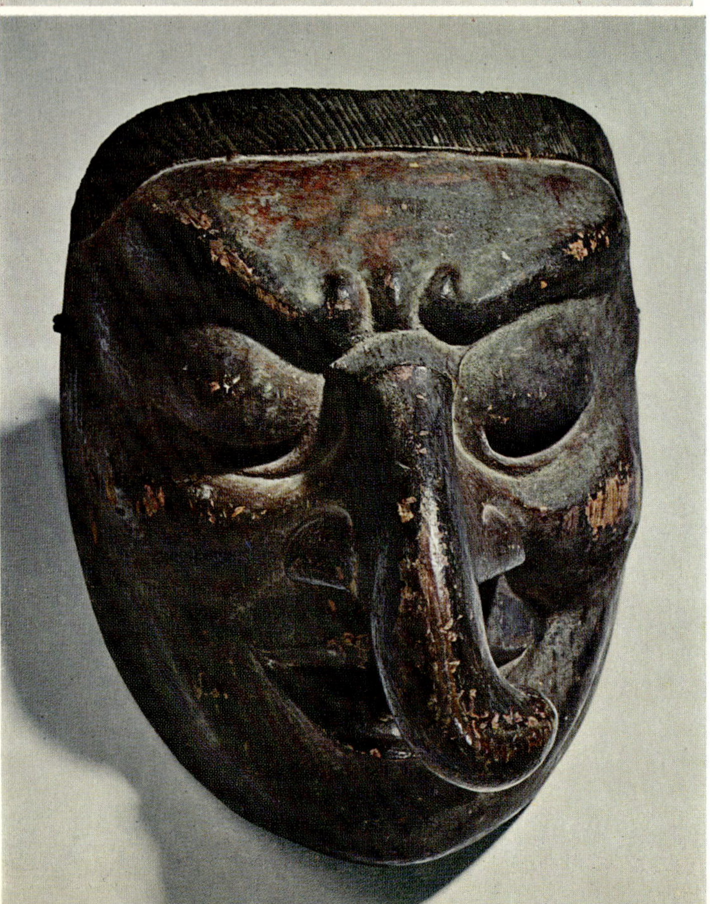

35. Kotokuraku. Japanese cypress with kaolin base and colors. H. 20.4, w. 16.7, dpt. 16.5 cm. Late tenth or early eleventh century. Hōryū-ji, Nara.
The twisted nose on this very early Kotokuraku does not move. The mask is deeply hallowed out and extends far over the ears when worn. Seemingly made by the same sculptor as the Sessen in plate 95, its swollen eyelids and peculiarly pliant lips are similar to those found in single-block Buddhist sculpture of the tenth and eleventh centuries. (See also pl. 37.)

36. Kotokuraku. Japanese cypress with kaolin base and colors. H. 21.6, w. 17.6, dpt. (including nose) 16.1 cm. 1160. Tamukeyama Shrine, Nara.
As the inebriated young barbarians *(kotokuraku)* dance in a jolly circle, their noses—carved separately and attached with a string—sway to the rhythm of the dance. The cast includes four or six young barbarians as well as the host, who brings out the wine cups, and the wine bearer. This well-carved mask vividly expresses the drunken abandonment of the barbarians. Much of its refinement comes from its gracefully rounded curves and balanced features. (See pl. 164 for inscription on back.)

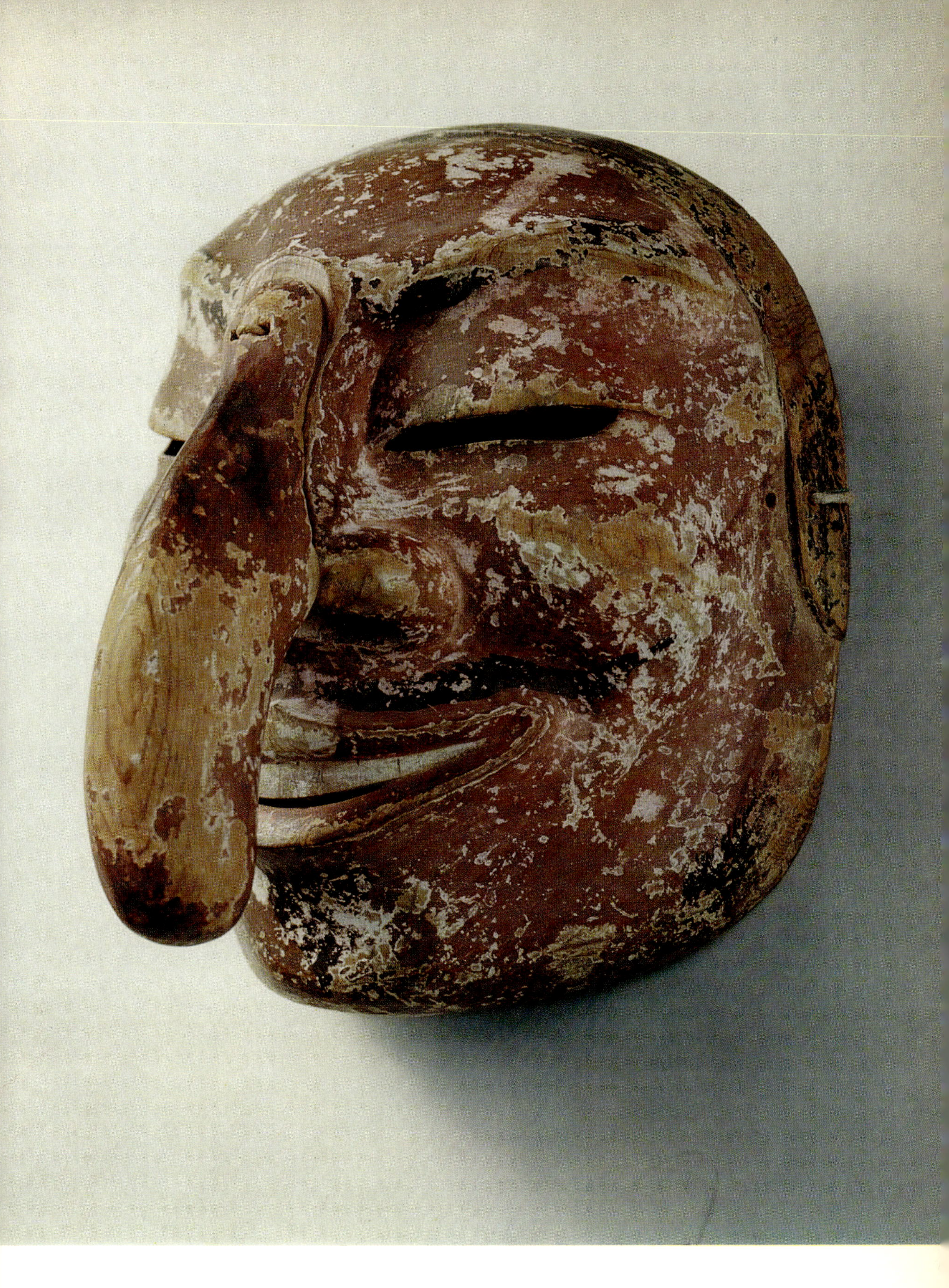

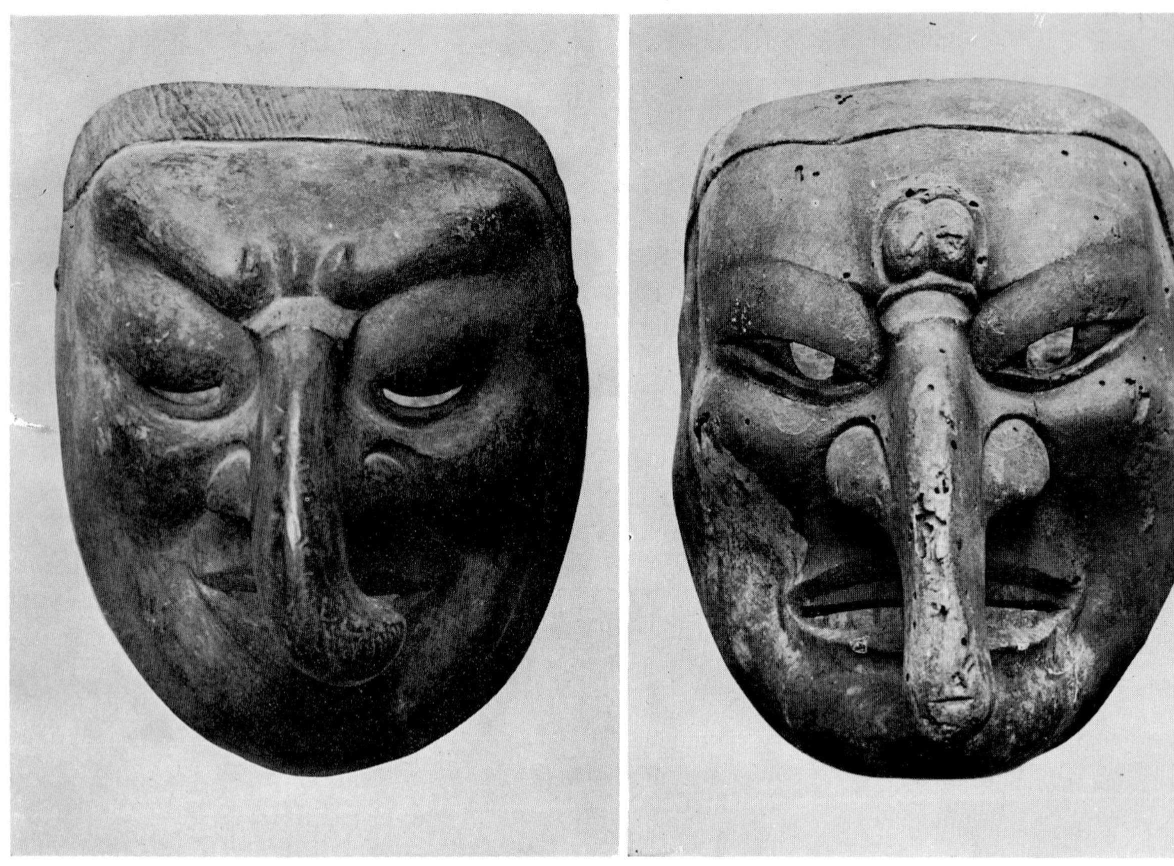

37. Kotokuraku. Late tenth or early eleventh century. Hōryū-ji, Nara Prefecture. (See also pl. 35).

38. Kotokuraku. Hōryū-ji, Nara Prefeture.

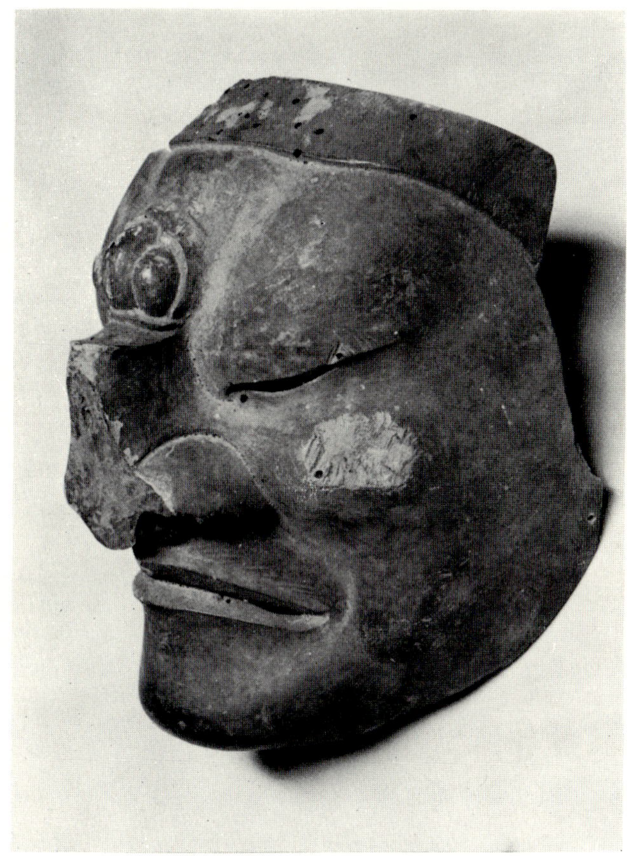

39. Kotokuraku. Hōryū-ji, Nara Prefecture.

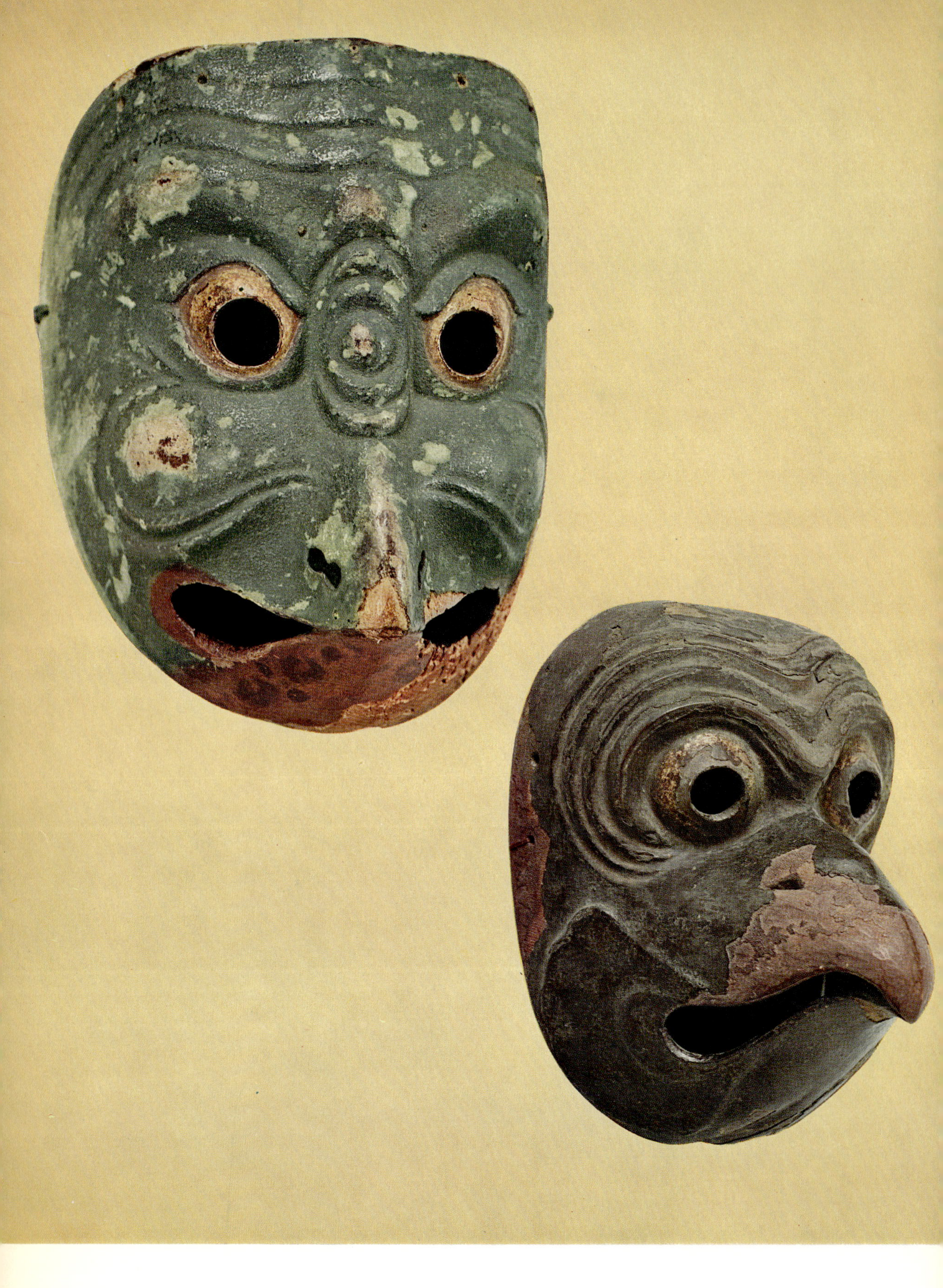

40. Korobase, probably by Inshō. Paulownia, cloth and *sabi urushi* priming, and kaolin base with colors. H. 19.3, w. 16, dpt. 10.1 cm. C. 1185. Kasuga Shrine, Nara.
In the elegant dance in which this mask was used, also known as the Crane Dance *(Tsurumai),* four men dressed in birdlike masks and large caps and blue net-covered robes circle the stage with cranelike movements. The shallow relief on this mask gives it a strong linear feeling. Originally fur was tacked on for eyebrows. The bell that was hung from the beak to suggest the crane's cry has been lost.

41. Korobase. *Kaya (Torreya nucifera),* cloth and *sabi urushi* priming, and kaolin base with colors. H. 18.7, w. 16, dpt. 13.9 cm. 1211. Masumida Shrine, Aichi Prefecture.
Compared to the mask in plate 40, this Korobase is more three-dimensional and has a remarkably large beak. Around the corners of the mouth, the flesh stands out in the shape of flower petals, and the forehead is covered with deeply engraved wrinkles. There is a charming drollness in the round eyes and tapered beak.

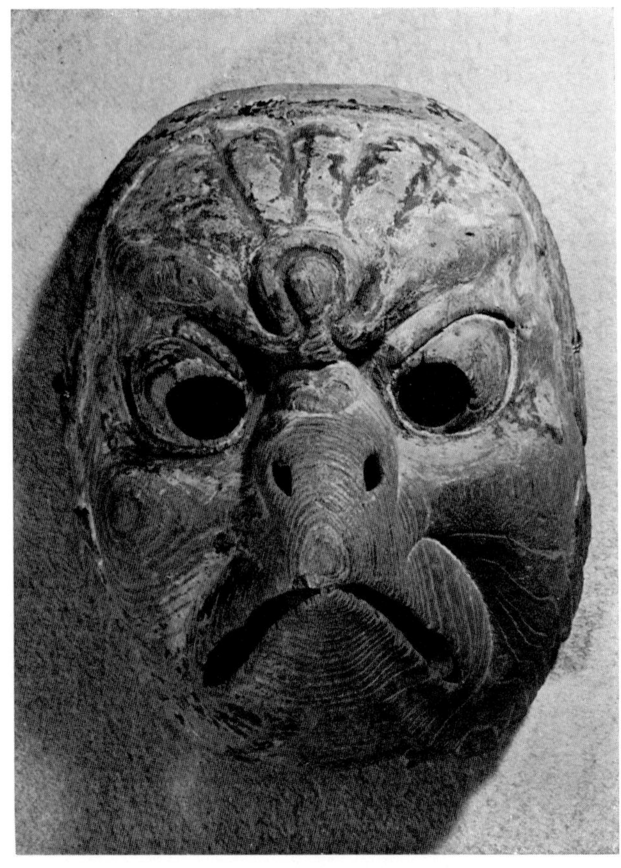

42. Korobase. 1042. Tamukeyama Shrine, Nara.

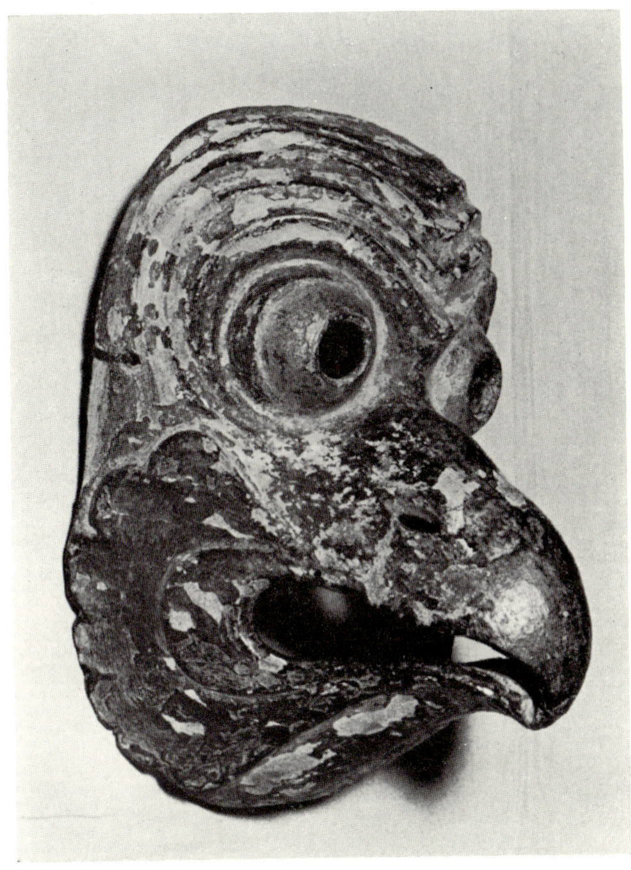

43. Korobase. Restoration date 1178. Atsuta Shrine, Nagoya.

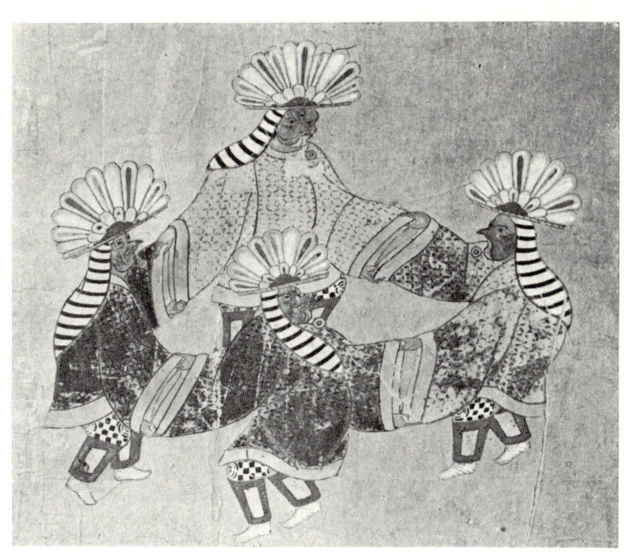

44. *Korobase.* Detail from *Bugaku Screens,* by Tosa Tōō. A six-fold screen. Colors and gold-leaf on paper. Mid-Edo period. Private collection, Japan.

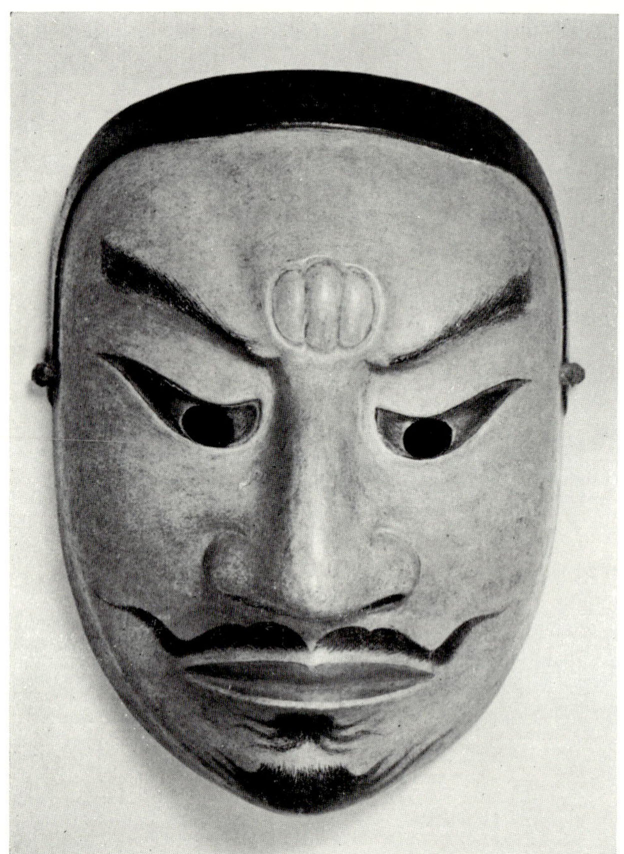

45. Ōnintei. Repainted. 1042. Tōdai-ji, Nara.

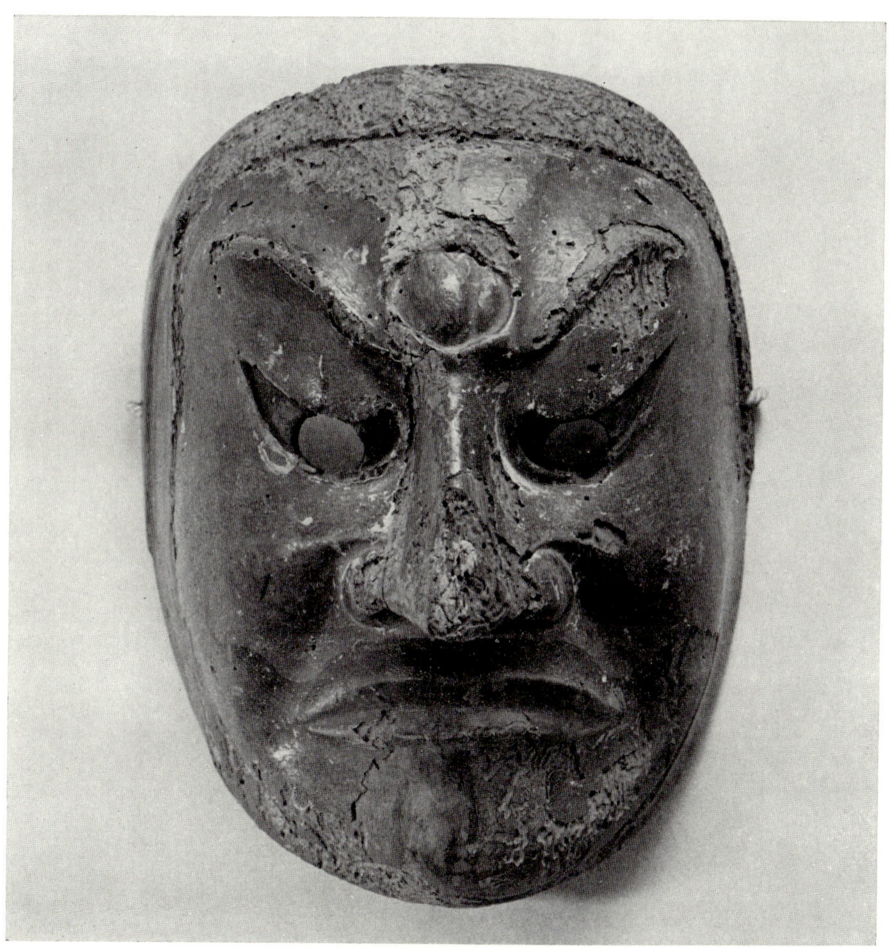

46. Ōnintei, by Inshō. 1185. Kasuga Shrine, Nara.

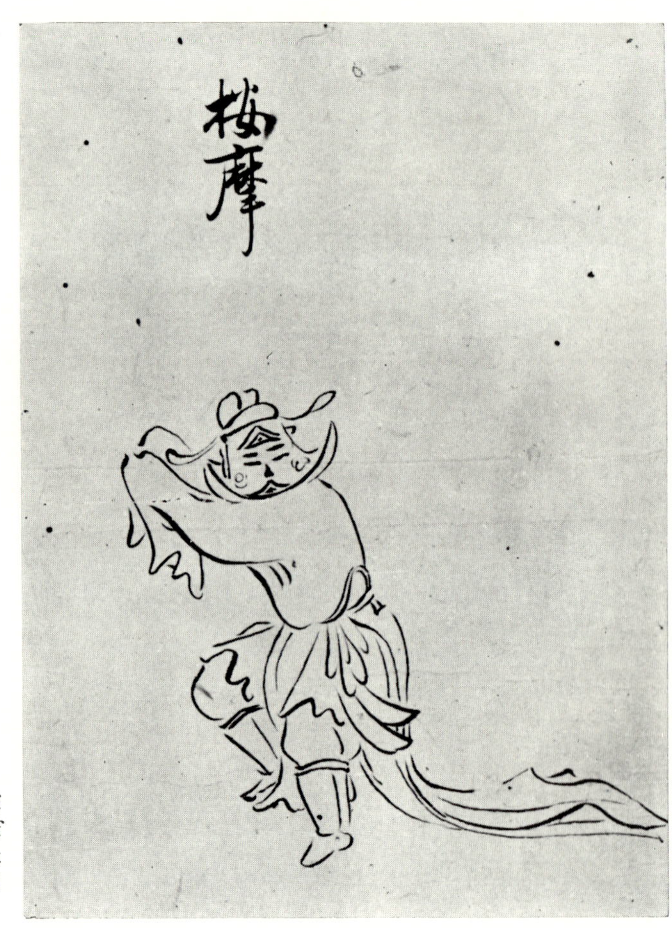

47. *Ama.* Detail from the *Shinzei kogakuzu* (Shinzei's Illustrations of Ancient Music). Monochrome ink handscroll. Twelfth century. Yōmei Bunko, Kyoto.

48. Soriko. Paper mask. Shitennō-ji, Osaka.

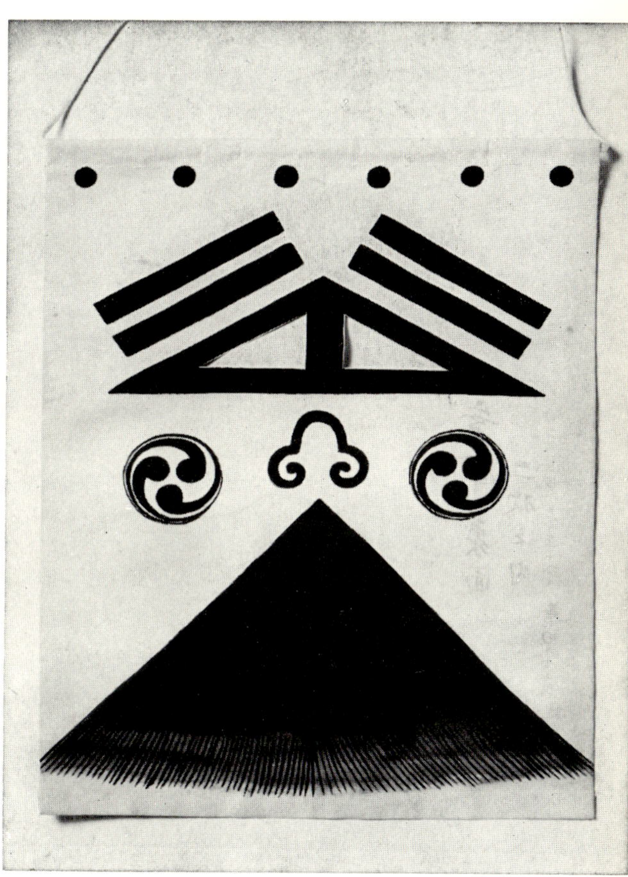

49. Ama. Paper mask. Shitennō-ji, Osaka.

52 (right). Saisōrō. Japanese cypress with kaolin base and colors. H. 19.5, w. 16, dpt. 10 cm. Latter half of twelfth century. Tamukeyama Shrine, Nara.
The only "old man's dance" in the Bugaku repertory, *Saisōrō* has to be performed by an old man of high rank. The dancer is expected to die within a year of presenting the piece, and today performances are rare. The contents of the dance, though not entirely clear, probably demonstrate the impermanence of life.

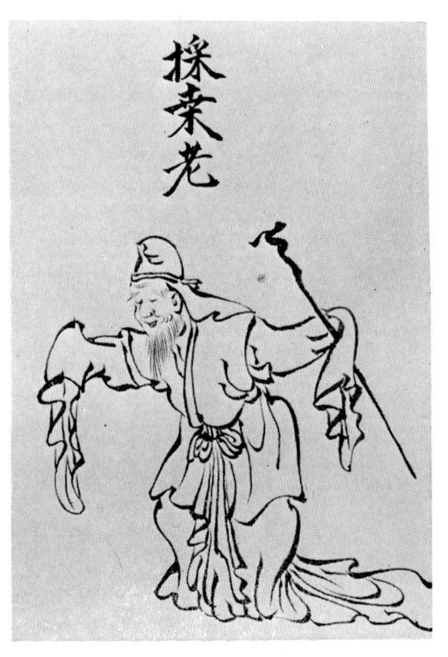


51 (left). Saisōrō. Unidentified wood, *sabi urushi* priming (cloth reinforcement on the back), and kaolin base with colors. H. 21.4, w. 15.9, dpt. 9.1 cm. 1249. Itsukushima Shrine, Hiroshima Prefecture.
Most Saisōrō are typological descendants of this mask, the second-oldest example. The wrinkles lining the forehead and cheeks, as well as the detached chin, resemble those of the Nō mask Okina (pl. 8). (See pls. 158–59 for details and pls. 176–77 for inscription on back.)

50. *Saisōrō*. Detail from the *Shinzei kogakuzu* (Shinzei's Illustrations of Ancient Music). Monochrome ink handscroll. Twelfth century. Tokyo University of Fine Arts.

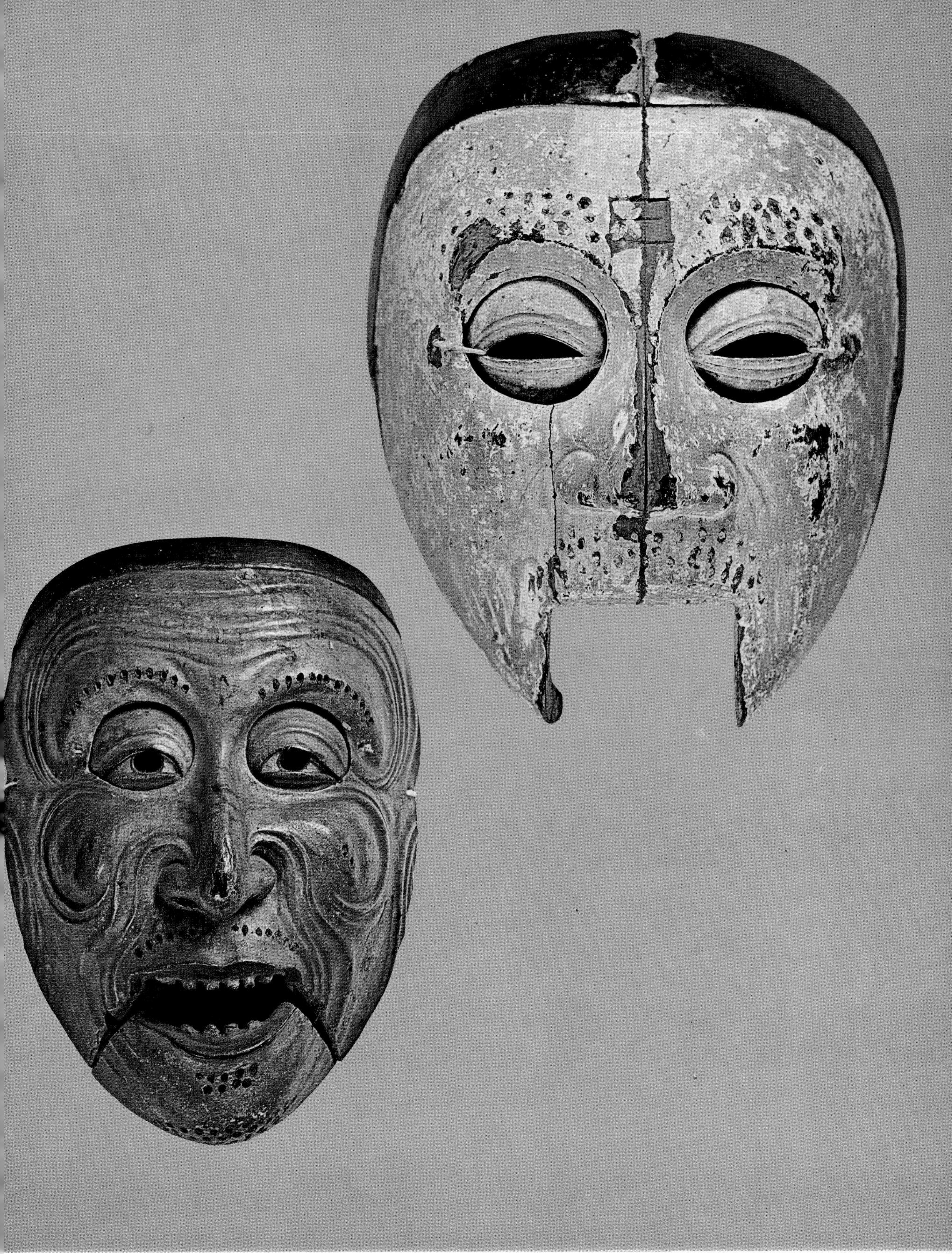

55. Ni-no-mai (Emi-men). 1211. Masumida Shrine, Aichi Prefecture.

56. Ni-no-mai (Hare-men). 1211. Masumida Shrine, Aichi Prefecture.

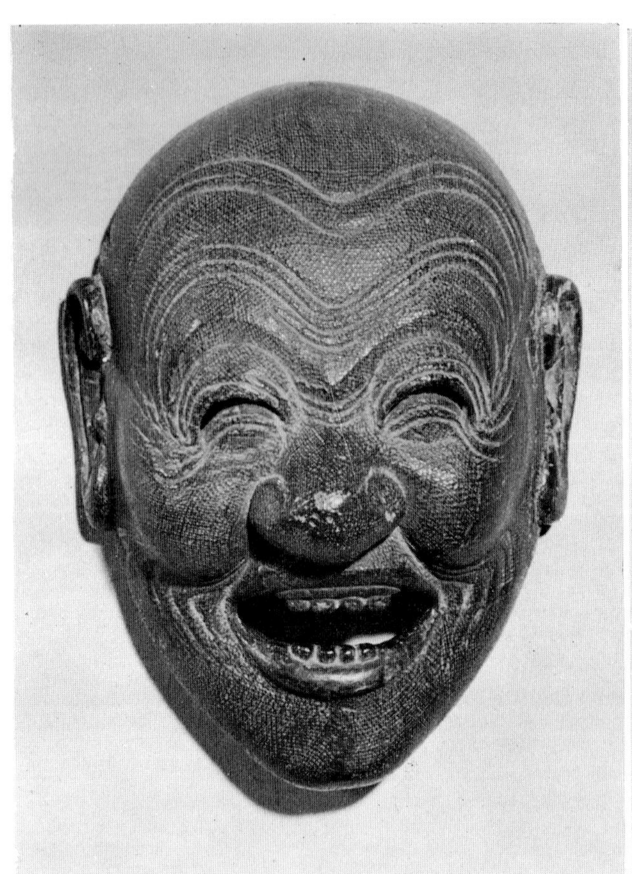

53. Ni-no-mai (Emi-men). Restoration date 1178. Atsuta Shrine, Nagoya.

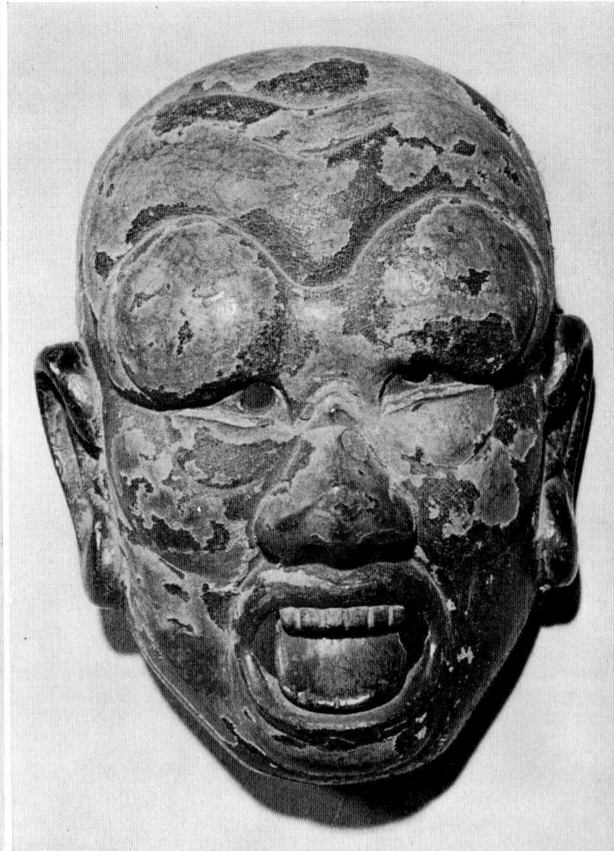

54. Ni-no-mai (Hare-men). Restoration date 1178. Atsuta Shrine, Nagoya.

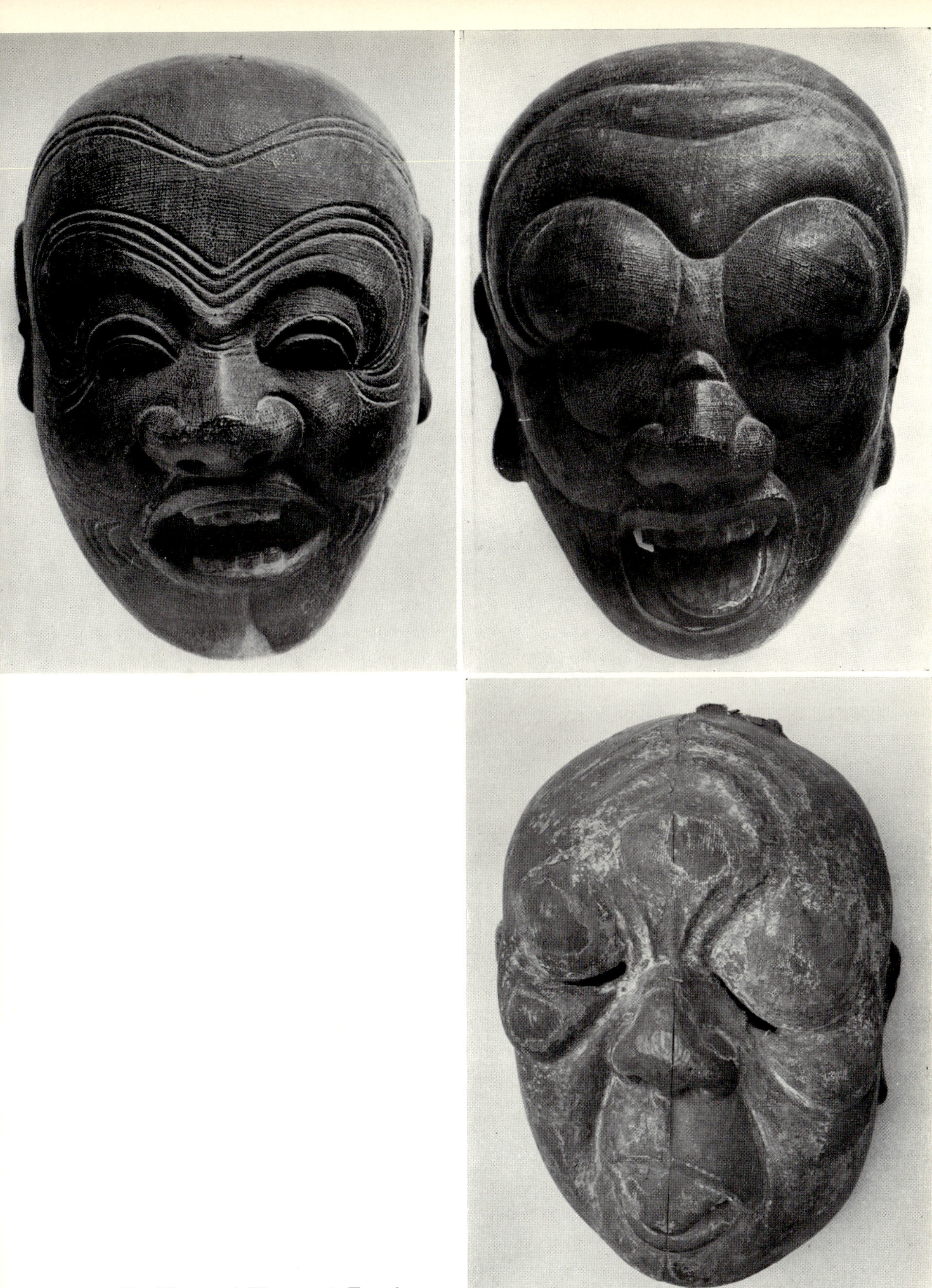

57. Ni-no-mai (Hare-men). Tamukeyama Shrine, Nara.

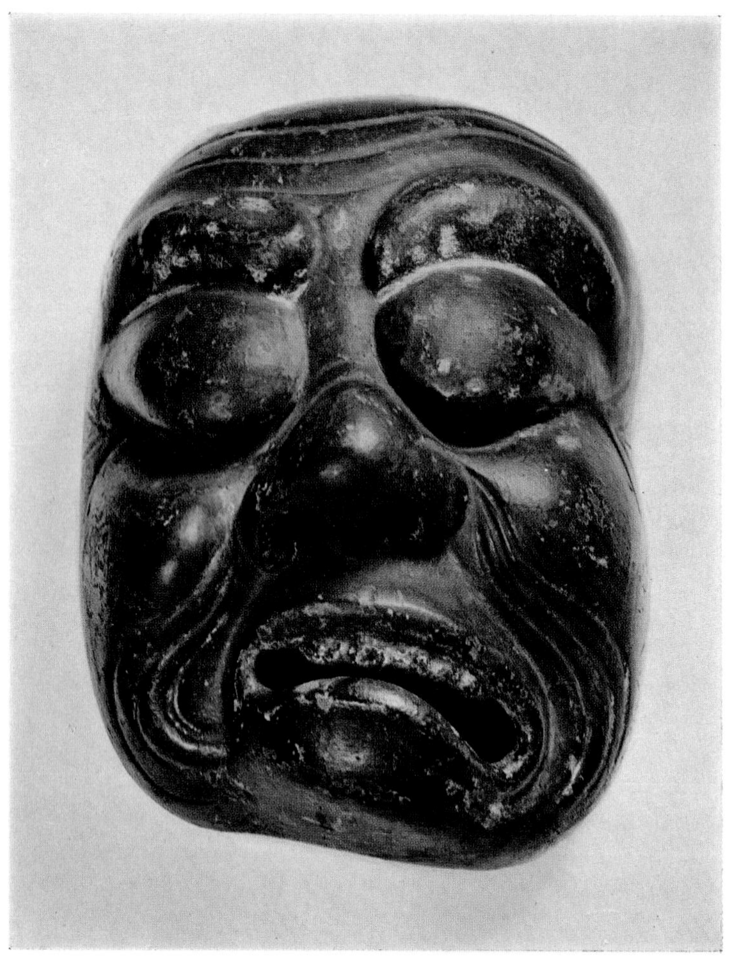

58–59. Ni-no-mai (Hare-men on left and Emi-men on right), by Gyōmyō. Japanese cypress, *sabi urushi* priming, and kaolin base with colors. Emi-men h. 26.6, w. 20.3, dpt. 13.5 cm. Hare-men h. 29.8, w. 21.9, dpt. 16.1 cm. 1173. Itsukushima Shrine, Hiroshima Prefecture.

The old man and the old woman of *Ni-no-mai* mockingly imitate the dancers of the preceding *Ama*. The comic gestures of their blundering dance remind one of clowns. The Japanese idiom "to do a *Ni-no-mai*," to imitate crudely, is derived from this performance. These two masks, the oldest surviving examples, are unparalleled masterpieces of refined, grotesque exaggeration. Humor pervades the curling grin, the puffed-up cheeks, and the distorted features. (See pl. 166 for inscription on Emi-men.)

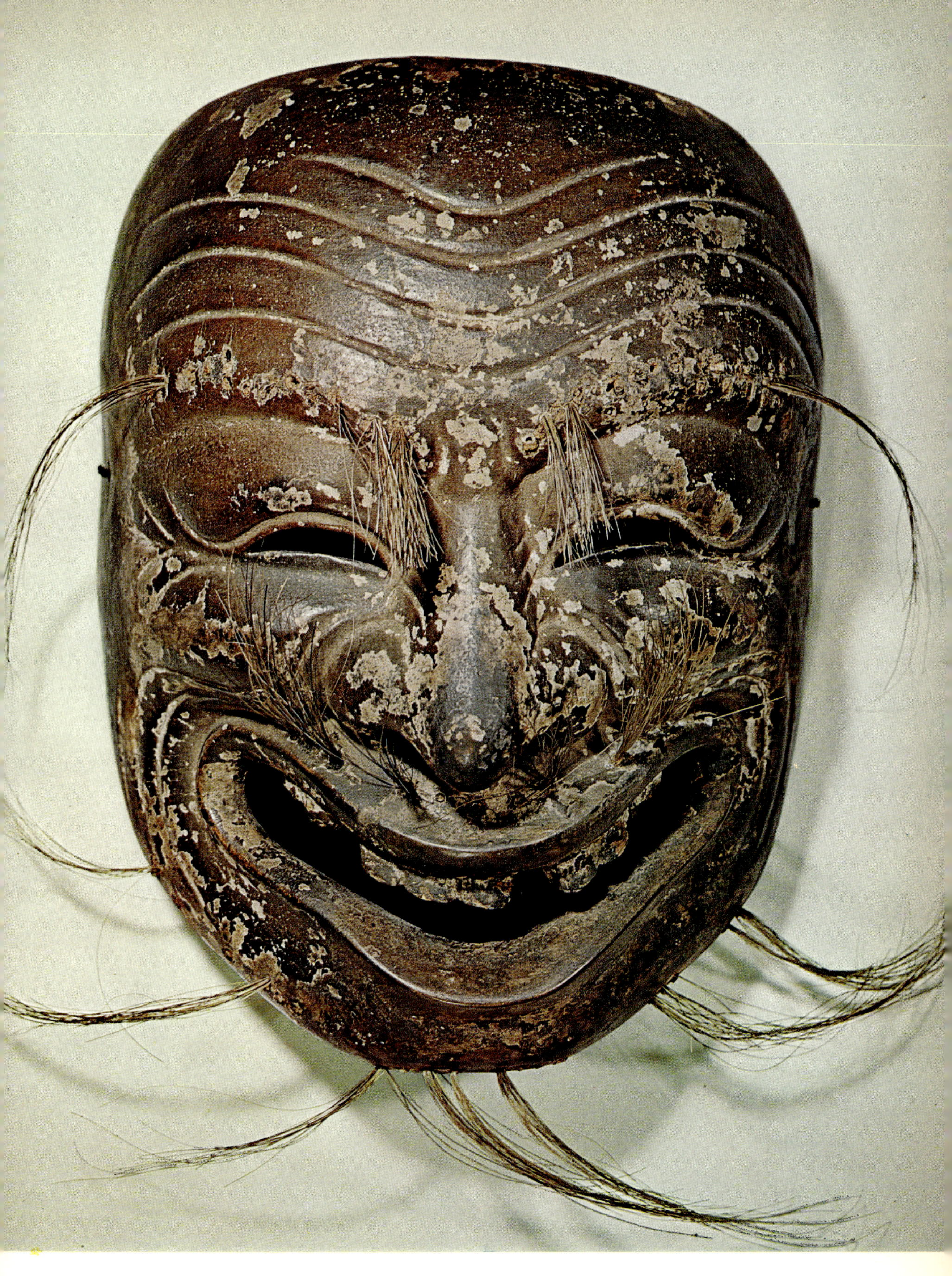

## Masks for Military Dances

### *Shinnō*

*Shinnō* was supposedly first choreographed in China during the reign of Emperor T'ai Tsung (r. 626–49) to commemorate the soldiers who supported the founding of the T'ang dynasty. In the Nara period as many as one hundred dancers dressed in full armor danced *Shinnō* as a representation of a battle scene. Although no longer performed today, *Shinnō* appears to have been danced customarily by four people facing each other, wearing gold armor and shin guards and holding shields and weapons (pl. 60).

*Shinnō* never seems to have been very popular, perhaps because it extolled a foreign emperor. Whatever the reason, the *Gakkaroku,* written in the early Edo period, already refers to it as lost. There are some records of its performance in the late Heian period at the Imperial Palace and as part of a memorial service at Toba Shōkōmyō-in in Ise Province (modern Mie Prefecture). According to the *Ippen shōnin eden* (Pictorial Biography of the Monk Ippen), a memorial performance of *Shinnō* was held for Ippen in 1287 at Kibitsu Shrine in Bingo Province (modern Hiroshima Prefecture). Emperor Nimmyō (r. 833–50) also seems to have been especially fond of this dance.

The single Shinnō mask remaining today belongs to Sumiyoshi Shrine in Osaka (pls. 66, 90). The inscription on the back of the mask, containing the date 1288, shows that it was originally one of four. Noteworthy for the skillfulness of both modeling and painting, particularly of the hair of the eyebrows and mustache, the mask is clearly a stylistic predecessor of such Nō masks as Tenjin and Beshimi.

Remarkably preserved in the same shrine are also belt (pl. 65) and shoulder ornaments used for *Shinnō*. Kept with the mask, they are inscribed in the same hand and with the same date. The belt ornament has the accompanying explanation "belt

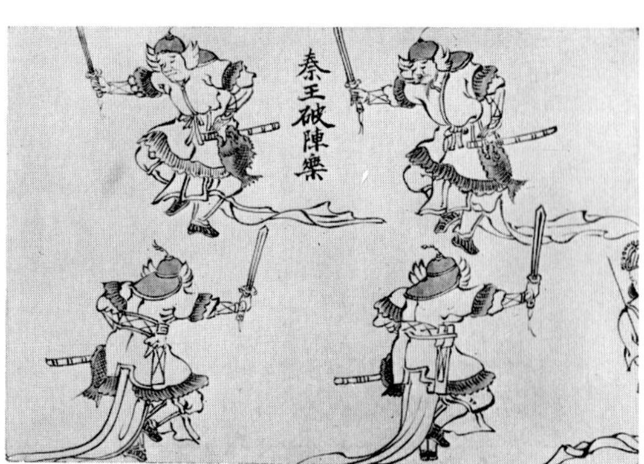


60. *Shinnō*. Detail from the *Shinzei kogakuzu* (Shinzei's Illustrations of Ancient Music). Monochrome ink handscroll. Twelfth century. Tokyo University of Fine Arts.

ornament for *Shinnō*" *(Shinnō kawame)*. There seem to have been four belt ornaments and eight shoulder guards. Four shields used in *Shinnō* are also still extant.

Each costume in Bugaku indicates rank and class by its headgear and accessories. Military dances like *Bushō Taiheiraku* and *Shinnō* have costumes resembling the garb worn by T'ang-period tomb figurines and figures of Buddhist guardians. They wear shoulder guards *(katakui,* "biting the shoulder"; pl. 64) and buckles *(obikui,* "biting the belt," or *kawame;* pl. 65) sculpted out of wood and then painted. A dragon's head forms the shoulder guard, so devised that the dancer can slip his arm through the open mouth and then fasten it at his shoulder. The buckle, made to clasp on to the front of the belt, depicts a goblin clenching the belt with its teeth. Most of the ornaments used in performances today come from the Meiji period (1868–1912) or from more recent times. Therefore these accessories from the Kamakura period are very special relics.

*Sanju*

The mask is red-faced with thick eyebrows, bold eyes, inflated nostrils, and a wide mouth. The main dancer, wearing a helmet and sword at his hip and carrying a halberd, dances in a vigorous, heroic style. Although the piece calls for six boy assistants, they are usually reduced to four and sometimes to only two. It is unclear from the records whether the boy assistants wore masks or not. If they did, there is no remaining evidence of such masks.

Various stories explain the origin of the dance. According to one, *Sanju* was both composed and danced by King Shishikutsu (Japanese reading) on the occasion of Śākyamuni's birth. According to another, it preserves a dance expressing jubilation at the retreat of the Silla (Korean) army, as performed by Isakawa Myōjin, a guardian god of mythological times.

There are two styles of Sanju masks. Almost all extant pieces belong to the first type, with a long face and thick, closed lips. The mask at Tōdai-ji (pl. 69) and that at Tamukeyama Shrine (pl. 62) have, or had, fur eyebrows and mustaches. On the back of the Tōdai-ji mask is an inscription (pl. 165) saying that Inken copied the mask from one at Hiyoshi Shrine in the year 1207. Another mask interesting for bearing traces of once having had tacked-on fur is the Sanju at Kushibiki Hachiman Shrine in Aomori Prefecture (pl. 71). A representative provincial example, it was made at the end of the Kamakura period. Other Sanju masks, including those at Masumida Shrine in Nagoya (dated 1211), Konda Hachiman Shrine in Osaka Prefecture (pl. 68), Ibuki Hachiman Shrine in Ehime Prefecture (dated 1305), and Itsukushima Shrine in Hiroshima Prefecture (pl. 67), are similar to the Tōdai-ji mask except for their painted eyebrows and mustache hairs. The mask at Itsukushima Shrine, of unsurpassed excellence, was presented as part of a gift from the Taira clan to their titulary shrine in 1173, along with the famous set of illuminated sutras known as the *Heike nōkyō*.

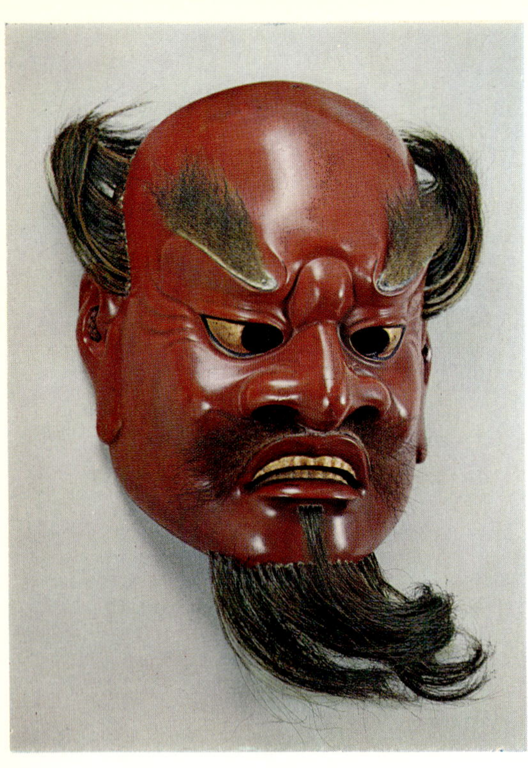

61. Sanju, by Jōkei. Japanese cypress with lacquer ground. H. 27, w. 21.3, dpt. 14.7 cm. 1184. Kasuga Shrine, Nara.
Copied by Jōkei from an older mask at Kōfuku-ji, this represents one type of Sanju mask. This Sanju is very large in scale, comparable to Gigaku masks, and is carved with realistic, dynamic fullness. The present lacquering and attached hair and fur are recent restorations. (See pls. 174–75 for inscription on back.)

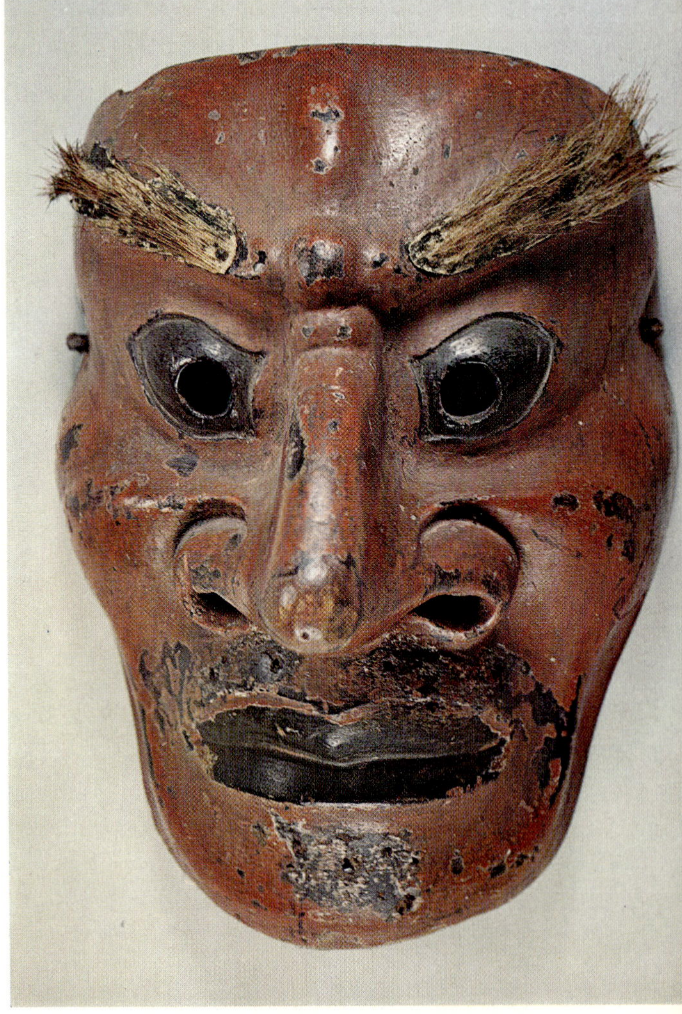

62. Sanju, by Inken. *Kaya (Torreya nucifera),* cloth and *sabi urushi* priming, and red lacquer. H. 23, w. 16.4, dpt. 14 cm. 1207. Tamukeyama Shrine, Nara.
This type of long-faced Sanju mask with enormous eyes, nose, and mouth is most common. The mask is hollowed out so as to be very thin and light, and the eyebrows and mustache are made of tacked-on fur. According to the inscription, Inken made the mask for the Kyoto temple Saishō Shitennō-in. When the temple burnt down, this mask and an identical Sanju (pl. 69) were removed to Tōdai-ji.

It is the oldest existing Sanju mask. Another Sanju mask, housed at Hōryū-ji and inscribed with the date 1430, seems to belong to the Tōdai-ji type; yet because of its rather round head, it bears a closer resemblance to the Kitoku at Tōdai-ji (pl. 92).

The other Sanju type is represented by a unique mask now at Kasuga Shrine (pl. 61), originally at Kōfuku-ji. Large in scale, it covers much of the head. Real hair has been used above the ears and on the chin. The brows gather above the slightly crossed eyes. Bared teeth flash from the grimacing mouth. Unfortunately the mask has been repainted, although in the traditional red color. From the incised inscription on the back (pls. 174–75) we know that this mask was copied by Jōkei in 1184 from a mask at Gangō-ji. There is an almost certain connection between this mask and a mask worn with a *hōkammuri* helmet mentioned in the section on *Sanju* in the *Kyōkunshō*. According to that document, during the reign of Emperor Gemmei (r. 707–15) there was a Sanju mask in the treasure house of Gangō-ji, and a copy of it was in the Yamashina-dera subtemple of Kōfuku-ji. When the Gangō-ji treasure house burnt down during the Bunji era (1185–90), another copy was made. There are no inconsistencies in these dates. The generous and confident carving of the mask copied from the Kōfuku-ji mask is close indeed to the Gigaku masks of the Nara period, making it highly possible that the mask was copied from an eighth-century mask. The carver was the eminent Jōkei, who, working at the beginning of the Kamakura period, belonged to the main line of the Kei school of sculptors situated in Nara, which revived the old Nara style of sculpture infused with a new realistic spirit.

*Kitoku*

Kitoku, like Sanju, represents a king: variously identified as either the Chinese marquis Kuei Te, king of the country of Su Shen, or the Hun king Jih Chu, also known as Marquis Kuei Te (Kitoku in Japanese). The dancer wears a helmet with a dragon perched on top, carries a sword at his hip, and dances with a long halberd (pl. 63).

Kitoku masks fall into two broad types, as noted in the *Kyōkunshō:* one kind has a human face, the other a mouth resembling a carp's, jutting out and opened to form a large, round, gaping hole. When the carp-mouth mask (Koikuchi) is used, two to six attendants *(banko)* accompany the dancer.

Early examples of the human-type Kitoku, which number about twenty-two, can be divided structurally into three types. The first type, illustrated by the mask now in the Fujita Art Museum (dated 1134) but thought to have originally come from Hōryū-ji, has an oval perimeter and glaring eyes that lend it dignity (pl. 72). The precise, sure carving of this mask establishes its superior quality. One mask at Tōdai-ji (pl. 92) and another at Tamukeyama Shrine belong to the same type. In their simple and realistic flavor they resemble thirteenth-century Buddhist sculptures of deva images, and can thus be dated to the early Kamakura period.

The second type is represented by the mask dated 1173 at Itsukushima Shrine made by Gyōmyō (pl. 73). Its remarkably long face is defined by a firmly set jaw and a flattened forehead. Also of this type are one mask at Atsuta Shrine (dated 1178) and another at Masumida Shrine (dated 1211).

The last type, comprising one mask dated 1228 at Konda Hachiman Shrine (pl. 74) and one originally from Amanosha Shrine but now in the Tokyo National Museum, has an exaggeratedly long face. The sharply delineated fold in the cheeks between nostrils and chin distinguishes the expression of these two masks. They are remarkably similar to Sanju masks, and in certain cases the only way to tell Kitoku and Sanju apart is by color: red for Sanju and green or flesh-colored for Kitoku. Although the two masks of this type are both inscribed "Kitoku," the one at Konda Hachiman Shrine is red and, like the Sanju mask at Tōdai-ji (pl. 69), has a beard and mustache made of leather, which are pasted on the mask and painted over with black lacquer; it might thus best be considered a Sanju mask.

The stylistic distinctiveness of each of the three types is all the more interesting since all can be ascribed to about the same period.

*Kitoku Koikuchi*

There are only five extant examples of Kitoku Koikuchi: one at Tsurugaoka Hachiman Shrine, one at Kasuga Shrine (dated 1537; pl. 75), one in the Tokyo National Museum (dated 1843), one at Hōryū-ji, and one at Tendai-ji in Iwate Prefecture. The beautiful

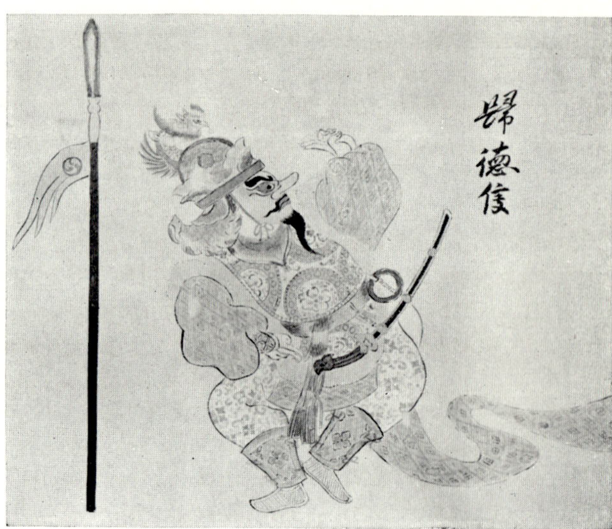


63. *Kitoku.* Detail from the *Ōei kogakuzu* (Illustrations of Ancient Music in the Ōei Era), by Tosa Mitsunobu. Handscroll in colors and ink. Edo-period copy of lost original. Tokyo National Museum.

mask at Tsurugaoka Hachiman Shrine, characterized by a deep structure and realistic carving, has a pursed mouth that makes the mask seem to be whistling (pl. 93). The mask at Tendai-ji, also of this whistling form, should be noted as an unusual provincial example, although it is a rather late product.

The other three masks all have rounded, open lips in the shape of a carp's mouth. The inscription on the mask in the Tokyo National Museum states that it is a copy of a Kitoku Koikuchi in the archives of the Kyoto Imperial Palace. Left unpainted, it was probably made simply in order to preserve the type rather than for use. The Hōryū-ji mask, probably of more recent date, is quite thick and simply constructed and therefore of interest more as a folk mask than as a true Bugaku mask. This is the only Kitoku Koikuchi painted with red lacquer.

*Kitoku Banko*

The attendants *(banko)* of Kitoku are masked only when the main dancer is wearing a Koikuchi mask. Then, according to the *Kyōkunshō,* they dance in unison, and the "first man, standing at the front right, wears a yellow mask, while the last man, standing at the back left, wears a dark mask." When the dancer wears a human-faced Kitoku mask, the attendants wear hats that are used only by unmasked dancers.

The only fully finished, authenticated Kitoku Banko mask is the mask at Sumiyoshi Shrine dated 1163 (pl. 91). It shows an old man with knitted brows and protruding eyeballs. His cheekbones are high, lips thin, and skin a reddish tan; wrinkles fan out from the eyes and cheeks. The thinness and refinement of the mask are to be expected in a late Heian piece. The inscription (pls. 168–69) indicates that this mask was one of a set of four.

The only other mask of this kind is housed in the Tokyo National Museum and is identical in form, though it has been left unpainted (pl. 76). It was made in 1843 by the same carver who copied the Kitoku Koikuchi at the same museum, and is likewise identified as a copy of a mask in the Kyoto Imperial Palace.

Although these are the only indisputable Kitoku Banko masks, another mask with the face of a youth should also be mentioned as being traditionally labeled "Banko." A Kamakura piece housed in the Tsurugaoka Hachiman Shrine, it represents a young boy with smiling eyes, an open mouth, an up-turned nose, and a shaven head (pl. 77).

This type of mask may have been used as a Kitoku Banko, for the *Kyōkunshō* mentions that a "smiling mask" could be used for the role of the attendant. On the other hand, the mask could possibly have been worn in the Bugaku piece called *Shishi* (Lion) by the young boys who escort the lion, since in the parallel Gigaku lion dance the attendant children wore masks with shaven heads and slight smiles. Some evidence, however, contradicts this interpretation. The *Shinzei kogakuzu* records that the two boys accompanying the lion wore their hair parted in the middle and tied in loops over their ears. A young boy's mask with such a hair-do is discussed next.

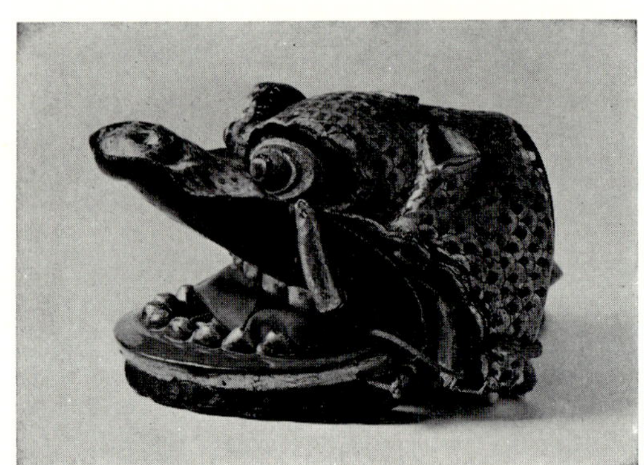

64. Shoulder guard. For use in *Taihei-raku*. Sumiyoshi Shrine, Osaka.

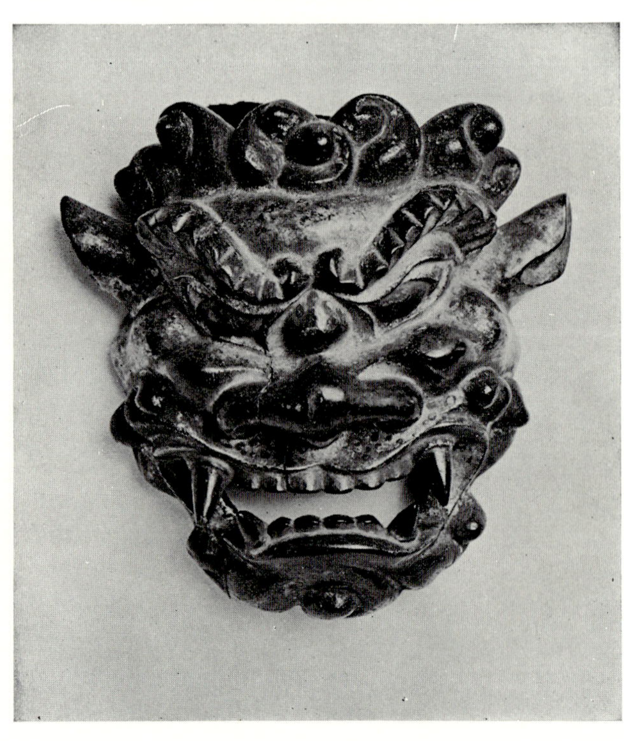

65. Buckle. For use in *Shinnō*. 1288. Sumiyoshi Shrine, Osaka.

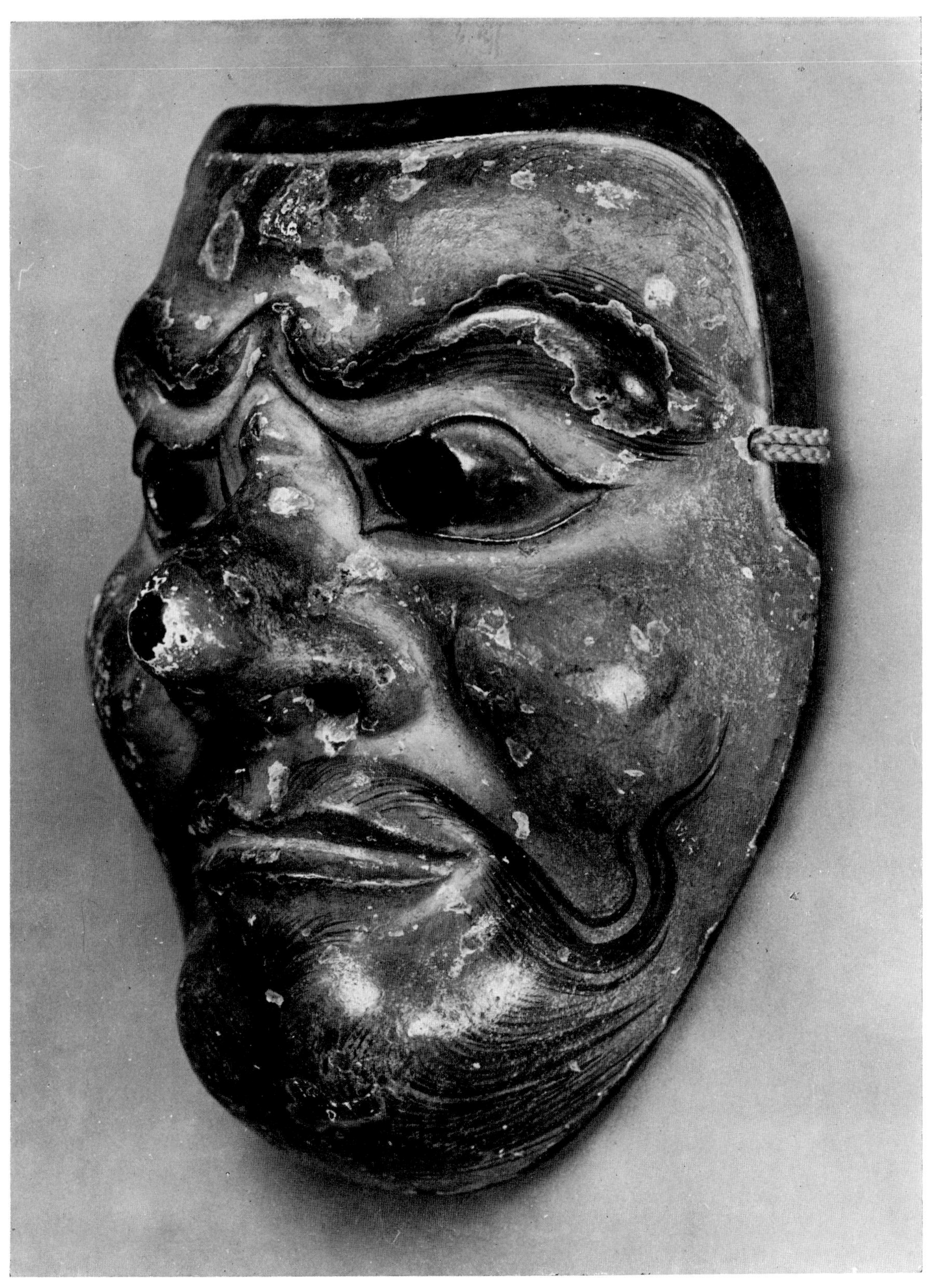

66. Shinnō. 1288. Sumiyoshi Shrine, Osaka. (See also pl. 90.)

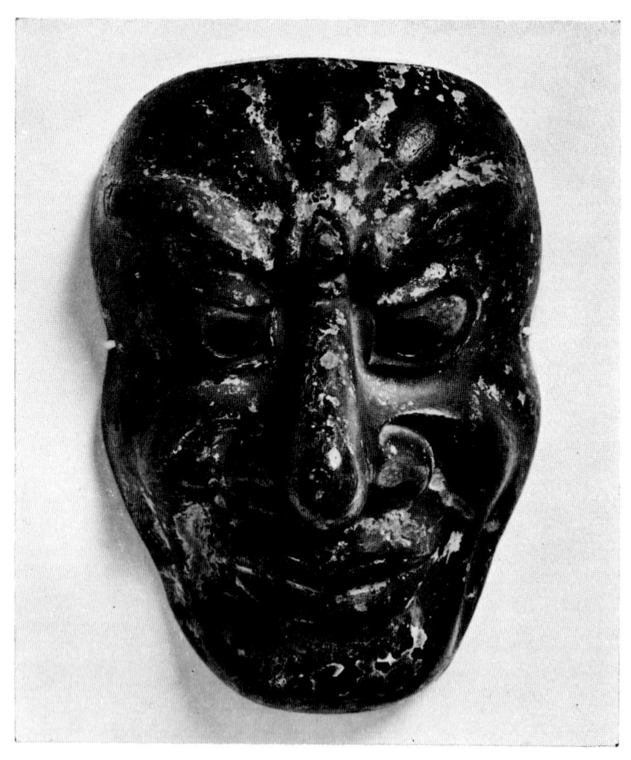

67. Sanju. 1173. Itsukushima Shrine, Hiroshima Prefecture.

68. Sanju, by Gyōen. 1288. Konda Hachiman Shrine, Osaka Prefecture.

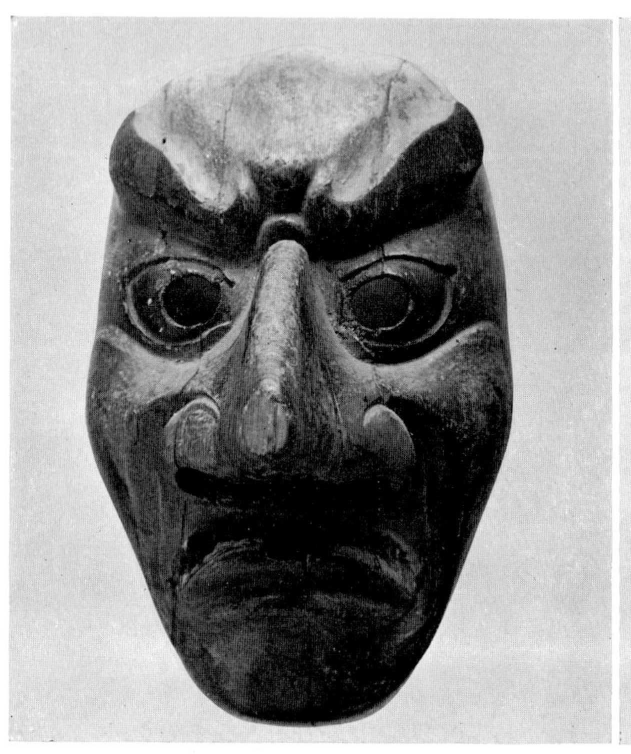

69. Sanju, by Inken. 1207. Tōdai-ji, Nara. (See pl. 165 for inscription on back.)

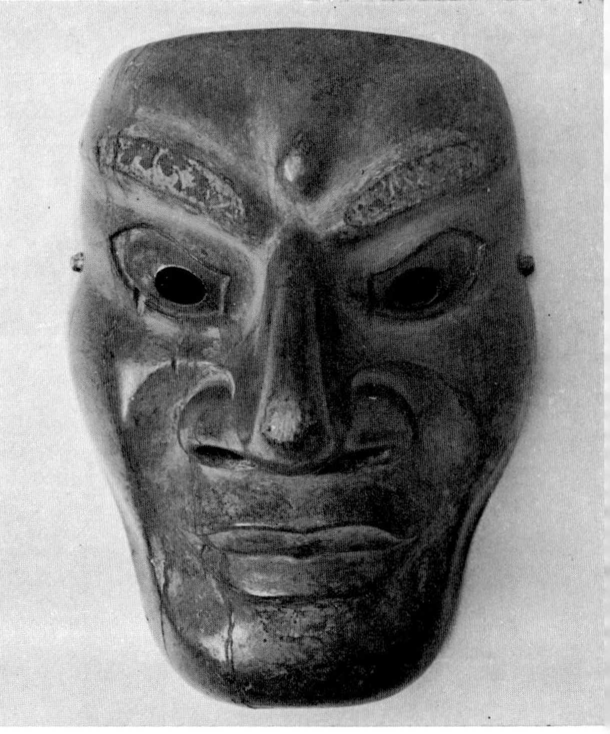

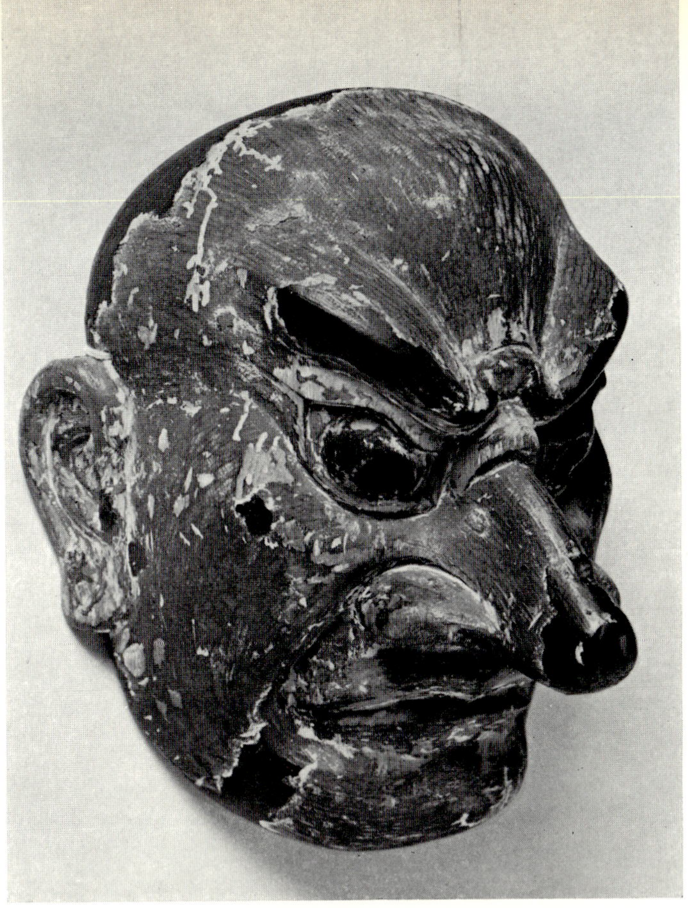

70. Sanju. Tsurugaoka Hachiman Shrine, Kamakura.

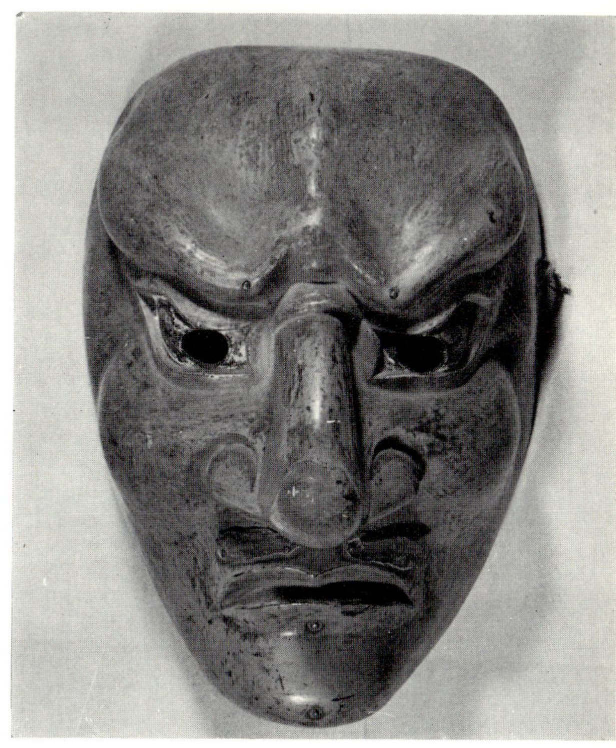

71. Sanju. Kushibiki Hachiman Shrine, Aomori Prefecture.

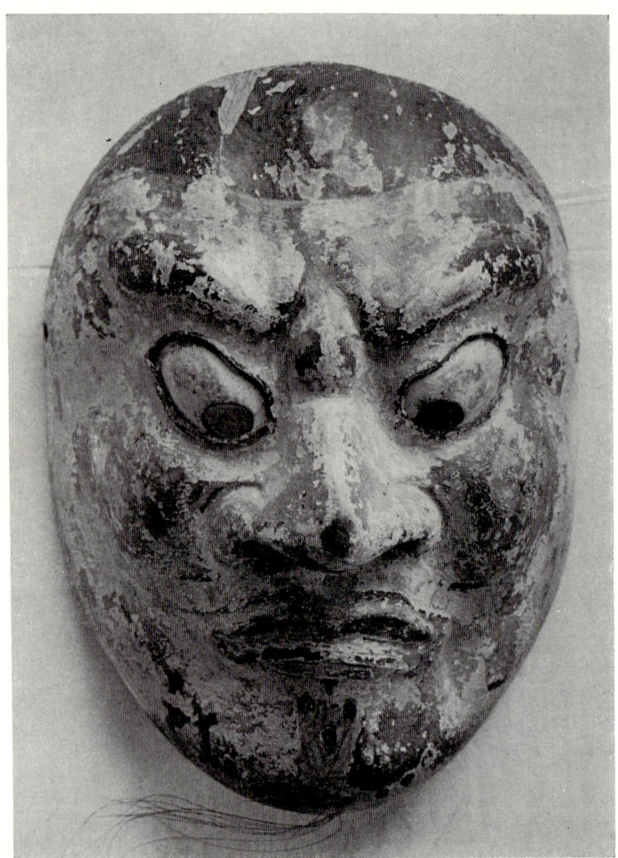

72. Kitoku. 1134. Fujita Art Museum, Osaka.

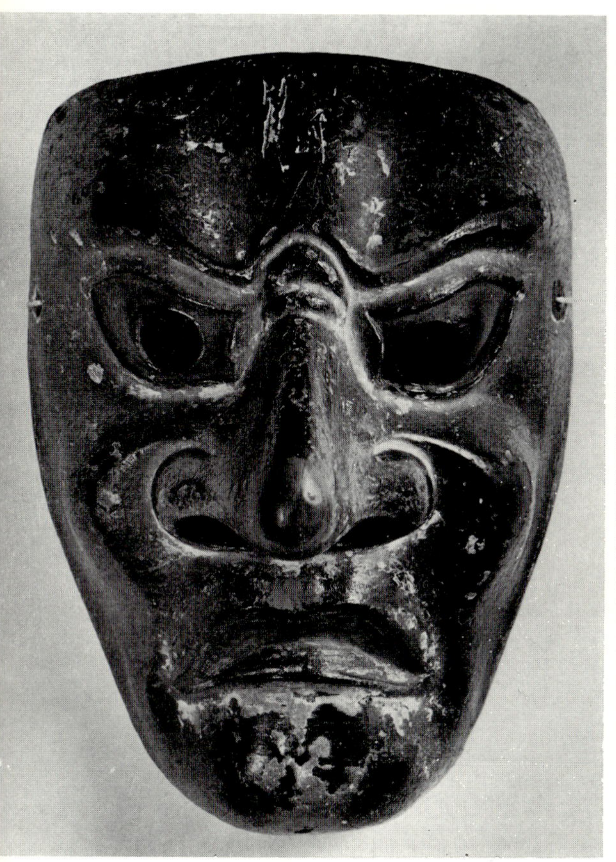

73. Kitoku, by Gyōmyō. 1173. Itsukushima Shrine, Hiroshima Prefecture.

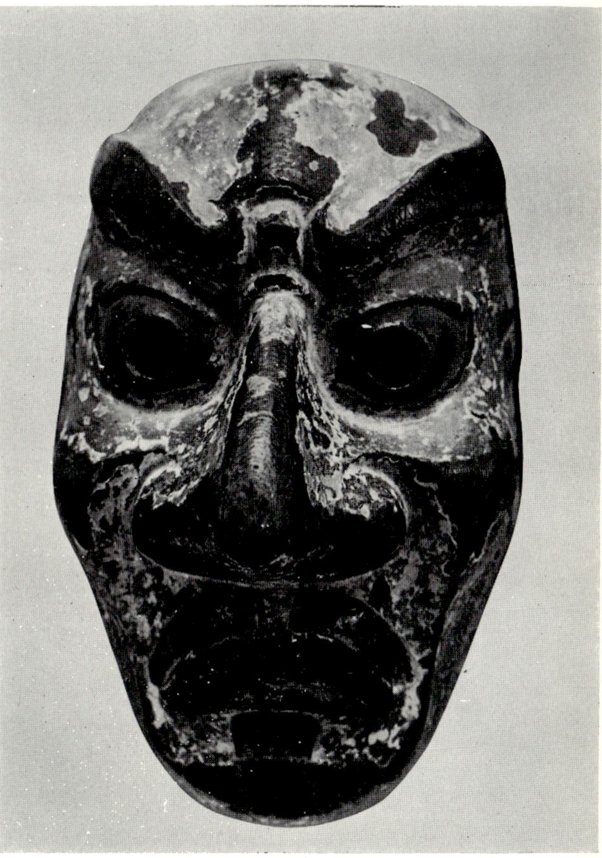

74. Kitoku, by Gyōen. 1228. Konda Hachiman Shrine, Osaka Prefecture. (See pl. 178 for inscription on back.)

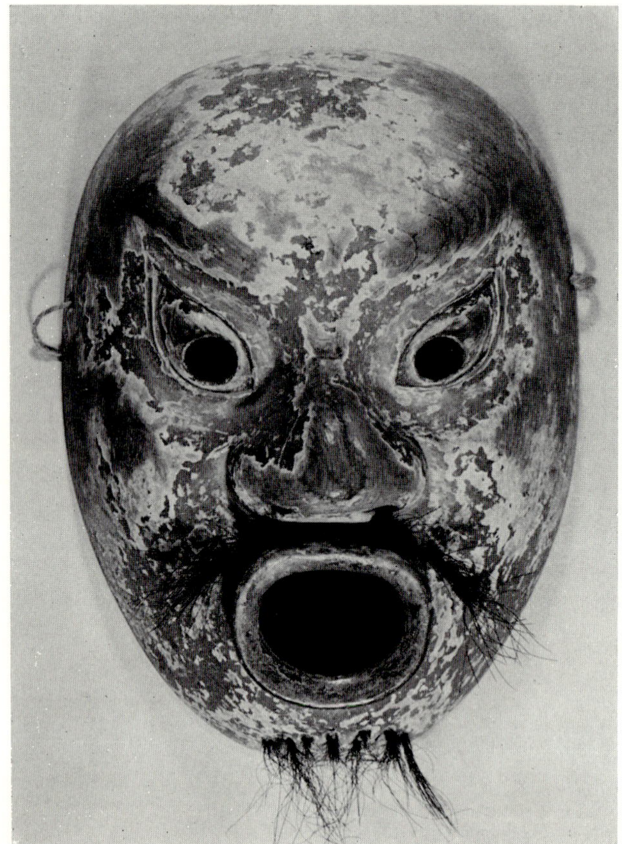

75. Kitoku Koikuchi. 1537. Kasuga Shrine, Nara.

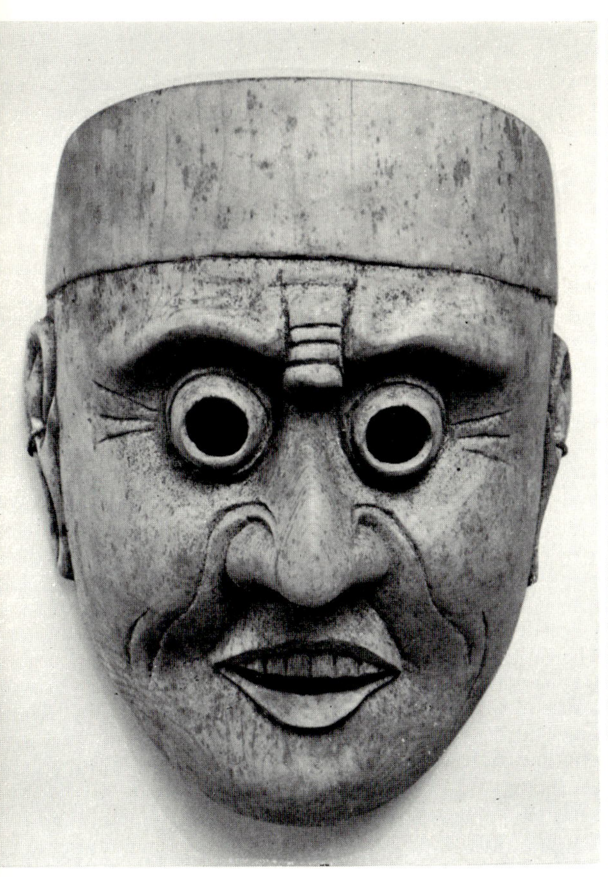

76. Kitoku Banko. 1843. Tokyo National Museum.

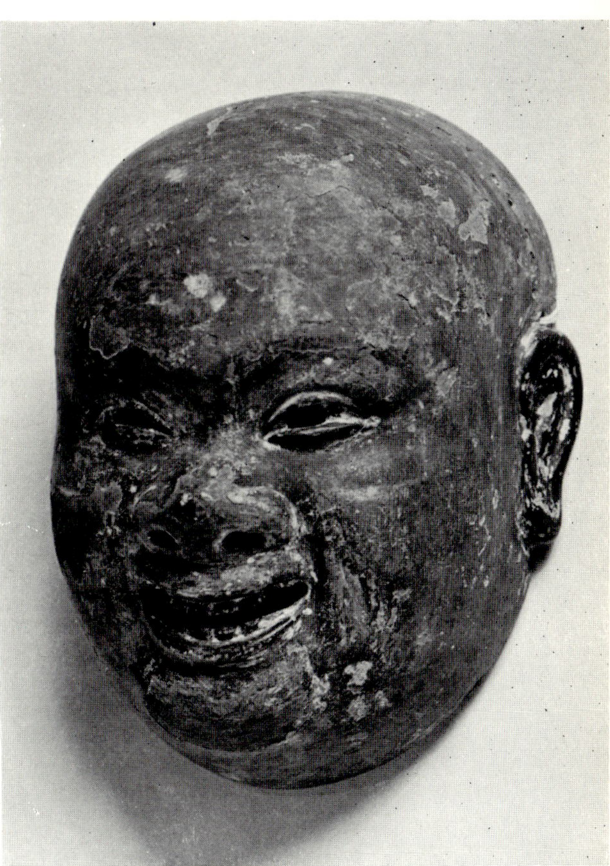

77. Kitoku Banko. Tsurugaoka Hachiman Shrine, Kamakura.

## Miscellaneous Masks

### *Tendō or Warabemai*

Three masks representing pretty young boys with hair parted down the middle resemble the famous statue in Hōryū-ji of Shōtoku Taishi at the age of seven. One mask (pl. 79), dated 1279 and housed in Konda Hachiman Shrine, is inscribed with the name "Tendō," though there is no corresponding *Tendō* dance in the Bugaku repertory. The other two extant masks (pl. 78), both at Masumida Shrine and dated 1211, are labeled by the shrine "Warabemai" (Children's Dance). Possibly these three masks were worn by the child attendants in *Shishi,* the Bugaku version of the Gigaku lion dance.

The name *Warabemai* refers to a number of Bugaku dances performed by young boys or girls. Masks, however, are not generally used in these dances, and therefore no concrete basis exists for calling these masks Warabemai. Performances of *Warabemai* are known to have been frequent from the late Kamakura period on, and even today the Bugaku repertory includes two or three lovely children's pieces, such as the *komagaku* piece *Kochō* (Butterfly).

Records indicate a variety of large-scale children's performances. In 1235 sixteen children participated in the program for raising the center pole of the pagoda at Enkyō-ji on Mount Shosha, Hyōgō Prefecture. At that time five pieces were danced, *Ryō-ō, Nasori, Genjōraku, Batō,* and *Rindai,* presumably without masks. Again, for a memorial service held in 1370, also at Enkyō-ji, the number of children participants expanded from the customary sixteen to twenty-two. In addition to the standard repertory, they performed such pieces as *Karyōbin* and *Kochō.* During the thirteenth and fourteenth centuries, Hōryū-ji and its related temples and shrines held Bugaku performances that included dancers sent from Shitennō-ji and featured performances called the *Shitennō-ji Warabemai.* There is no evidence that any of the various children's dances listed in such historical records used masks. Thus the purpose to which the Tendō and Warabemai masks were put in Bugaku remains a puzzle.

### *Bushō Taiheiraku*

While *Bushō Taiheiraku* is listed in the thirteenth-century *Kyōkunshō* as being performed with a mask, the seventeenth-century *Gakkaroku* states that "today the mask is not used." At some time the mask must have been discarded. No examples remain today, but the similarity of the dance to *Shinnō* and *Sanju* makes it likely that the mask was of a similar heroic type.

### *Kotoriso*

No mask remains that can be definitely described as a Kotoriso. A statement in the seventeenth-century *Gakkaroku* indicates that masks for *Kotoriso* had ceased to be worn in performances by that time.

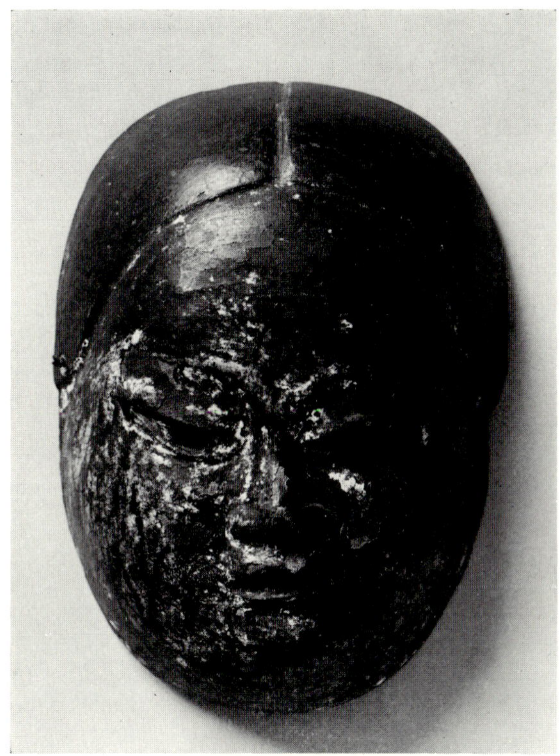

78. Warabemai. 1211. Masumida Shrine, Aichi Prefecture.

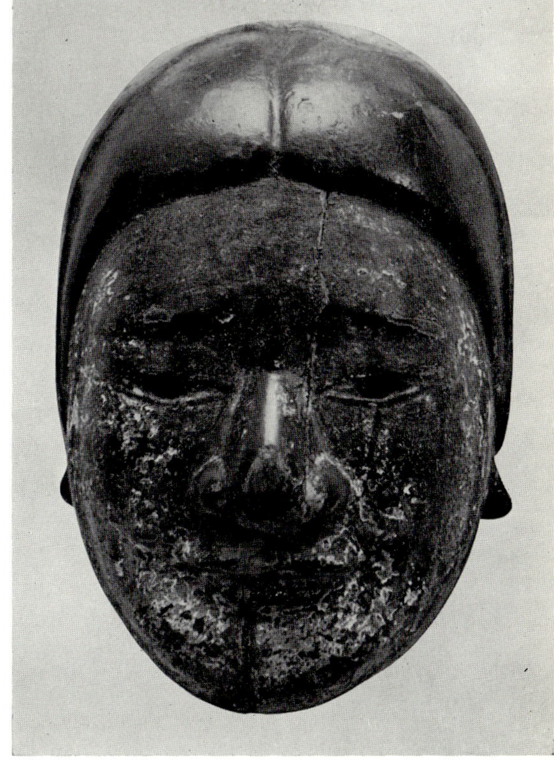

79. Tendō. 1279. Konda Hachiman Shrine, Osaka Prefecture.

*Kotoriso* closely resembles *Shintoriso*. In place of large hats, however, the dancers wear military helmets, and they dance with long swords at their waists rather than with the swatters used in *Shintoriso*.

*Shishi*

*Shishimai,* based on a Gyōdō (temple procession) piece and even today an extremely popular folk performance, has its counterparts in almost every Asian country, such as the Chinese lion dance and the Balinese Barong dance. Usually two or three people dress in a lion's costume, one holding the large lion mask and manipulating its mouth, the others acting as the hind legs and maneuvering the body. At times the lion is accompanied by boy attendants or an old man.

The Gigaku version of the lion dance had two forms: *Shishi* and *Shishiko* (Lion Cub). Although no dance remains, records indicate that at one time a *Shishi* Bugaku dance was performed as well, apparently primarily in connection with certain temple ceremonies. The only indication we have today of what the performance might have been like is from old pictures such as those shown in the *Shinzei kogakuzu* (pl. 80), which depict a man leading a lion by a rope and accompanied by two children and musicians. These representations demonstrate features held in common by Bugaku and Gyōdō, for Gigaku *Shishiko* and the Gyōdō *Hae-harai* (Fanning Away Flies) also include children, while the Gyōdō *Tsunabiki* (Rope Pulling) centers on a man dragging a palanquin by a rope in the same manner that the lion must have been led in the Bugaku *Shishi*.

The exact appearance of the Bugaku Shishi mask is unknown. The Shōsō-in treasury at Tōdai-ji contains a Nara-period Gigaku mask, and the Hōryū-ji a late Heian mask used in a Gyōdō performed on the anniversary of the death of Shōtoku Taishi. There are many Shishi masks made after the Kamakura period, but most are used in Gyōdō processions, while the rest are worn in what has become a separate, independent *shishi* dance.

*Sohōhi*

The dance *Sohōhi* is now no longer performed, and no clearly attributable masks remain. The early popularity of the dance in Japan, however, is indicated by a jacket inscribed "child's costume for *Sohōhi*" found among the treasures given to the Shōsō-in in 756, and the dance is known to have been performed at the dedication of the Great Buddha image at Tōdai-ji in 752. According to the *Kyōkunshō,* the actor was dressed like a Chinese temple lion *(shishi)* and wore a doglike mask. The performance would seem to have been closer to Gyōdō than to Bugaku, for the child actor, wearing the doglike mask and gesticulating, did not dance on stage but merely paraded at a stately pace accompanied by a palanquin (pl. 81).

80. *Shishi*. Detail from the *Shinzei kogakuzu* (Shinzei's Illustrations of Ancient Music). Monochrome ink handscroll. Twelfth century. Yōmei Bunko, Kyoto.

81. *Sohōhi*. Detail from the *Shinzei kogakuzu* (Shinzei's Illustrations of Ancient Music). Monochrome ink handscroll. Twelfth century. Yōmei Bunko, Kyoto.

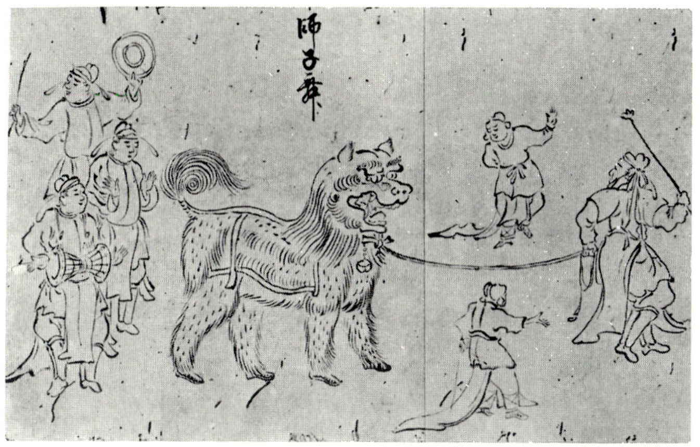


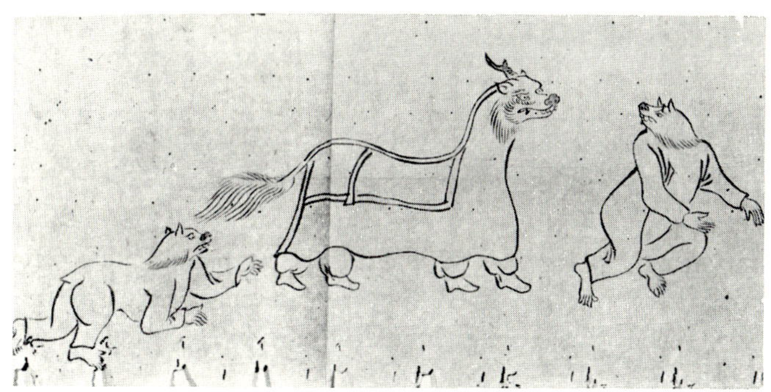

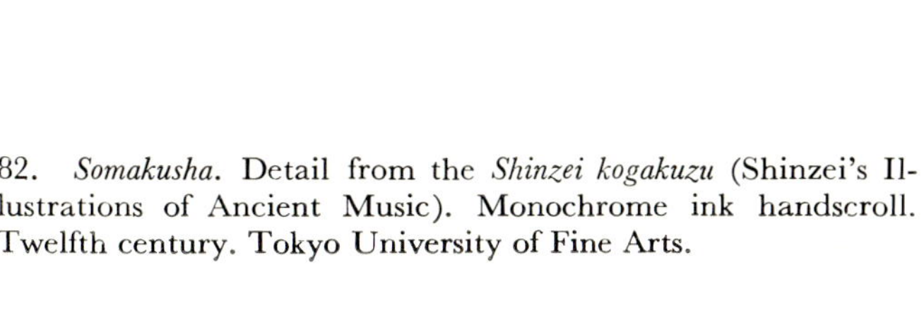

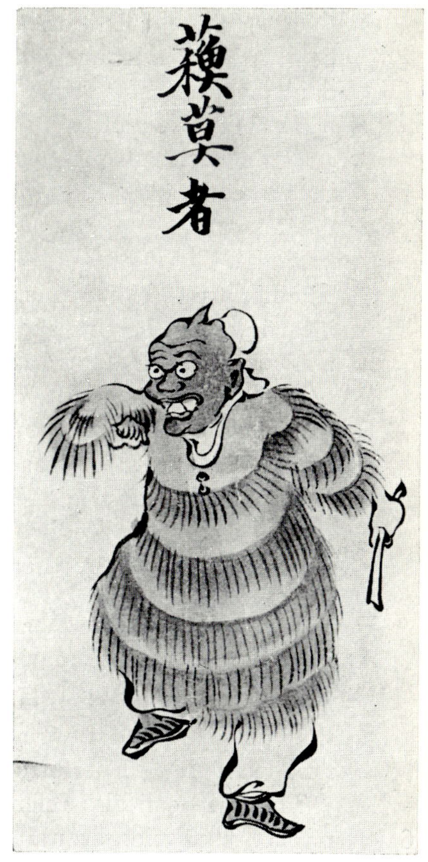

82. *Somakusha*. Detail from the *Shinzei kogakuzu* (Shinzei's Illustrations of Ancient Music). Monochrome ink handscroll. Twelfth century. Tokyo University of Fine Arts.

*Somakusha*

Two stories form the background to *Somakusha,* the music for which, but not the dance, is still performed today in such places as Shitennō-ji and Itsukushima Shrine. One relates that when the legendary mountain ascetic En no Ozunu (active latter half of seventh century), having completed his devotions, came down from Ōmine mountain playing his flute, the god of the mountain danced for him to commemorate his accomplishment. The other story claims that after Shōtoku Taishi (574–622) had forded the Kamenose rapids in Kawachi Province (present-day Osaka), he played on his *shakuhachi* and summoned the god of Mount Shigi to dance in accompaniment. In performance this is represented by a flute player coming on stage dressed in a Chinese-style hat to play the introductory *ranjo* and *netori* movements and by a masked dancer representing the god of the mountain.

For *Somakusha,* as for *Shishi* and *Sohōhi,* there is no indisputably attributable early example. The so-called Somakusha masks at Itsukushima Shrine and Shitennō-ji (pl. 83), with black monkeylike faces, lolling tongues, and long white implanted hair, bear little resemblance to the horned Somakusha depicted in such illustrated books of dances as the *Shinzei kogakuzu* (pl. 82). On the other hand, the old mask in the Shōsō-in sometimes designated as Somakusha, with a beastial face, glaring eyes, fangs, and a single horn jutting out of its forehead (pl. 84), resembles most closely the mask illustrated in plate 82.

*Bosatsu*

The Bosatsu mask represents a bodhisattva, a being who, in Buddhism, devotes his last incarnation to helping mankind. Despite the many examples of Bosatsu masks, only a few are designated as Bugaku masks, the rest being used for Gyōdō processions. Due perhaps to the strongly religious character of the piece, the Bosatsu dance seems to have enjoyed its greatest popularity during the Nara period and to have died out soon after. In 752 it was performed as a part of the consecration ceremony of the Great Buddha at Tōdai-ji. The statement in the thirteenth-century *Kyōkunshō* that *Bosatsu* was acknowledged to be extinct indicates that this dance had disappeared almost completely by the Kamakura period, having been absorbed into the Gyōdō procession.

The term "Gyōdō" refers to three separate ceremonies. The earliest in origin is a circumambulation ritual performed by Buddhist monks who chant sutras while circling the temple building or the main image of worship. Such practices may well have their origins in India, where rituals often take the form of circumambulation. A Japanese example still performed today is the Hana Festival at Yakushi-ji in Nara.

The term can also refer to a memorial service for the dead *(kuyō)* that includes a masked procession around the temple precincts. Lastly, in the Jōdo sect, which came into prominence in the twelfth century, Gyōdō forms part of a reenactment of the *raigō,* Amida's descent to welcome the dead to the Western Paradise of Pure Land Buddhism. This ceremony was a visual enactment of the doctrine that Amida (Amitābha), leading a procession of bodhisattva *(bosatsu),* will come to greet the dying believer and lead him to the Pure Land. The figures, dressed in brocade with uncannily lifelike masks covering their entire head (pls. 6–7), and each carrying a heavenly musical instrument, parade slowly along a raised bridge from the Amida hall to a subsidiary building, and then return to the Amida hall. Amida and Jizō (Kṣitigarbha) lead the procession, gesticulating as they walk. This gives the startling impression of statues come alive. Even today some temples such as Taima-dera in Nara and Sennyū-ji in Kyoto perform this type of Gyōdō as annual events. The Amida *raigō* is also illustrated in Pure Land painting.

The great majority of the many extant examples of Bosatsu masks are used today only in Gyōdō processions. Certain Bosatsu, however, such as the one at Tsurugaoka Hachiman Shrine in Kamakura, belong to a set of Bugaku masks, and they may once have been used in the Bugaku dance *Bosatsu.* All the superior examples of Bosatsu are Gyōdō masks, such as the eight at Hōryū-ji (of which one is dated 1102), the six at Tōdai-ji (two dated 1158), and the twenty-five at Jōdo-ji in Hyōgo Prefecture (pl. 86).

*Sessen*

Nothing at all is known about the content of the dance *Sessen.* The *Kyōkunshō* states that the dance had died out by the thirteenth century. In 1135 a single man performed *Sessen* in the Imperial Palace, but when a contemporary dancer, Ō no Hisayuki, decided to learn the piece, he could find no one who remembered it accurately, and was unable to reconstruct the dance.

Despite the lack of knowledge about the dance itself, two old masks can be identified indisputably as Sessen. The one kept at Hōryū-ji (pl. 95) is marked "Sessen mask" on the back. The face is natural and human without any distinctive exaggeration. It has a fine profile and is hollowed out so deeply that it covers the ears of the dancer. Raised eyebrows, open eyes, and tight nostrils, all precisely carved, give the mask a cheerful, masculine expression. Its resemblance to Shintō sculpture of the tenth century suggests that it is a product of the mid-Heian period, as do similarities in carving between this mask and the curved-nose Kotokuraku at Hōryū-ji (pl. 35). Such an early date would put this Sessen mask among the oldest examples of Bugaku masks.

The other Sessen mask (pl. 85) belongs to Chōgo Sonshi-ji in Nara. Though similar in general form to the mask at Hōryū-ji, the mask is shallower, the modeling is less skillful, and the overall execution shows a certain perfunctoriness. Both sides have broken off. This mask is most likely an early Kamakura piece.

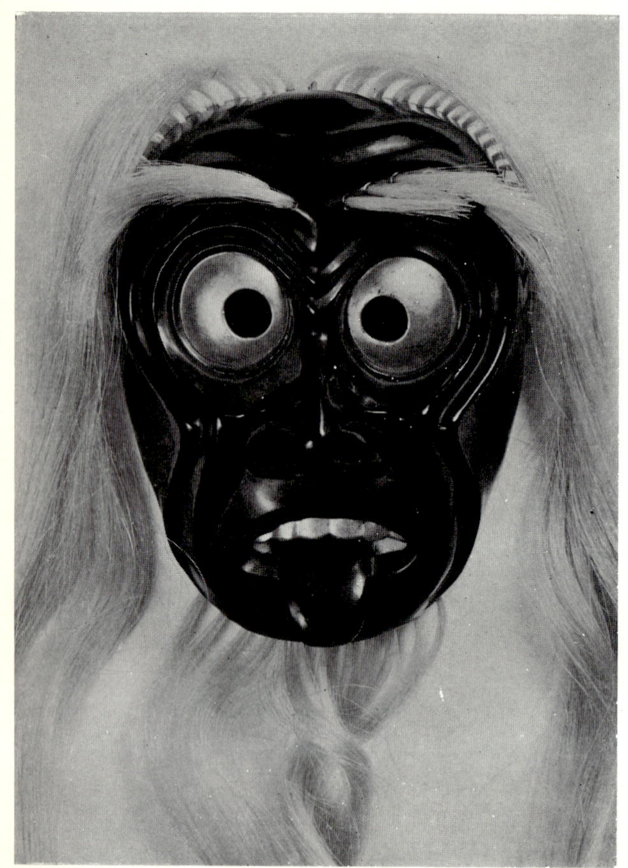

83. Somakusha. Shōwa period (1926–). Shitennō-ji, Osaka.

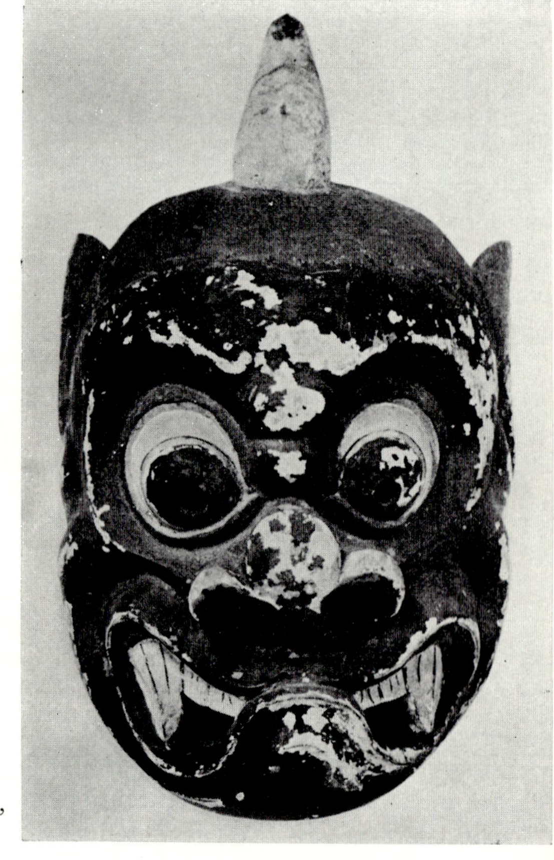

84. Old mask, thought to be Somakusha. Shōsō-in, Nara.

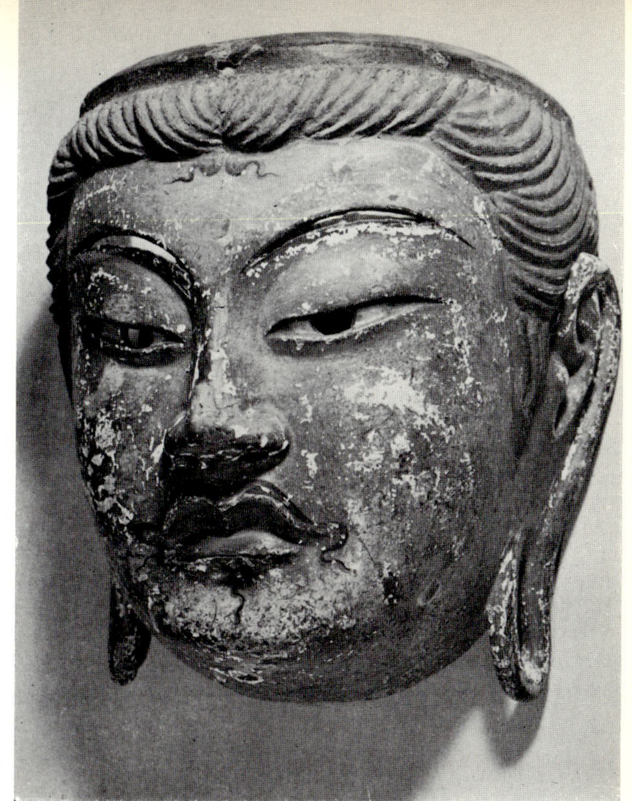

86. Bosatsu. Gyōdō mask. Jōdo-ji, Hyōgo Prefecture.

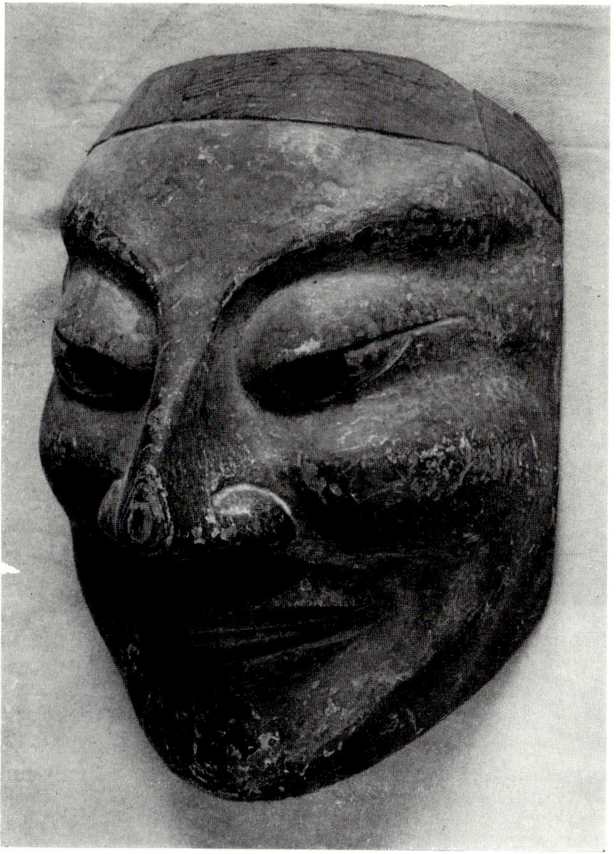

85. Sessen. Chōgo Sonshi-ji, Nara Prefecture.

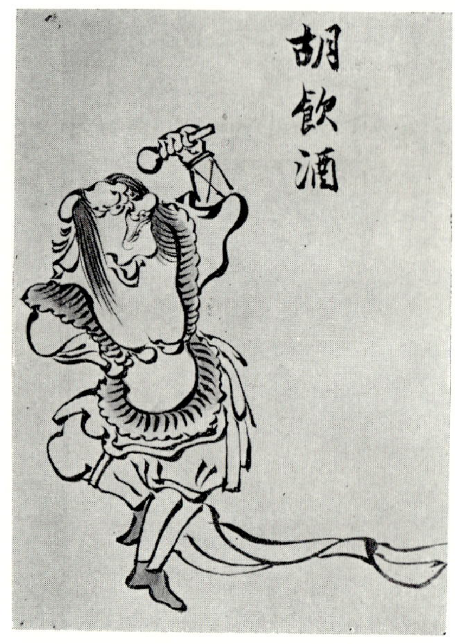


87. *Konju.* Detail from the *Shinzei kogakuzu* (Shinzei's Illustrations of Ancient Music). Monochrome ink handscroll. Twelfth century. Tokyo University of Fine Arts.

## Masks for Dynamic Dances

### *Konju*

*Konju,* tradition says, was composed in China as a representation of a drunk barbarian. The likelihood of a Chinese origin for *Konju* is supported by the other *tōgaku* pieces with such names as *Suiko Kokyoko* (Short Piece about a Drunken Barbarian) and *Suiko Tōtai* (Drunken Barbarian Advance Corps), as well as a Gigaku piece called *Suiko.* There is another story, however, not definitively supported, that the piece was created in Japan by imperial command in the early ninth century, with choreography by Ōto no Manawa and music by Ōto no Kiyokami, two members of the official troupe. *Konju* was described in the thirteenth-century *Kyōkunshō* as being a long-standing piece in the secret traditions of the Ō guild of dancers at Iwashimizu Hachiman Shrine in Kyoto. Down to the present the highly respected Ō family has transmitted this dance, as well as *Saisōrō,* as a celebrated part of their repertory.

According to the *Kyōkunshō,* the dancer customarily drinks a cup of sake before putting on his costume for the role. On stage he shakes a stick representing a sake ladle and dances with broad, sweeping movements (pl. 87). At the end of the piece, befuddled by drink, he retires by a different staircase from the one by which he entered.

Only one old example of a Konju mask remains. Thought to be from the late Kamakura period, it is housed at present in Tamukeyama Shrine in Nara (pl. 88). The mask is quite ingeniously carved, so that at first glance the expression appears ferocious, but on closer inspection, the wide-open eyes look bleary with drink. Thick brows rise into an imposing forehead. The large curved nose, the tense frowning mouth, and the implanted forelocks, neatly parted down the center, make for a curious physiognomy. The original color must have been dark red, but most of it has peeled off, exposing a black lacquer base.

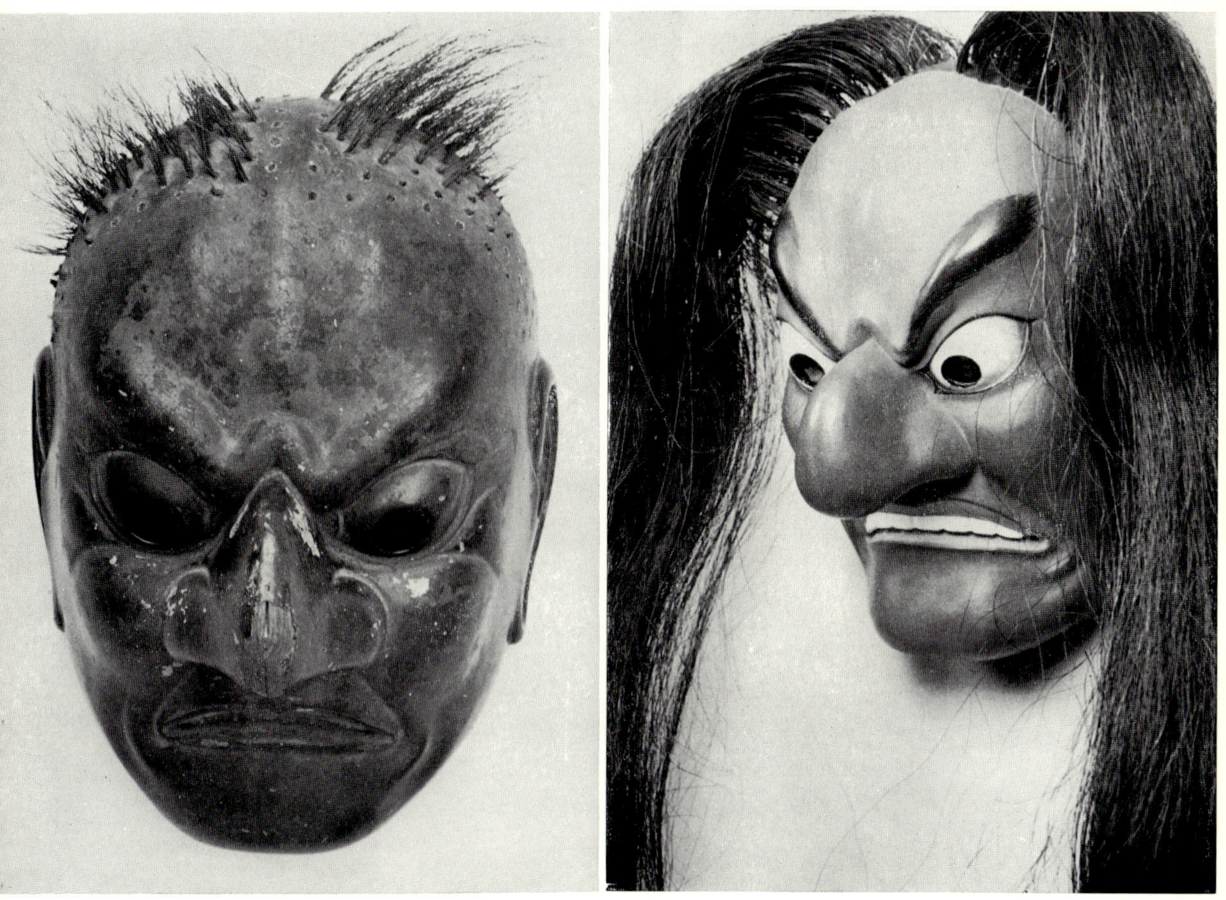

88. Konju. Tamukeyama Shrine, Nara.

89. Konju. 1912. Atsuta Shrine, Nagoya.

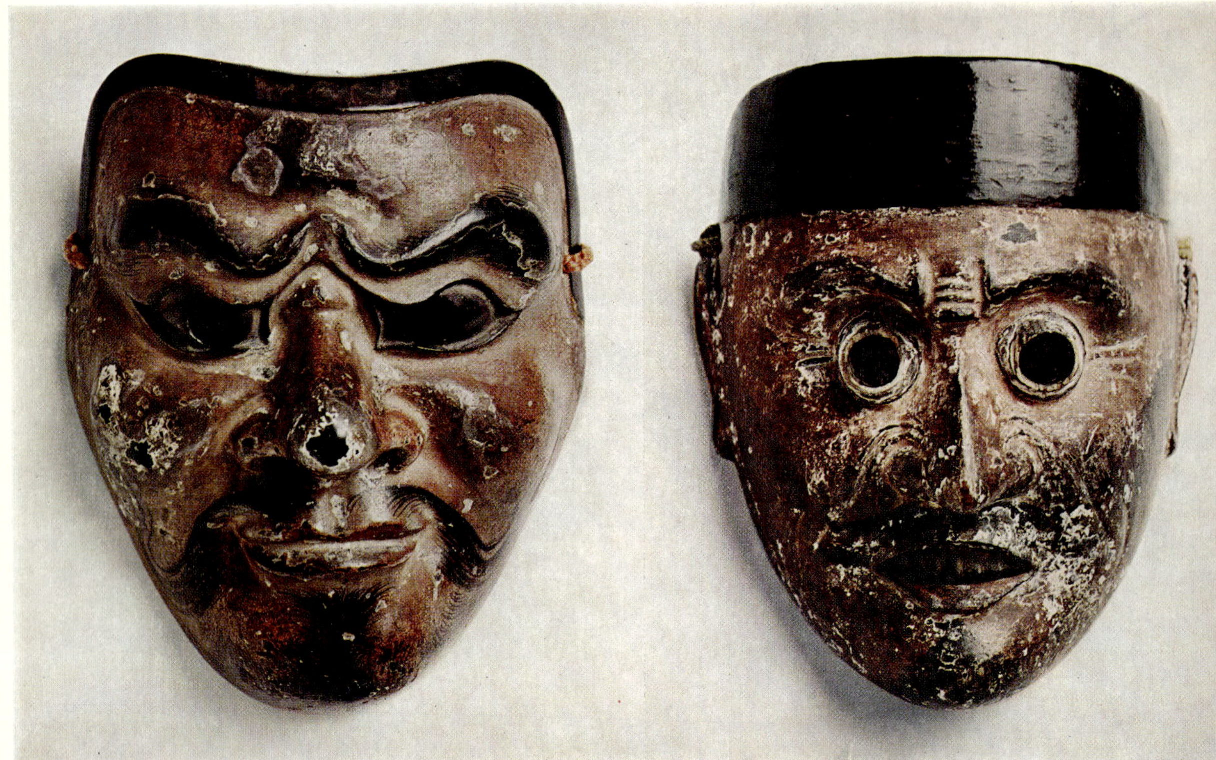

90. Shinnō. Japanese cypress, kaolin base with colors, and *sabi urushi* on back. H. 19.5, w. 15.5, dpt. 9.2 cm. 1288. Sumiyoshi Shrine, Osaka. This sole remaining example of a Shinnō mask is shallowly hollowed out. The careful attention to detail in the carving and the painting, the hair-by-hair brushwork in the eyebrows and mustache, and the small scale of the mask are all suggestive of Nō masks made a century or two later. (See also pl. 66.)

93. Kitoku Koikuchi. Japanese cypress, *sabi urushi* priming, and kaolin base with colors. H. 25.8, w. 19.5, dpt. 18.6 cm. Thirteenth century. Tsurugaoka Hachiman Shrine, Kamakura. A variant of the Kitoku mask, the "carp-mouth" Kitoku has rounded projecting lips. In this early version, the oldest extant example of its type, the pursed lips are only slightly rounded, as if whistling.

91. Kitoku Banko. Japanese cypress, cloth and *sabi urushi* priming, and kaolin base with colors. H. 20.6, w. 18.3, dpt. 11.6 cm. 1163. Sumiyoshi Shrine, Osaka. The four attendants of Kitoku Koikuchi wear this mask and dance in unison. There are very few specimens of Banko, and this priceless example is the only one that is dated. (See pls. 168–69 for inscription on back.)

92. Kitoku. Japanese cypress, *sabi urushi* priming, cloth pasted on edges, and kaolin base with colors. H. 21.8, w. 16.4, dpt. 12.3 cm. Early thirteenth century, Tōdai-ji, Nara.
As a king, Kitoku wears a dragon helmet, carries a sword at his hip, and dances with a halberd. This mask's distinctly realistic sculpturing exhibits strong similarities to the Buddhist statues of guardian beings made during the Kamakura period.

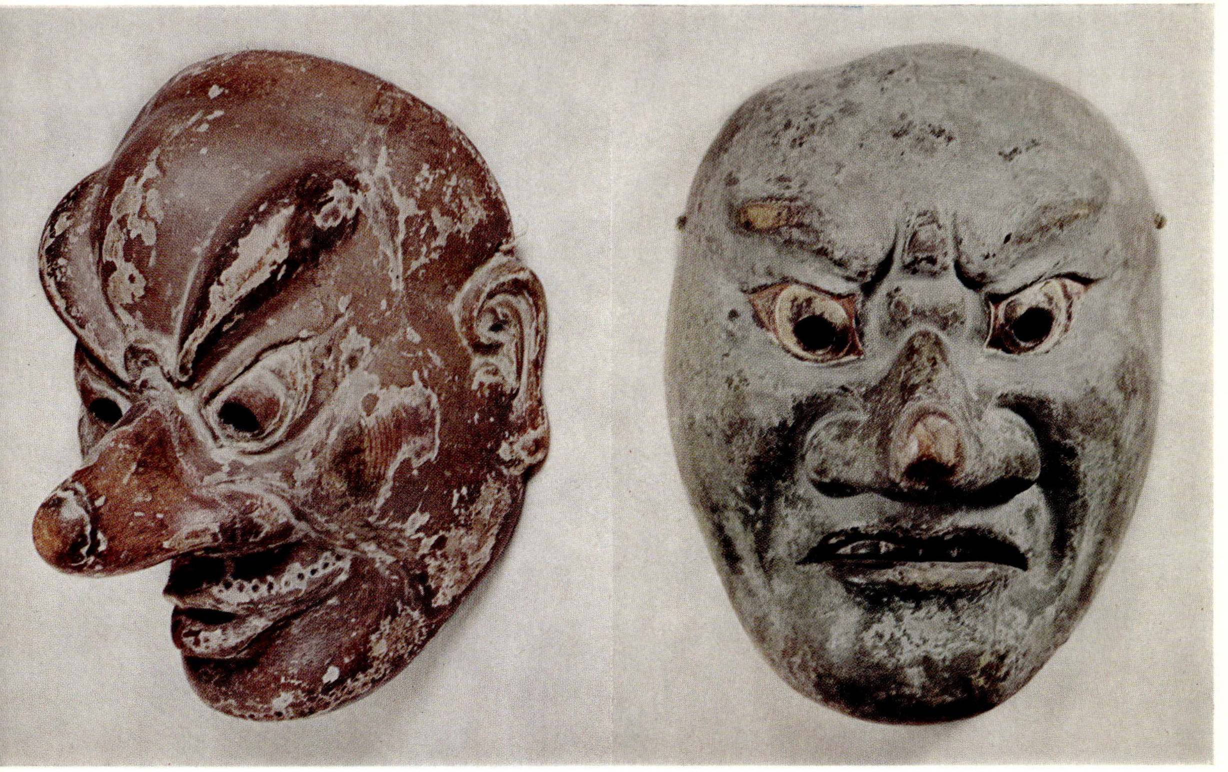

A recent copy of Konju is owned by Atsuta Shrine in Nagoya (pl. 89). According to the inscription on the back, Takeuchi Kyūichi, a member of the Imperial Art Committee *(teishitsu gigei-in)*, copied it in 1912 from an old mask owned by Ō Tadamoto of the Ō family for use in a Bugaku performance at Atsuta Shrine. In both form and size this mask closely resembles that in Tamukeyama Shrine, though it has been painted a yellowish brown. Even though it is a modern mask, it retains the interest of an older style.

*Batō*

The *Batō* dancer circles the stage in jerky leaps, kneeling periodically to throw his heavy corded hair forward and rake it with clawlike hands (pl. 94). Some say this represents the joy of a barbarian upon killing the wild beast that devoured his father. Others claim the dancer tears his hair in bitter pain and sorrow while searching the mountains for the body of his father, who has been eaten by a tiger. Still another story has it that the dance is based on a myth from the Sanskrit Ṛgveda in which a white horse kills a poisonous snake, and that the cords dangling from the mask represent the horse's mane. Regardless of its precise content, the dance, set to a fast tempo, expresses tense, mounting emotion as the dancer shakes his mane of disheveled hair.

A Brahmin monk is reputed to have introduced *Batō* into Japan, making it quite an early import. The early and continued popularity of the dance can be inferred from an account in a twelfth-century diary telling how the courtier Takasue borrowed an old Batō mask from the barracks of the Right and kept it in his house. Startled by a dream commanding him to return the mask immediately, Takasue looked carefully at the back and found an inscription stating that the mask has been made in 802 for the office of *sumō* wrestling. The mask was presumably worn in a victory dance at one of the court contests. For many generations *Batō* has been a part of the repertory of the Shiba family of dancers in Nara. Even now the Shiba family is supposed to possess an old, traditional Batō mask. Although today *Batō* is danced only by one person, in ancient times it was also performed by four dancers.

The most common way of writing *Batō* (抜頭)—meaning "pulling head"—must refer to the dance movement of raking long strands of cord, but one of the alternate character-combinations read with the same pronunciation (鉢頭) aptly describes the mask as "bowl-head" or "crown-head." The prominent forehead is a conspicuous feature of the ruddy face, with its popping eyes, large hooked nose, and tapered jutting chin. The mask strongly resembles Konju. The major difference is that the hair—unlike Konju's real hair implanted in clean straight rows and parted down the middle—is made of twisted navy-blue silk cords planted densely, but randomly, over the crown of the head. Analyzed in close detail, Batō can be further distinguished from Konju by the eyebrows, which do not run together into a V shape over the bridge of the nose, but rather grow out of a double-lobed bulb. The eyes of Batō are distinctly

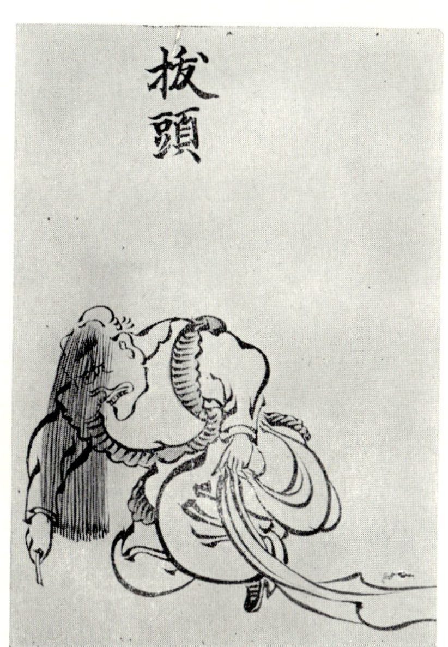


94. *Batō.* Detail from the *Shinzei kogakuzu* (Shinzei's Illustrations of Ancient Music). Monochrome ink handscroll. Twelfth century. Tokyo University of Fine Arts.

crossed while those of Konju look outward, and Batō bares both rows of teeth while Konju displays only the upper teeth.

Today there are at least twenty old masks dispersed around Honshu and Shikoku, including famous examples at Hōryū-ji (dated 1144; pl. 97), at Sumiyoshi Shrine in Osaka (dated 1161; pl. 98), at Itsukushima Shrine, made by Gyōmyō (dated 1173; pl. 96), at Atsuta Shrine (pl. 99), and at Masumida Shrine (one dated 1211). The well-known mask at Hōryū-ji (pl. 97) is the oldest, but regrettably the hair is new and the front and back have been relacquered. As a masterpiece of invention, the mask at Itsukushima Shrine (pl. 96), though slightly damaged, is unexcelled for restrained technique and malicious expression. The unusual sunken cheeks and tapered chin of the Sumiyoshi Shrine mask (pl. 98) suggest a grim austerity, but unfortunately a part of the surface has been repainted and the hair has been replaced.

A newly discovered mask from Seto Shrine in Yokohama (pl. 100) deserves notice for its red lacquer inscription, which tells that the mask was made in 1219 following a revelation in a dream to the carver, Unkei, the leader of the Kei school of Buddhist sculptors. The precise, confident carving technique that characterizes this large and rather unusually modeled mask make the date quite plausible. The thick sculpting of the muscles and bulging veins is similar to the image of Kongō Rikishi at Tōdai-ji, also made by the Kei school. The handwriting of the inscription is convincingly old. Regardless of the truth of the attribution to Unkei, this novel mask is a noteworthy work among the extant examples of Batō.

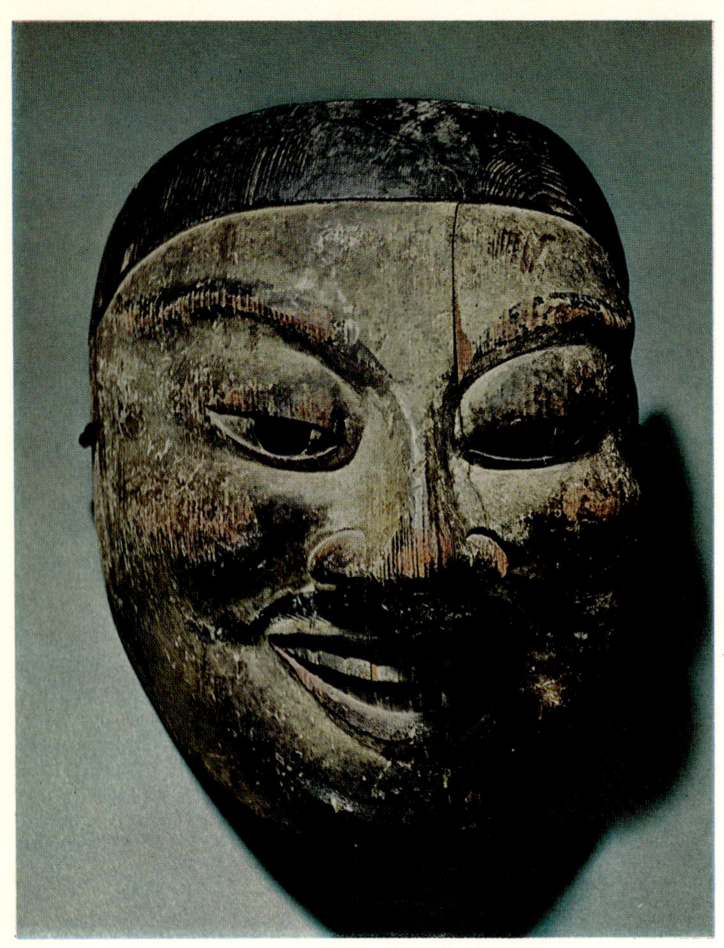

95. Sessen. Japanese cypress with kaolin base and colors. H. 20.8, w. 16.5, dpt. 12 cm. Late tenth or early eleventh century. Hōryū-ji, Nara Prefecture.
The full silhouette, the three-dimensionality, and the simple carving of this mask resemble early Shintō sculpture. The contents of the dance, which had died out by the Kamakura period, are completely unknown.

96. Batō, by Gyōmyō. Japanese cypress, *sabi urushi* priming (cloth reinforcement on the back), and red lacquer. H. 29.7, w. 21.8, dpt. 15.5 cm. 1173. Itsukushima Shrine, Hiroshima Prefecture.
Lashing long blue cords of hair against his red lacquered mask, the dancer of *Batō* expresses the bitter remorse of a young barbarian on discovering his father was eaten by a tiger, or, according to another story, the revengeful glee of having vanquished the wild beast that killed his father. This thinly carved mask, produced at the height of Bugaku mask making, expresses repressed malice in its crossed eyes and sharply curved nose and eyebrows. (See pl. 167 for inscription on back.)

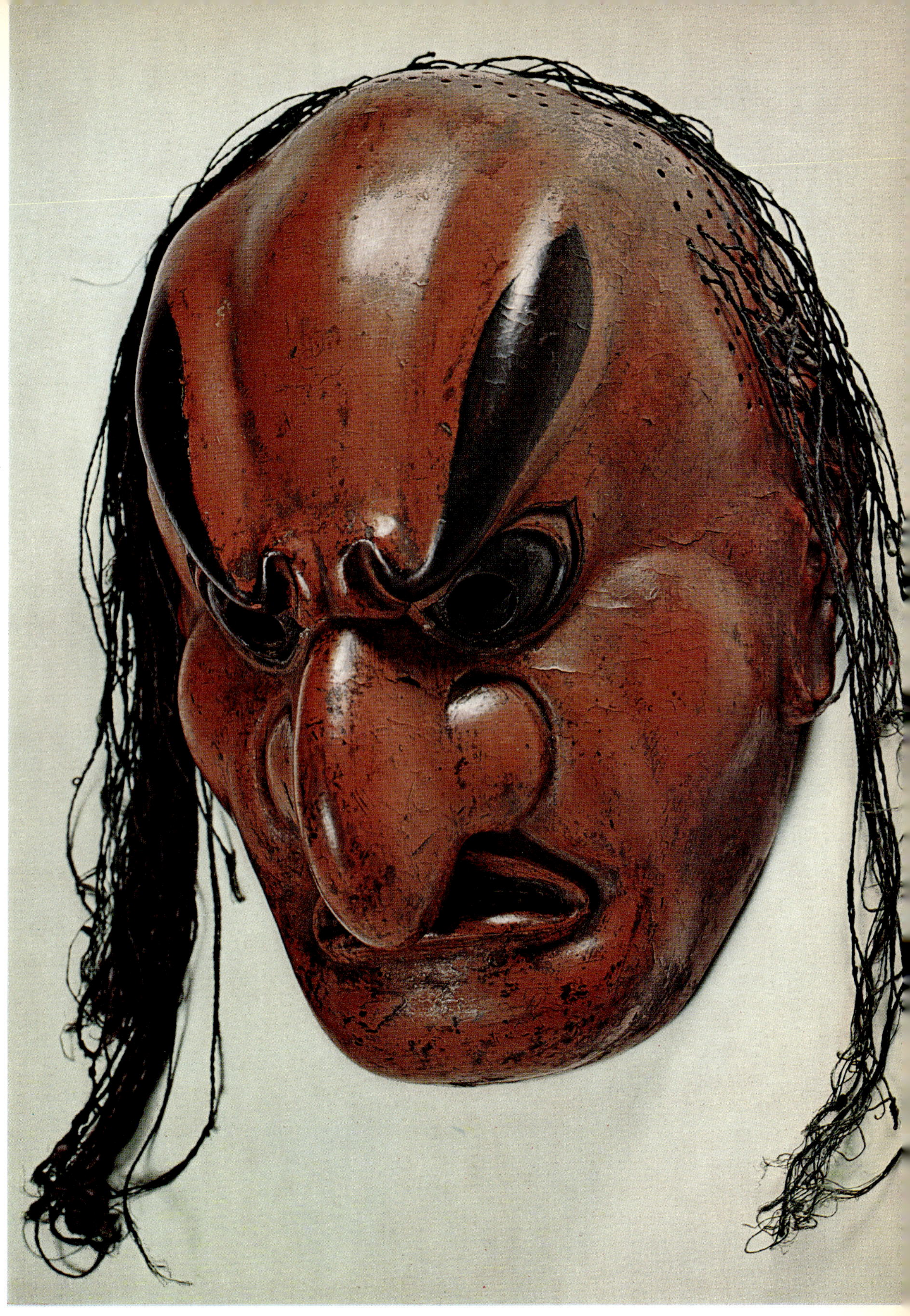

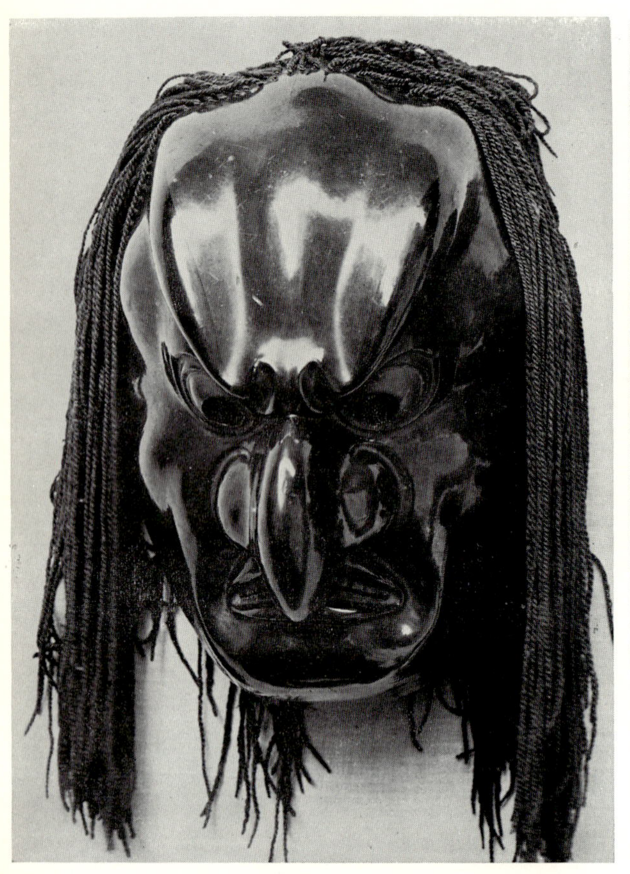

97. Batō. Repainted. 1144. Hōryū-ji, Nara Prefecture.

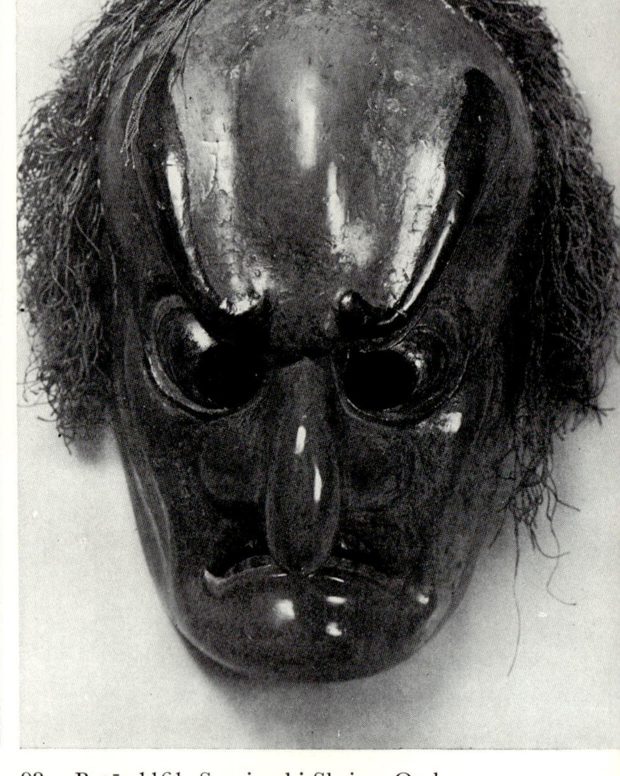

98. Batō. 1161. Sumiyoshi Shrine, Osaka.

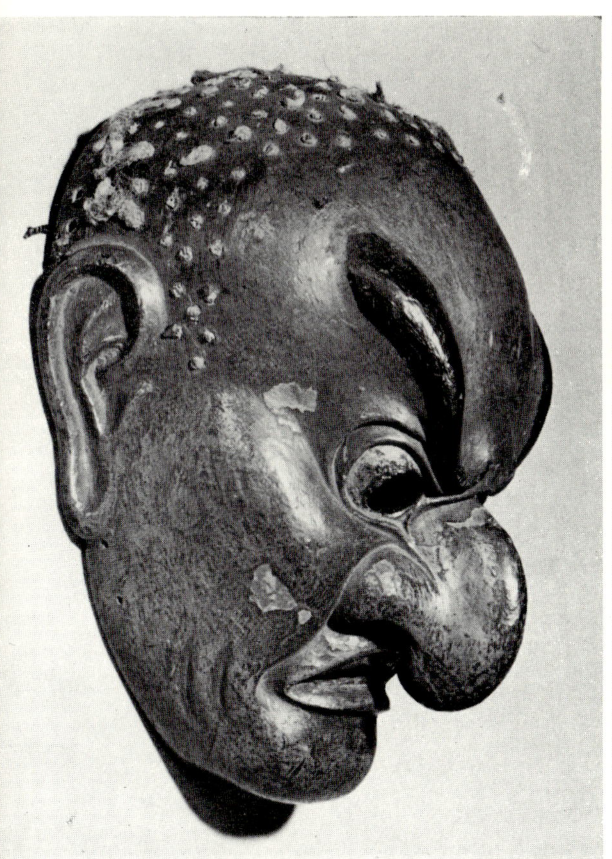

99. Batō. Restoration date 1178. Atsuta Shrine, Nagoya.

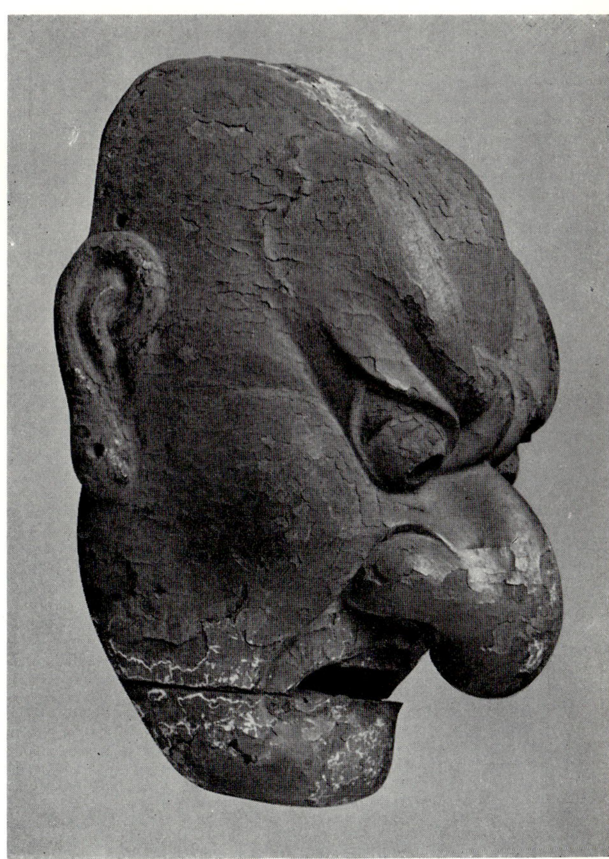

100. Batō, possibly by Unkei. 1219. Seto Shrine, Yokohama.

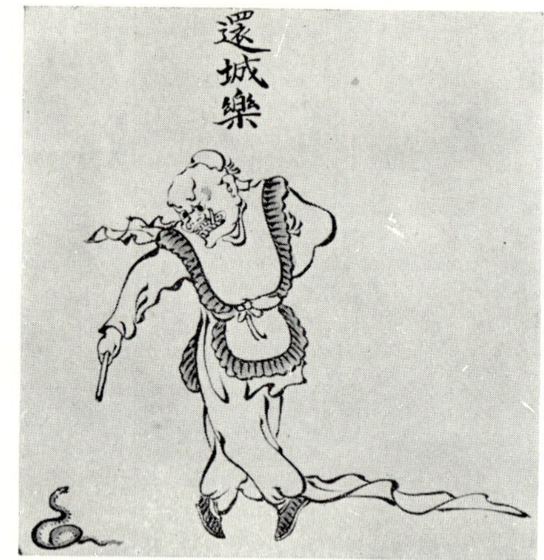


101. *Genjōraku.* Detail from the *Shinzei kogakuzu* (Shinzei's Illustrations of Ancient Music). Monochrome ink handscroll. Twelfth century. Tokyo University of Fine Arts.

*Genjōraku*

Two very dissimilar stories seem to have been combined in the dance *Genjōraku,* as can be inferred from the alternate names of the dance. In one interpretation it expresses the delight of a "western barbarian" at finding a snake, one of his favorite dishes. The rejoicing dancer rotates around a wooden model of a coiled snake placed in the middle of the stage—at one point picking up the snake and dancing with it. Plates 12, upper right, and 102 are illustrations of *Genjōraku.*

The snake dance is thought to have originated in India, but it seems to have merged with a Chinese dance called *Genkyōraku* (Return-to-Capital Dance) or *Genjōraku* (Return Visit of a High Personage), which celebrates the safe return of Emperor Hsüan Tsung (r. 712–56) to the capital after supressing a rebellion led by Empress Wei. In Japan *Genjōraku* (Return-to-the-Castle Dance) retained the connotation of a victory dance; in a notable instance it was performed in 1333 upon the arrival of Emperor Godaigo at Enkyō-ji on Mount Shosha, where, returning from exile, he was to establish a temporary palace in the lecture hall.

*Genjōraku* was performed in Japan as early as the Nara period, for it is mentioned as *Kenjaraku* (Snake-Viewing Dance) in the *Saidai-ji shizaichō* (Register of Saidai-ji Treasures) in 780. From an early date it was a companion dance to *Batō,* and although it is treated as a dance of the Right, the music is actually the *tōgaku* typical of dances of the Left.

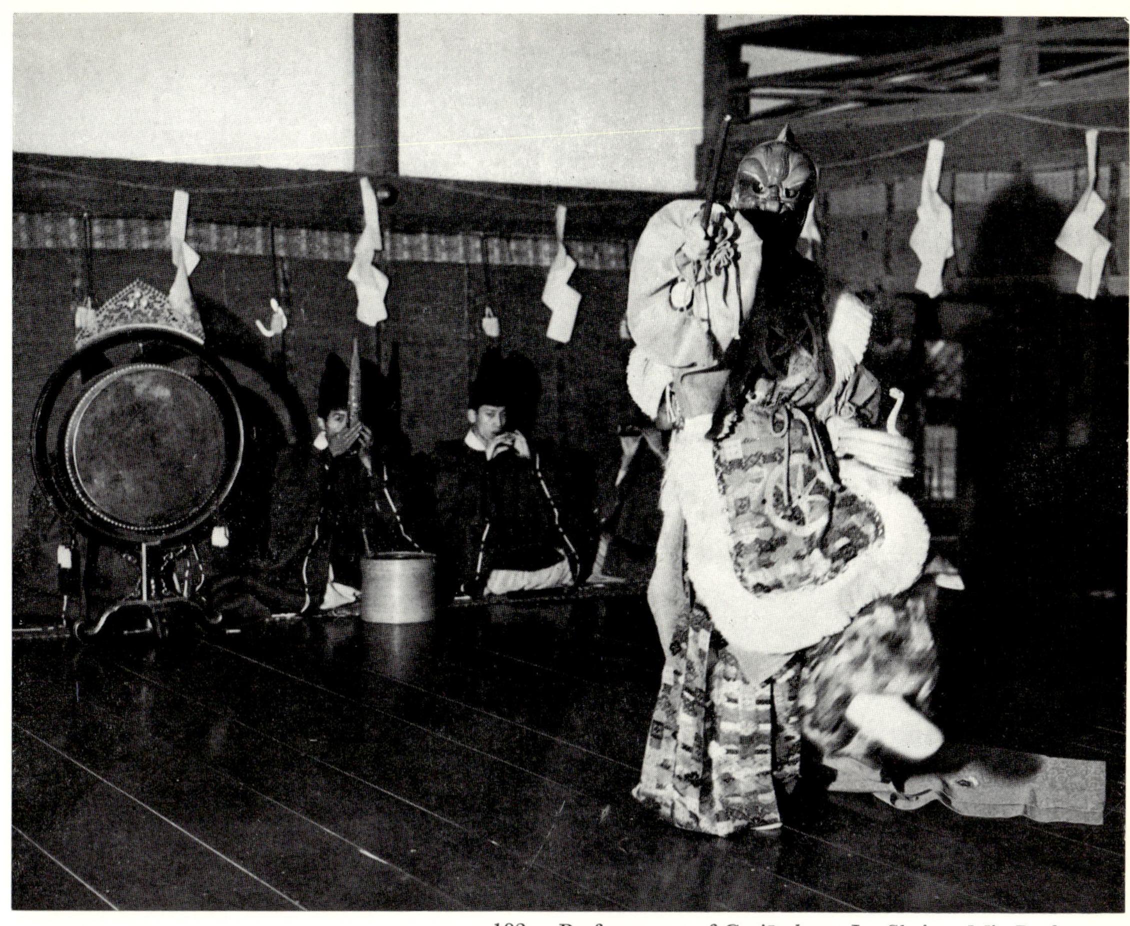

102. Performance of *Genjōraku* at Ise Shrine, Mie Prefecture.

The mask for *Genjōraku,* like that for *Batō,* is painted in red lacquer and has a prominent bowllike forehead. Veins swell over the muscles in the forehead of this strange, frightening face; the thick eyebrows bulge out, and finely carved wrinkles line the cheeks. The pug-nose, the close-set eyes, and the snarling upper lip give it a somewhat beastial appearance. The chin and lower teeth are carved as a separate cup *(tsuriago)* and dangle loosely. The central section of the face—eyes, nose, cheeks, and upper lip—is also carved out of a separate piece of wood and hung under the visorlike eyebrows in such a way that it jiggles up and down. This construction, unique to Genjōraku, is the most complex device found among Bugaku masks.

Some twenty examples of Genjōraku remain today. Among the finest are those at Hōryū-ji (dated 1144; pl. 103), Itsukushima Shrine (dated 1173; pl. 106), Atsuta Shrine (dated 1178; pl. 105), and Masumida Shrine (dated 1211). The Hōryū-ji and Itsukushima Shrine masks are outstanding. The large, bulging sinews of the forehead, covered with protruding blood vessels, and the deeply carved wrinkles in the cheeks lend these masks a gruesome aspect. The masks at Atsuta Shrine and Masumida Shrine are quieter, the crown of the head broader and the sinews comparatively less prominent. The fragment of a Genjōraku mask preserved at Iwakisan Shrine in Aomori Prefecture shows fine provincial workmanship (pl. 104). Judged to be a product of the Kamakura period, it has bulging sinews similar to those of the Hōryū-ji mask.

*Ryō-ō*

Chinese tradition traces the origin of *Ryō-ō* to the ancient country of P'o-hai (present-day Manchuria), where there lived a young prince called Ranryō (Lan Ling or Ch'ang Kung in Chinese). He had handsome, delicate features that he hid under a grotesque mask when he went into battle. So awesome was his appearance that he always succeeded in crushing his enemy. The performance of *Ryō-ō,* in commemoration of his victory over the Chou, celebrates the advent of peace and prosperity.

According to a separate story, a young Chinese prince fighting a pitched battle was aided by the ghost of his father, the king, who appeared wearing a dragon's head and a long beard. In either case, the dance celebrates a warrior's triumph.

Still other stories claim that *Ryō-ō* derives from an old Indian play, *The Joy of the Serpents* (*Nagananda* in Sanskrit), or that the form of the mask comes from the image of Shagara (Sāgara in Sanskrit), one of the eight dragon kings *(hachidai ryū-ō)* of Buddhist iconography. The connection between *Ryō-ō* and the dragon king is borne out in the folk use of the dance as a rain prayer. Especially popular under the name *Ryū-ō,* the dance was believed to incarnate the water-dragon god. In 1315 it was danced at Hōryū-ji in Nara to break the late summer dry spell, and other records testify to its frequent performance during the Kamakura period. Even today *Ryō-ō* is danced as a rain prayer in numerous places throughout the country.

Perhaps this shamanistic use of the dance accounts for its overwhelming popularity, for records show that *Ryō-ō* has been the most frequently performed Bugaku dance. The large number of extant masks throughout the country, sixty-four, indicates that it also had the widest distribution of any Bugaku piece. According to the *Gakkaroku,* this popularity began when the dancer Owari no Hamanushi returned to Japan in 839 from a four-year trip to China, but other evidence shows that the piece was in existence at least a century earlier. Among the Shōsō-in treasures are fragments of cloth from the year 752 marked as costumes for the "old Chinese dance of *Raryō-ō.*" Ryō-ō is also mentioned as one of the *tōgaku* masks in the *Register of Saidai-ji Treasures,* written in 780.

The Ryō-ō mask can be identified easily by the dragon perched on top. Even when the dragon is missing, the prominent eyes, the pointed nose, the profuse wrinkles engraved into the face, and the carved hair parted down the middle distinguish the mask. The eyebrows, mustache, and beard are made of real hair stuck into the wood. The face is painted gold and the dragon on top, sitting with raised head, is also in gold. The body of the dragon is sometimes decorated with red and green scales painted in shaded stripes, while the feathers of the wings are carved in relief and painted in shaded patterns of blue, red, rust, and vermilion. These bright colors lend the mask a gaudy yet heroic appearance. The bulging movable eyes *(dōgan)* and the dangling ring-shaped chin *(tsuriago)* are carved out of separate pieces of wood and set into the mask with connecting cords so that they sway in time with, and accent, the rhythm of the dance.

There are two types of Ryō-ō masks. The example in plate 111, from Itsukushima Shrine in Hiroshima Prefecture, in which the dragon on the top has small wings and raises its chest in the air, typifies the first. Made at the height of Bugaku mask production in the twelfth century, this mask is an unqualified masterpiece. The clean, precise chiseling of the hair and the wrinkles on the face has a free-flowing excellence. The modeling of the dragon perched calmly on top of the head is perfect. Among the many other examples of this type are masks at Masumida Shrine (dated 1211), Atsuta Shrine (dated 1284; pl. 108), and Tōdai-ji (dated 1259; pl. 113).

The second type is exemplified by the Ryō-ō at Himuro Shrine in Nara (pl. 109). Here the dragon on the top crouches low, spreading its wings to form a helmet. Masks at Tsurugaoka Hachiman Shrine in Kamakura (pl. 112), at Seto Shrine in Kanagawa Prefecture, and at Kanzeon-ji in Fukuoka Prefecture belong to the second group, as does the mask at Shitennō-ji in Osaka (pl. 110).

A mask at the Fujita Art Museum in Osaka (pl. 114), belonging to the second type, deserves special mention. Although unknown by specialists until quite recently, this mask, made with the dry-lacquer technique that flourished among Buddhist sculptors during the Tempyō period (711–81), is important as the only dry-lacquer Bugaku mask still in existence. In the dry-lacquer technique, a rough form is made by building layer upon layer of coarse hemp cloth with *mugi urushi* (barley mixed with lacquer) as an adhesive. The finer details are then modeled on top of this with *kokuso urushi,* a sawdust kneeded with *mugi urushi* to give a plastic, easily worked material that dries into a hard finish. The technique was widely used during the eighth century, and examples can be found among Gigaku and folk masks, indicating the possibility that Bugaku masks of the same period were also made with dry lacquer. This newly discovered, unique dry-lacquer Ryō-ō mask is said to have come originally from Ryōsen-ji in Nara. The mask is now badly damaged: both the dragon on the top of the head and the nose are missing, while the movable eyes and dangling chin are later additions carved from paulownia wood. Still, this mask with its mature, placid expression so typical of the flexible and flowing dry-lacquer technique is an unquestioned treasure from the Tempyō period.

### *Nasori*

*Nasori* rivals its partner dance *Ryō-ō* in popularity, and its masks are as widely distributed about the country, represented by as many as sixty-three old examples. *Nasori* was a very early import, the *Register of Saidai-ji Treasures* referring to it as early as the late eighth century. Perhaps because of its vigorous movements, it was often used as a victory dance following the skill competitions of the Heian period. Although the quick, free-flowing movements of *Nasori* are said to represent frolicking dragons, the content of the dance is, for the most part, unknown.

The grotesque mask has a long blunt nose, not unlike that of Ryō-ō, as well as round bulging movable eyes, rippling creases decorating the entire face, and hair implanted

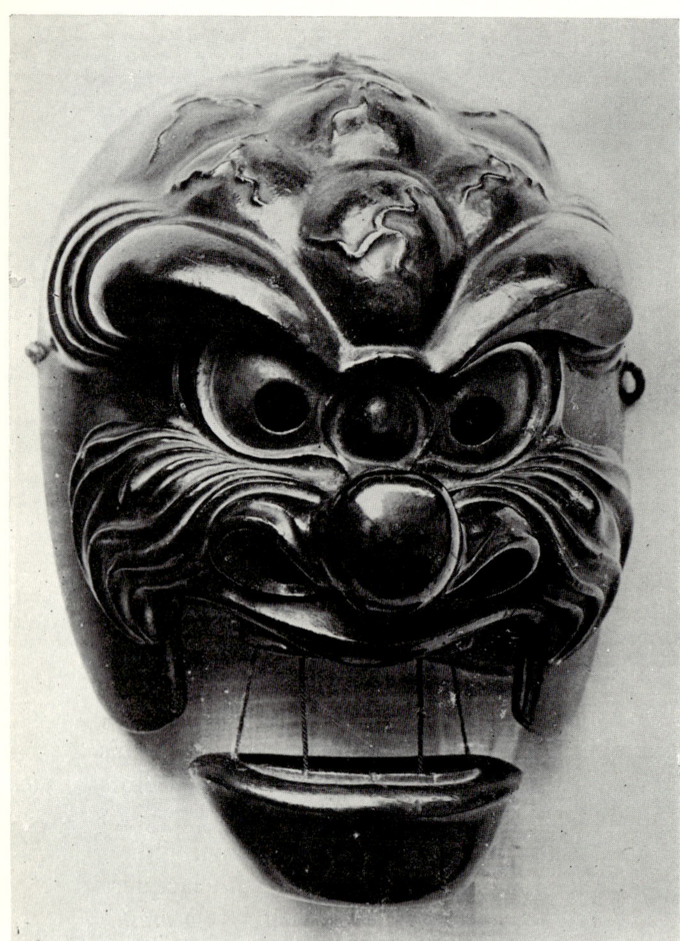

103. Genjōraku. 1144. Hōryū-ji, Nara Prefecture.

104. Genjōraku (fragment). Iwakisan Shrine, Aomori Prefecture.

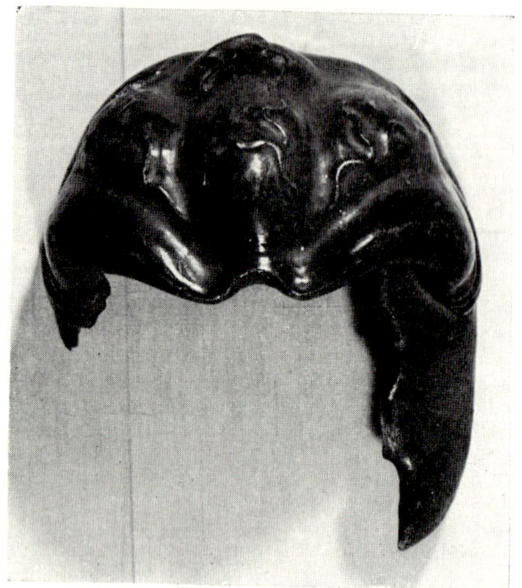

for the eyebrows, mustache, and beard. For Nasori, however, the hair on the head is real, and tusks jut out of the lower and upper jaws. The gold or white of the teeth and eyeballs make a striking contrast to the rust-green or ultramarine face. The dangling chin is of somewhat different construction from that of Genjōraku or Ryō-ō: it does not form a complete, separate ring, but rather is three-sided and slides neatly between the low-hanging cheeks.

Old and typical Nasori masks include one each at Itsukushima Shrine (dated 1173; pl. 115), Kasuga Shrine (latter half of twelfth century; pl. 118), Atsuta Shrine (about 1178; pl. 116), and Masumida Shrine (dated 1211). The mask at Itsukushima Shrine, which unfortunately has a restored chin, is the best among these. It was most likely made by Gyōmyō, since the handwriting in what is left of the inscription is identical with his other signed masks at Itsukushima Shrine. The masks at Tamukeyama Shrine (pl. 117) and in the Ise Repository (pl. 140), both originally from Tōdai-ji and dated 1259, follow these in quality. Two masks at Kanzeon-ji, although probably from the late Kamakura period at the earliest, adhere closely to the earlier models. Many examples found in outlying areas of Japan are interesting for demonstrating the process of provincial modification of the type. One local mask worth noting here is found in Chiryū Shrine in Aichi Prefecture, dated 1256.

105. Genjōraku. 1178. Atsuta Shrine, Nagoya. (See pls. 170–71 for inscription on back.)

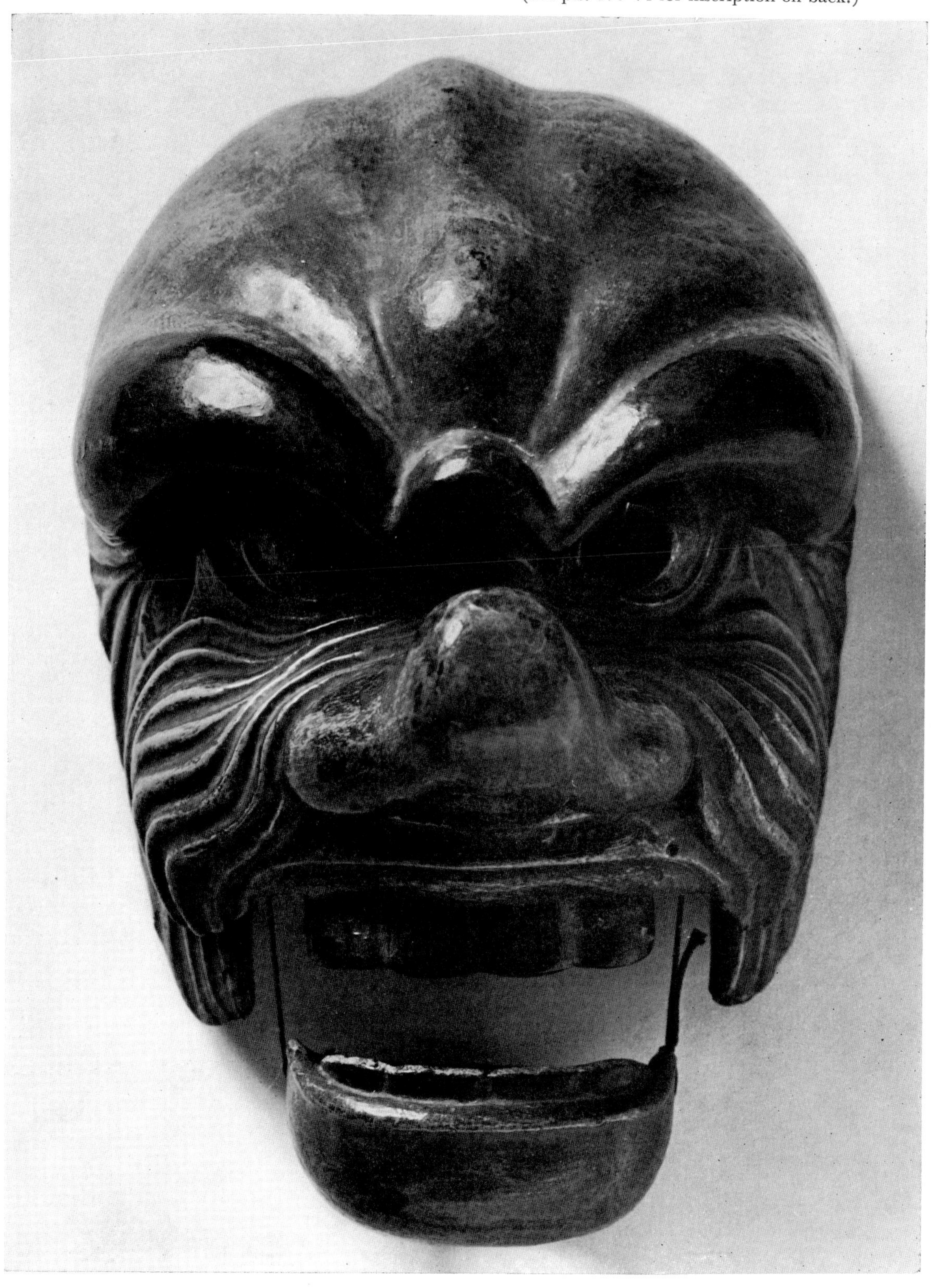

106. Genjōraku, by Gyōmyō. Japanese cypress, *sabi urushi* priming, and red lacquer. H. 20.7, w. 17.5, dpt. 13.3 cm. 1173. Itsukushima Shrine, Hiroshima Prefecture.

Rejoicing at having caught his favorite delicacy, a snake, a barbarian from the west dances around a wooden model of a snake placed in center stage. He wears a frightening mask with bulging sinews on the forehead. The eyes, cheeks, and nose, carved from a separate piece of wood and attached by cords, shake as he dances. This example has long been treasured as one of the gifts of the Taira clan to Itsukushima Shrine. (See also pls. 160–61.)

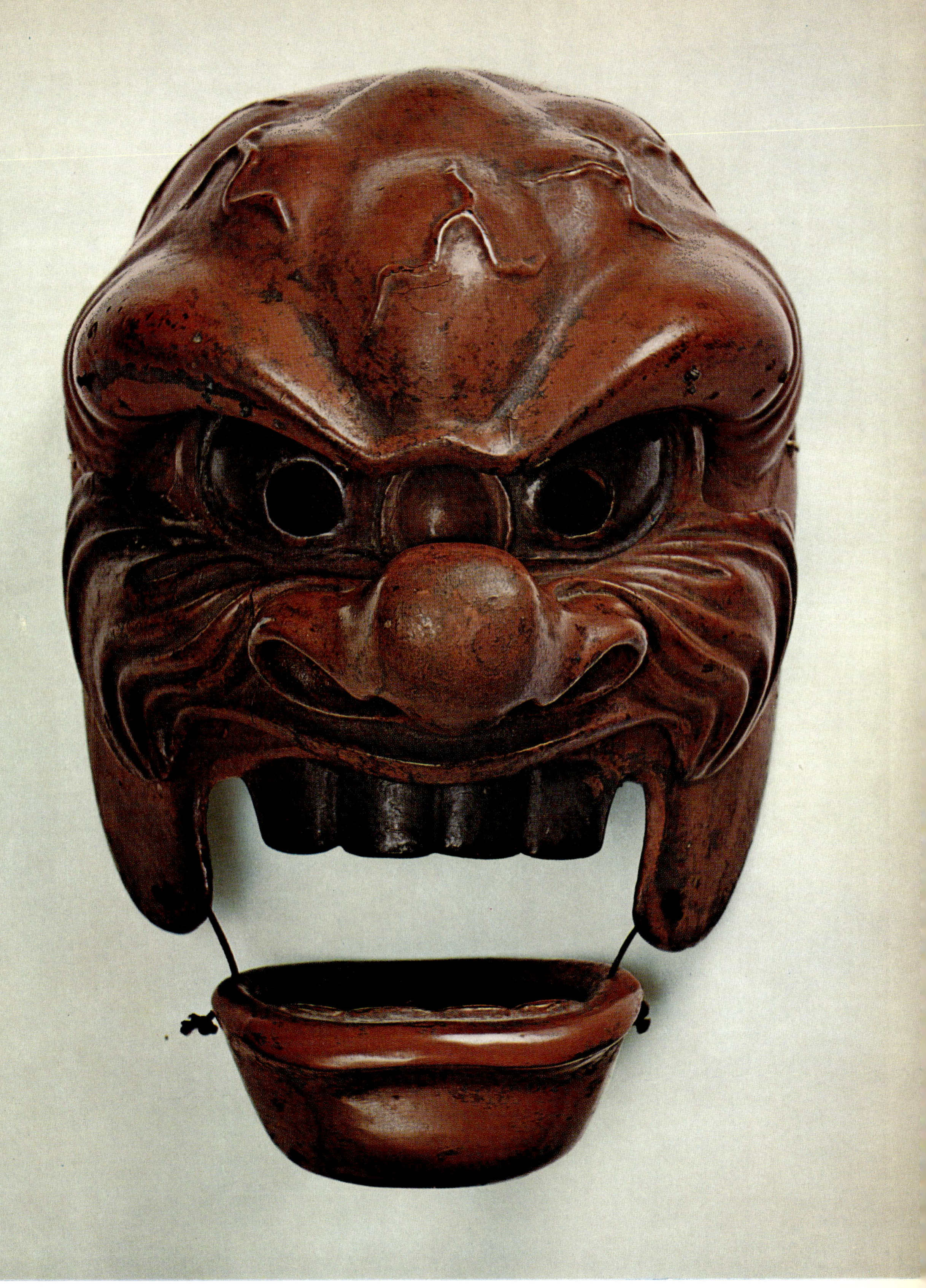

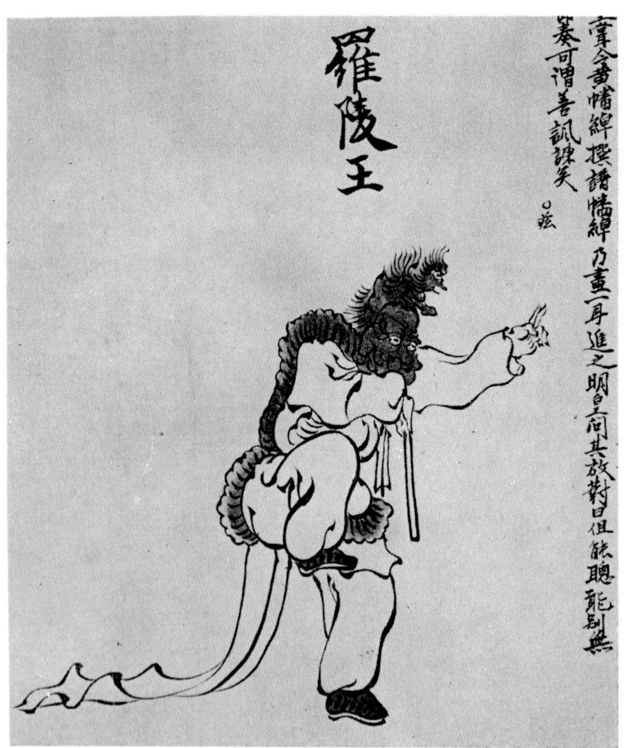


107. *Ryō-ō*. Detail from the *Shinzei kogakuzu* (Shinzei's Illustrations of Ancient Music). Monochrome ink handscroll. Twelfth century. Tokyo University of Fine Arts.

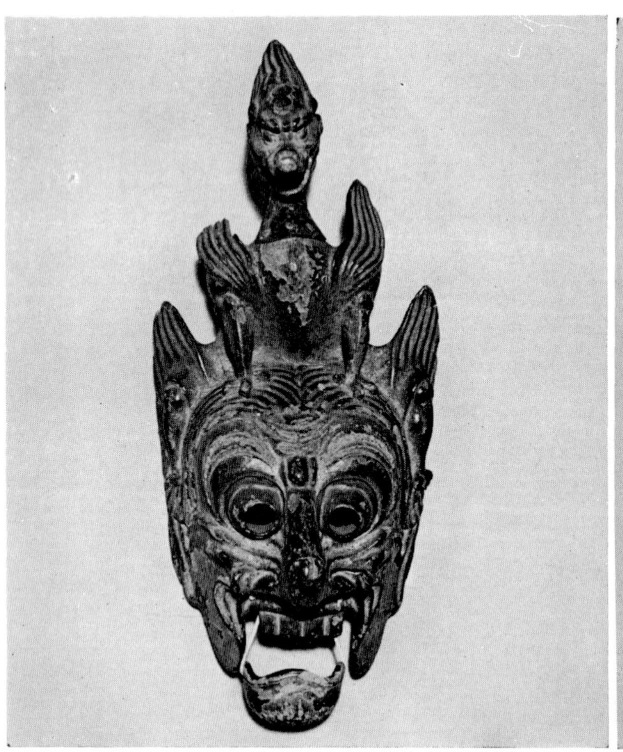

108. Ryō-ō. Restoration date 1284. Atsuta Shrine, Nagoya.

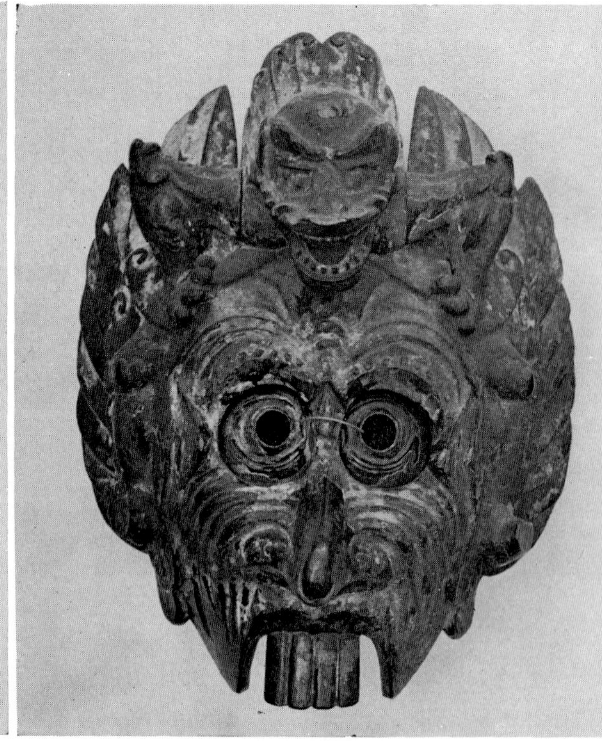

109. Ryō-ō. Himuro Shrine, Nara.

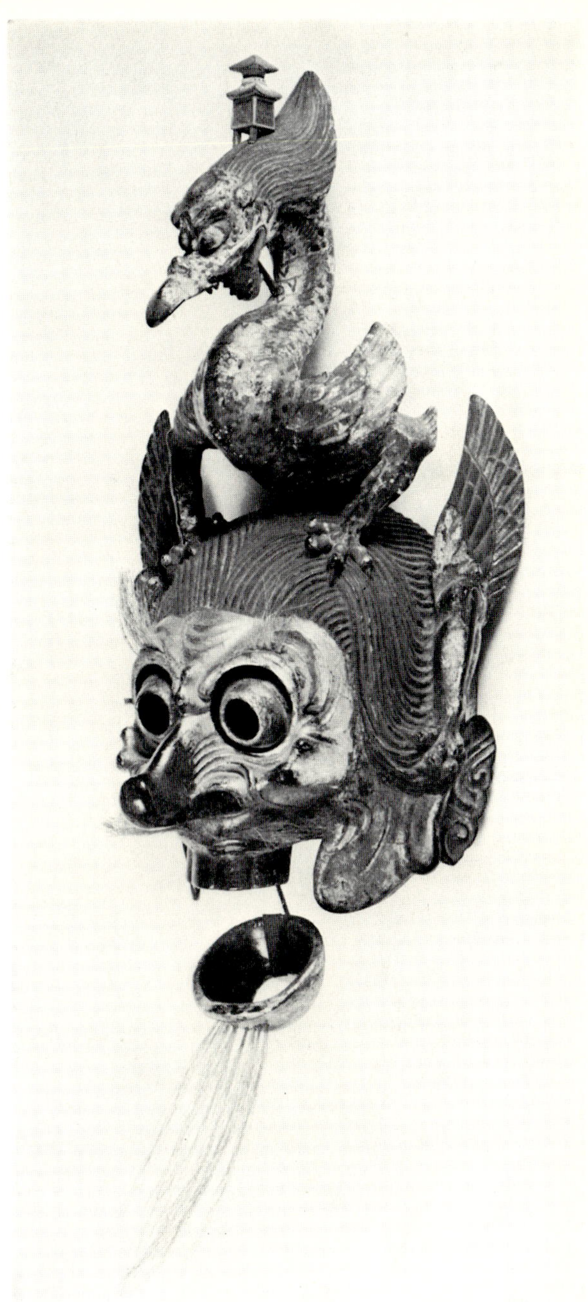

111. Ryō-ō. Late twelfth century. Itsukushima Shrine, Hiroshima Prefecture.

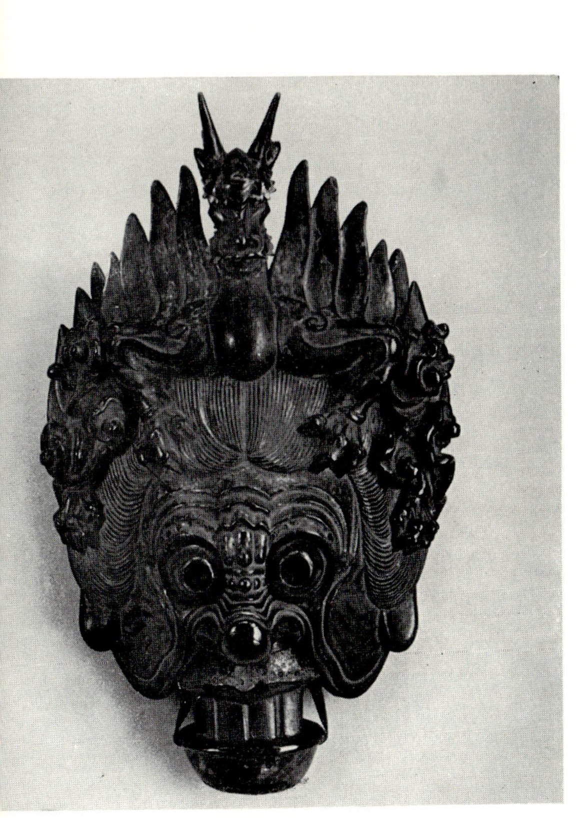

110. Ryō-ō. Shitennō-ji, Osaka.

112. Ryō-ō. Japanese cypress, cloth and *sabi urushi* priming, gilded and painted. H. 33, w. 24.3, dpt. 17.9 cm. Thirteenth century. Tsurugaoka Hachiman Shrine, Kamakura.
The dragon on this Ryō-ō mask crouches low, clutching onto the forehead and ears of the mask and spreading out its feathery wings to form a protective helmet. The menacing expression and muscular body of the dragon greatly contribute to the ferocity of the mask.

113. Ryō-ō, by Shōjun. Japanese cypress, cloth and *sabi urushi* priming, gilded and painted. H. 34.8, w. 20.3, dpt. 14.5 cm. 1259. Tōdai-ji, Nara.
Although this mask dates from the late Kamakura period when Bugaku was no longer at its height, it is a very fine work. The dragon perched on the top has small wings and raises its chest like the one on the mask at Itsukushima Shrine (pl. 111).

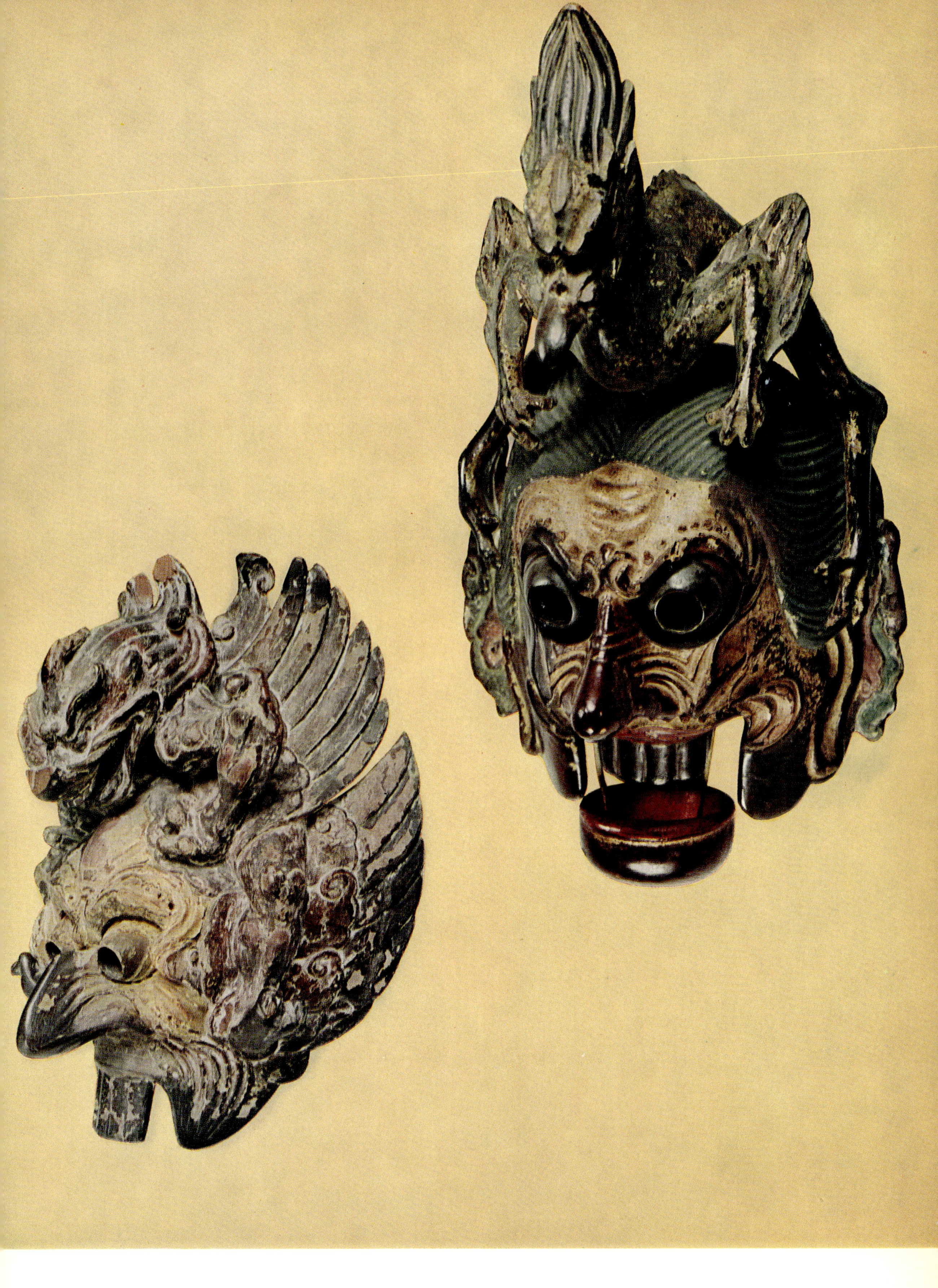

114. Ryō-ō. Dry lacquer. Fujita Art Museum, Osaka.

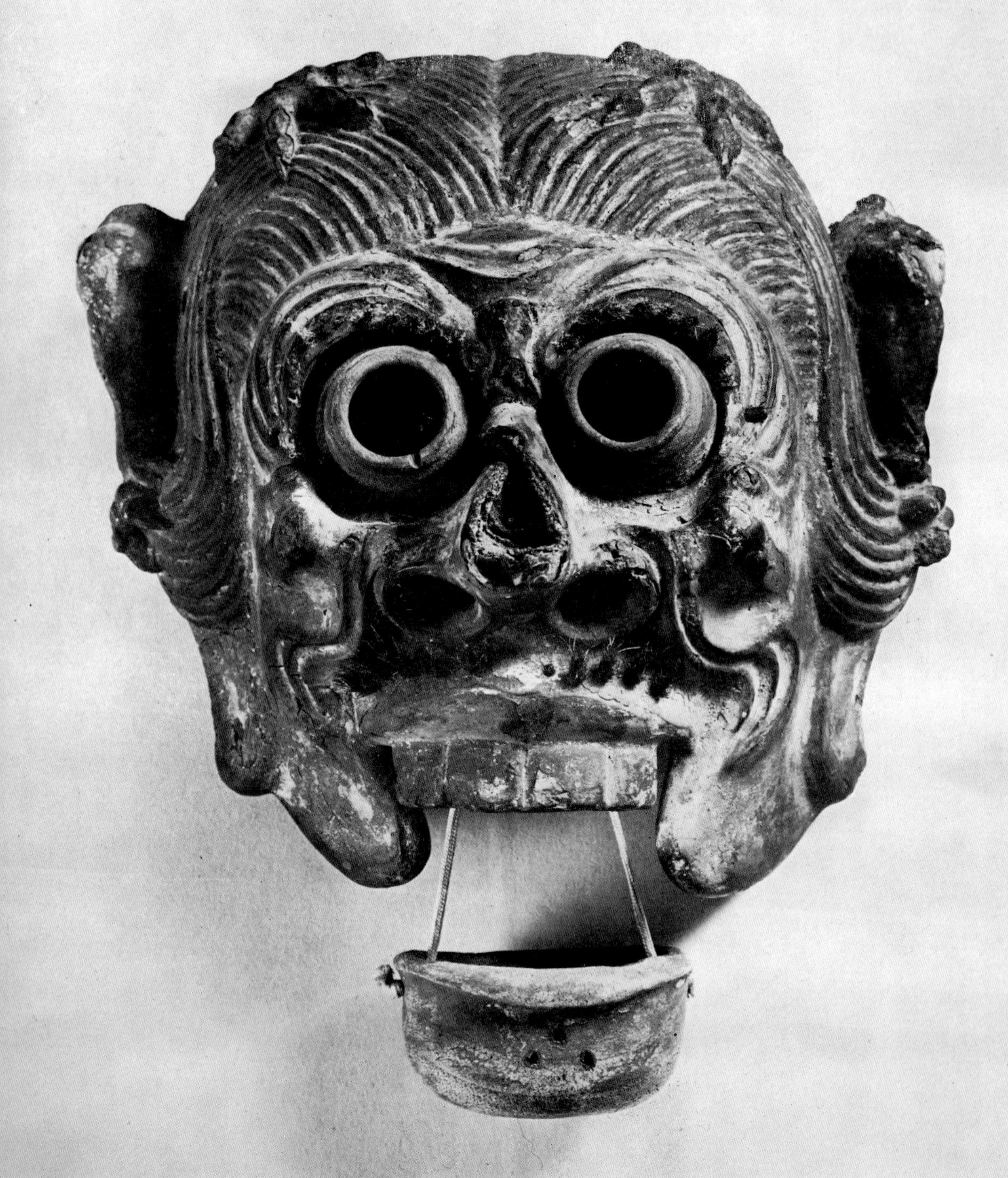

115. Nasori, by Gyōmyō. 1173. Itsukushima Shrine, Hiroshima Prefecture.

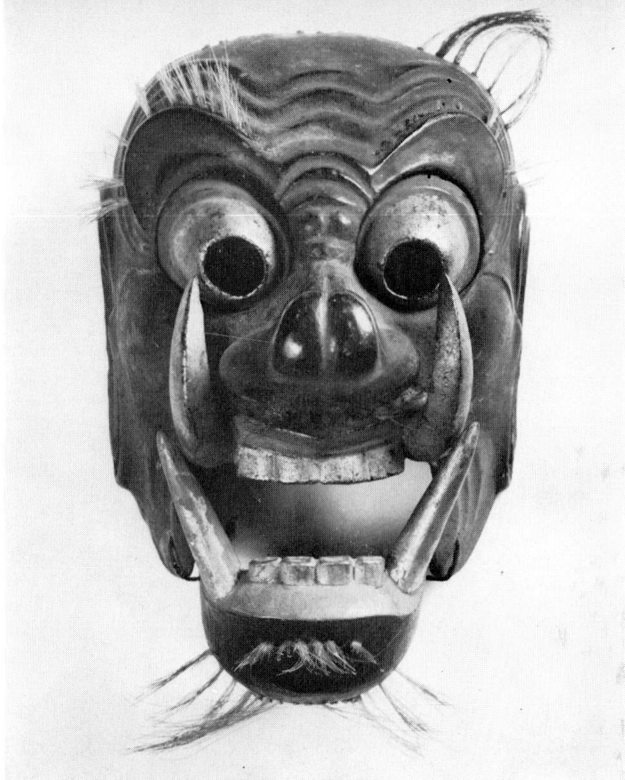

116. Nasori. Restoration date 1178. Atsuta Shrine, Nagoya.

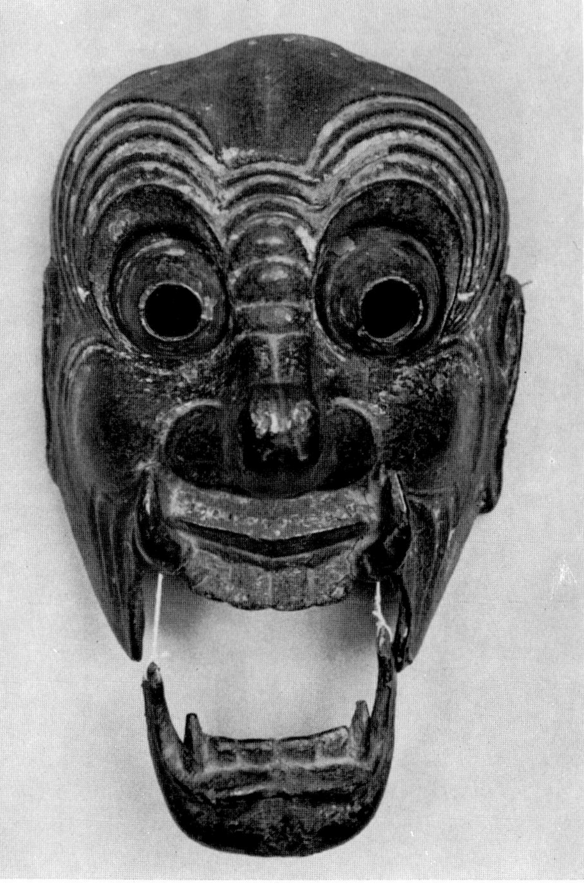

117. Nasori, by Shōjun. 1259. Tamukeyama Shrine, Nara.

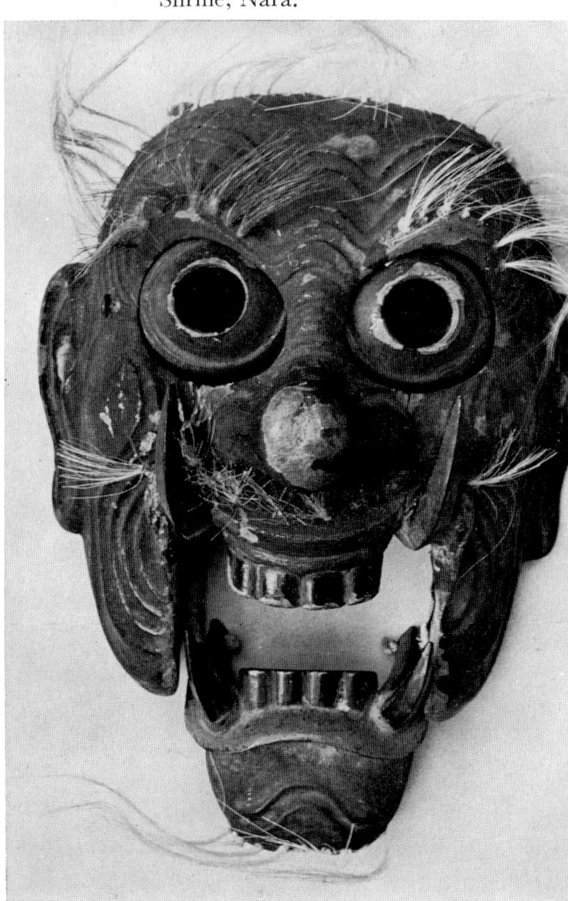

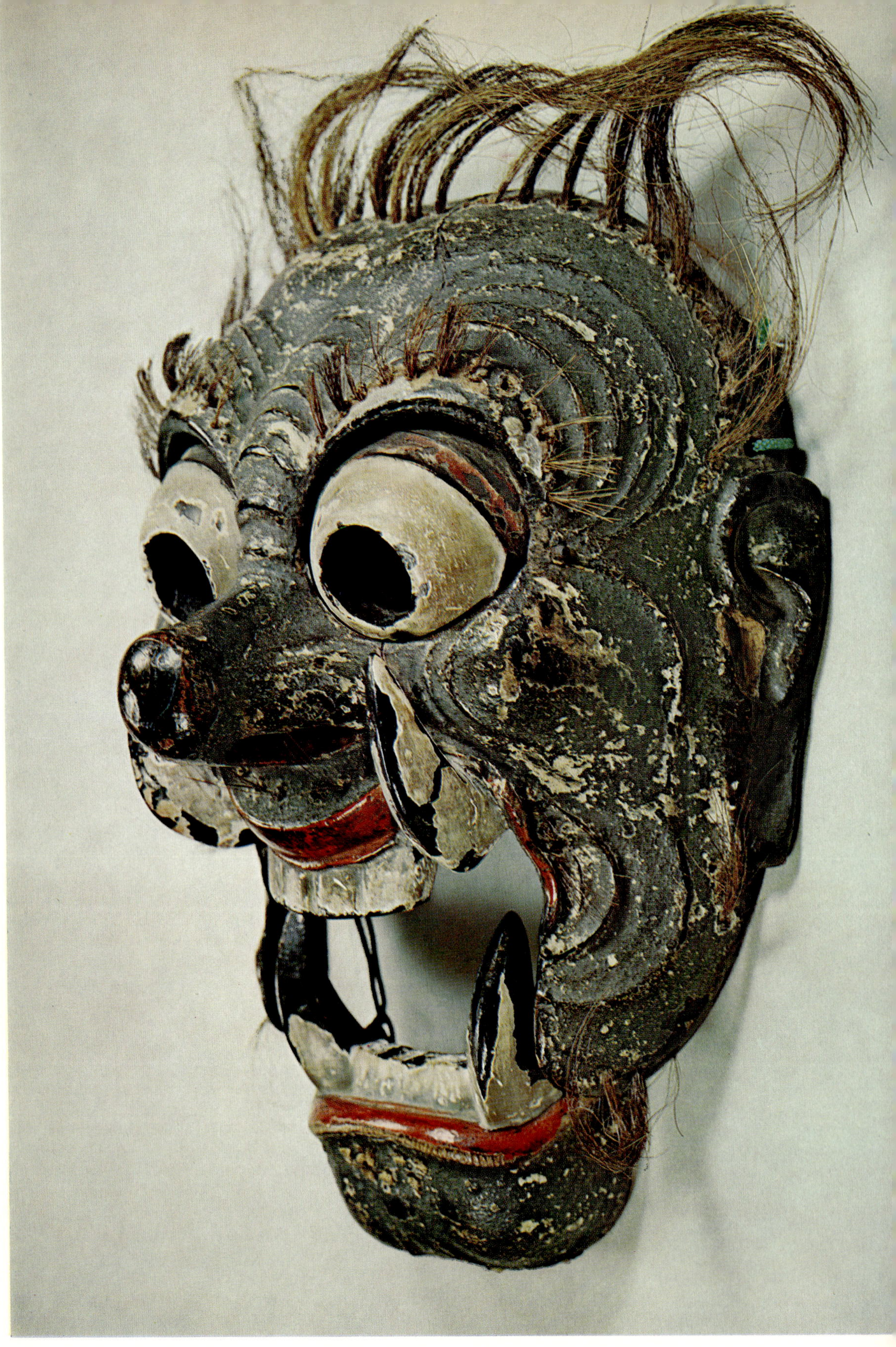

118. Nasori. Japanese cypress, *sabi urushi* priming (cloth reinforcement on back), and kaolin base with colors. H. 18.7, w. 16.5, dpt. 13.2 cm. Latter half of twelfth century. Kasuga Shrine, Nara.

*Nasori,* often danced by two as a partner dance to *Ryō-ō,* may represent two dragons at play. Its widespread popularity resulted in many examples of the mask. The one shown here is typical, with green wrinkled face, tusks, and eyes that rotate within their sockets.

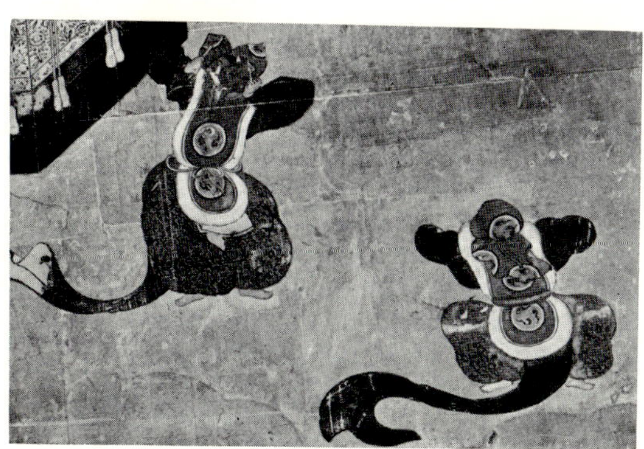

119. *Nasori.* Detail from *Bugaku Screens,* by Tosa Tōō. A six-fold screen. Colors and gold-leaf on paper. Mid-Edo period. Private collection, Japan.

# 3

# MASKS IN THE PROVINCES

The temples and shrines around the old cultural centers (Kyoto, Nara, Osaka, Nagoya, Hiroshima) that still give Bugaku performances today use faithful copies of the traditional Bugaku masks, and the dances themselves seem not to have changed radically since the Heian period. In marked contrast, the dances and masks that spread to the countryside were liberated from traditional forms. They come down to us mixed with other provincial traditions and performing arts, their form and content having been changed freely in accordance with provincial taste.

Not all types of Bugaku masks were adopted in the provinces, only those that could be easily adapted for use in such folk-religious practices as exorcism or in prayers for securing harmony. Masks such as Nasori and Ryō-ō, used in rain dances, were particularly popular. These two masks are by far the most widely dispersed, with a total of more than sixty examples. A mere indication of the number of masks is not conclusive, of course, since many must have been lost through damage and removal; yet it does show the basic trend in diffusion of Bugaku from the cultural centers to the provinces. Masks of the more lively and amusing pieces, particularly those with mysterious or mystical powers, such as Ryō-ō, Nasori, Ni-no-mai, Sanju, Batō, Kitoku, and Genjōraku (all of dynamic features), are distributed widely throughout the main islands. The number and variety of these masks indicate the extent to which Bugaku prospered in the provinces from the Kamakura period onward.

Most of the provincial masks of the thirteenth and fourteenth centuries are well-made, faithful examples of their types. Many still retain the standard technique of finishing the wood surface by covering it with an application of cloth and *sabi urushi* as priming before painting it with kaolin. Typical of these early provincial masks are those at three shrines in Aomori Prefecture: Ōboshi Shrine (pls. 120, 123–25), Kushibiki Hachiman Shrine (pls. 122, 126), and Iwakisan Shrine (pl. 121). The Kamakura-period masks at these shrines, along with masks made in the Muromachi period, represent the full range of types to be found in the provinces. In addition, these three shrines house many folk masks of uncertain identity.

As time estranged the carvers from the models and attitudes of the cultural centers, the techniques and forms of the masks underwent a radical transformation. The complex devices that characterized Bugaku masks—movable eyes, dangling chins—were dispensed with, to be replaced by devices such as gilded copper plates inlaid on the eyes and teeth. The use of a simple kaolin or *gofun* base (a technique also prevalent in the Muromachi period for finishing Buddhist statues and for painting Nō masks) came to substitute for the time-consuming lacquer priming. The form of the masks grew less and less recognizable until some, notably the Nasori (pl. 142) and the Ryō-ō (pl. 134) at Amanomiya Shrine, bore little resemblance to their types in anything but name.

The evolution of the provincial Ryō-ō mask is indicative of many of the changes. Two fine orthodox Ryō-ō dating from the end of the Kamakura period and made with standard, unmodified techniques can be found in Tesshū-ji in Shizuoka Prefecture (pl. 128) and in Ōboshi Shrine (pl. 120). The Ryō-ō at Ōto Shrine in Chiba Prefecture (pl. 129), however, inscribed with the date of 1328, has already dispensed with the movable eyes: they are carved as an inseparable part of the mask. Despite its crude carving, this mask is orthodox in form. Similarly, the eyes of the Muromachi-period Ryō-ō at Kushibiki Hachiman Shrine in Aomori Prefecture are immobile. Further disintegration is apparent in the surprisingly artless masks at Tendai-ji (pls. 130–31), not far from Kushibiki Hachiman Shrine: large teeth seem to spring out of their mouths, and the hair of one mask flares upward like the flaming hair on statues of the Buddhist deity Myō-ō. Of course, their eyes do not move.

The two Ryō-ō at Hakusan Shrine in Niigata Prefecture (pl. 132) and at Nagahama Hachiman Shrine in Ishikawa Prefecture (pl. 133) have kaolin painted directly on the surface, replacing the priming of *sabi urushi.* Still further modification can be found in the Ryō-ō at Amanomiya Shrine (pl. 134), which would hardly be recognizable without the separately made coiled dragon that seems to have been worn on top of the head like a helmet (not illustrated). A ripple pattern of parallel horizontal lines represents the facial wrinkles of this shallow oval mask.

The technically difficult movable eyes disappeared as quickly from Nasori masks as from Ryō-ō. The Nasori at Ōto Shrine in Chiba Prefecture, made by the same carver who made the Ryō-ō there, no longer has movable eyes; nor do the two Nasori at Tendai-ji (pl. 141). Interestingly, the edge where the now lost chin was severed from the body of the mask in plate 141 resembles that found in masks using a detached chin *(kiriago),* normally found only in Saisōrō, more than the dangling chin *(tsuri-ago)* typical of Nasori masks.

The Nasori at Amanomiya Shrine (pl. 142) has both movable eyes and a dangling chin, but since the lower jaw is merely tied to the upper jaw by cords, the essential element has been lost: the swing of the chin no longer induces the eyes to roll. Although the wrinkles of this mask have been carved according to traditional circular patterns, the total lack of fleshiness makes the face look like a skeleton. The triangular sawlike teeth help give this mask the raw attraction of certain South Pacific folk masks.

Simplification of the complex movable central plate *(dōbō)* of Genjōraku took many forms. The Genjōraku at Gokuraku-ji in Kamakura (pl. 136) retains only the dangling chin, whereas a mask at Tendai-ji that is undoubtably a Genjōraku (pl. 138) has dispensed with even that feature (the present separation of the chin from the body of the mask is due to damage). Most interesting, however, is the solution found in the Genjōraku at Kushibiki Hachiman Shrine (pl. 137), a fourteenth-century mask finished with cloth and *sabi urushi* priming under a red lacquer surface. In place of the *dōbō,* the crown of the head has been carved separately and placed over the head like a helmet. The dancer first dons the "central plate" like a mask, then places over his head the bowllike wooden cap with long sideburns. The two sections are joined by cords strung through holes in the mask. The eyes of this mask, like those of Ryō-ō, are carved separately so that they can move, but they are not attached to the dangling chin.

While the construction of provincial Bugaku masks gradually grew simpler, the techniques and devices perfected in early Bugaku masks were adopted by other kinds of masks. A demon *(oni)* mask used for exorcism (dated 1296), originally from Hōryū-ji and now in the Tokyo National Museum (pl. 139), has incorporated the typical Genjōraku device of the *dōbō.* Two demon masks at Katashiba Shrine in Fukui Prefecture imitate the movable eyes of Bugaku masks; inscriptions show that they were repaired in 1346. The demon mask at Amanomiya Shrine used in the exorcist rite called *tsuina* has both movable eyes and a dangling chin.

Metal inlay found on the teeth and eyes of many Nō masks can be considered an adaptation from Bugaku masks. This technique first appears on the Nasori mask dated 1259 that was originally at Tōdai-ji and is now in the Ise Shrine Repository (pl. 140). It has tusks and irises of silver-plated copper. Gold-plated copper inlays brighten the eyes and teeth of the Muromachi-period Ryō-ō (pl. 135) at the Sumiyoshi Shrine in Katō County, Hyōgo Prefecture, and those of the Genjōraku (pl. 136) and Batō at Gokuraku-ji in Kamakura. Eyes of gold-plated copper appear also on the demon mask dated 1296 mentioned above (pl. 139).

Later Bugaku masks show marked changes in form due to cross-influences with other sculptural traditions. The pair of Nasori at Amatsu Shrine in Niigata Prefecture (pls. 143–44), for example, imitate the convention (called *aun no ittsui*) used in the pair of guardian lions at the right and left of entrances to shrines and in the guardian kings enshrined in temple gates: one mask has its mouth open saying "ah," the other clenched shut saying "un." In the Buddhist tradition this expression is said to be symbolic of complete understanding and harmony, for as soon as one opens its mouth to speak, the other answers in accord.

Another example of influence from Buddhist sculpture is the modeling of the hair on the Batō mask at Iwakisan Shrine (pl. 148). In place of the blue cords that characterize Batō, this mask has sparse, wavy strands incised along the hairline in a manner similar to that found on Buddhist images. Although this mask appears at first glance to be of recent date, the use of *sabi urushi* as a priming on both front and back probably places it in the fourteenth century.

Hakusan Shrine in Niigata Prefecture houses a strange mask labeled "Nō Batō" (pl. 149), which bears no resemblance to a Bugaku mask, but rather recalls folk masks of the Edo period. Thick eyebrows shield the upward-slanting eyes and high nose. The mustache forms a large curve on both cheeks, twisting up at the ends. The author has not seen the dance performed, but it is probably a mixture of folk performances related to both Nō and Bugaku and of recent creation. A dance called *Nō Batō,* still performed at Amatsu Shrine in Niigata Prefecture, is similar to the Bugaku dance, but uses the Nō mask Akujō. That shrine has a separate piece called *Batō* that uses a mask looking like a monkey.

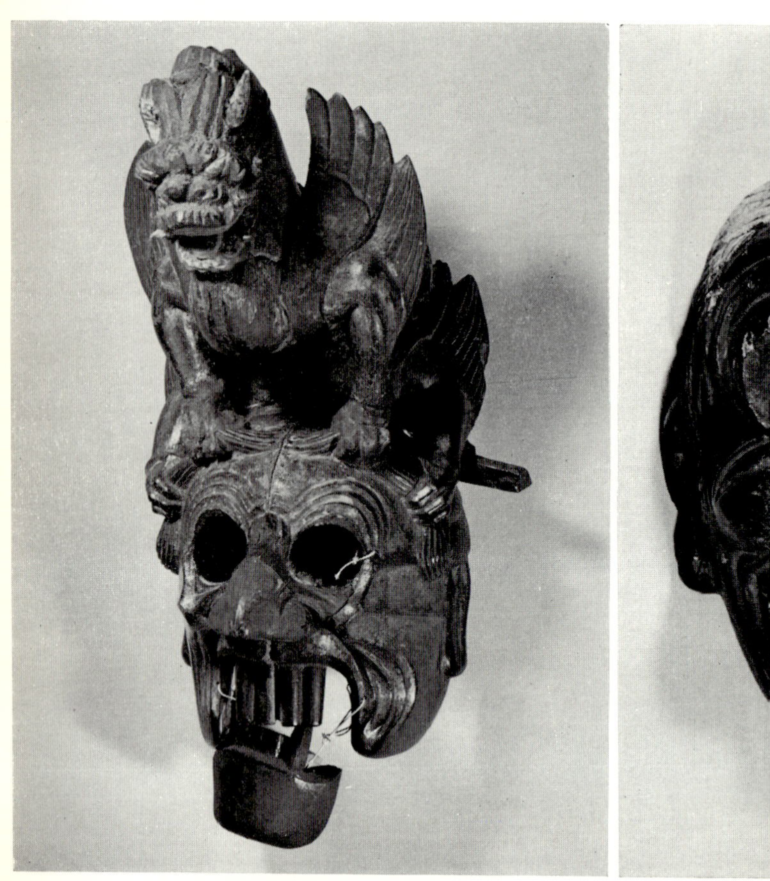

120. Ryō-ō. Ōboshi Shrine, Aomori Prefecture.

121. Ryō-ō. Iwakisan Shrine, Aomori Prefecture.

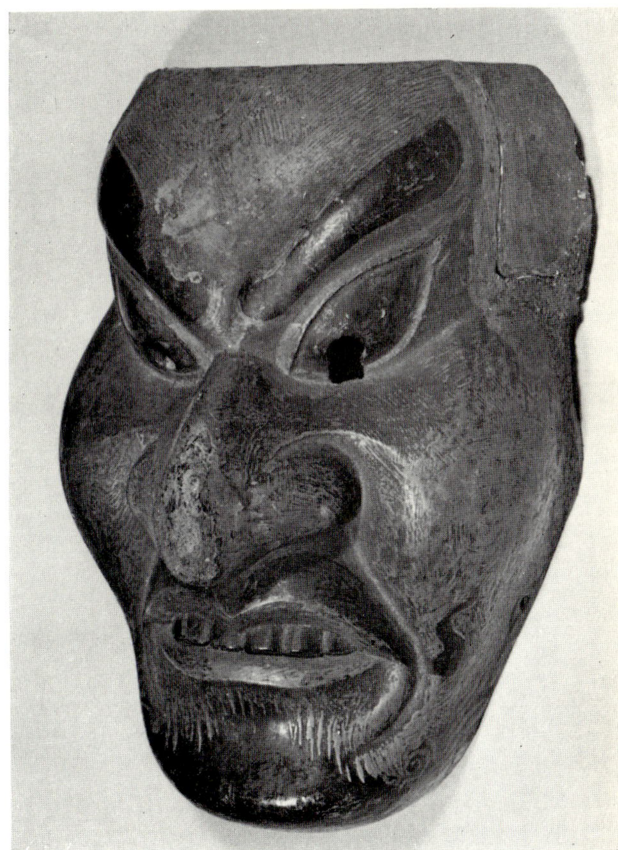

123. Sanju. Ōboshi Shrine, Aomori Prefecture.

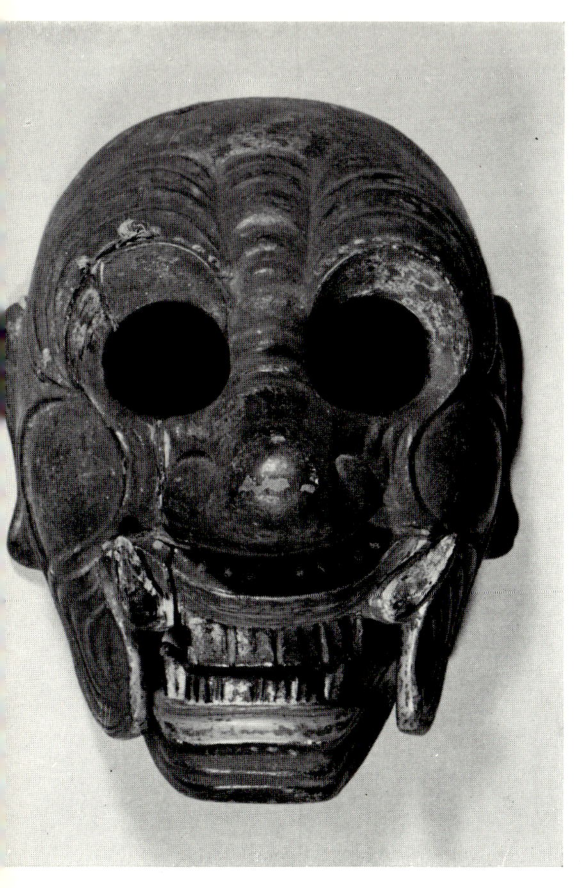

122. Nasori. Kushibiki Hachiman Shrine, Aomori Prefecture.

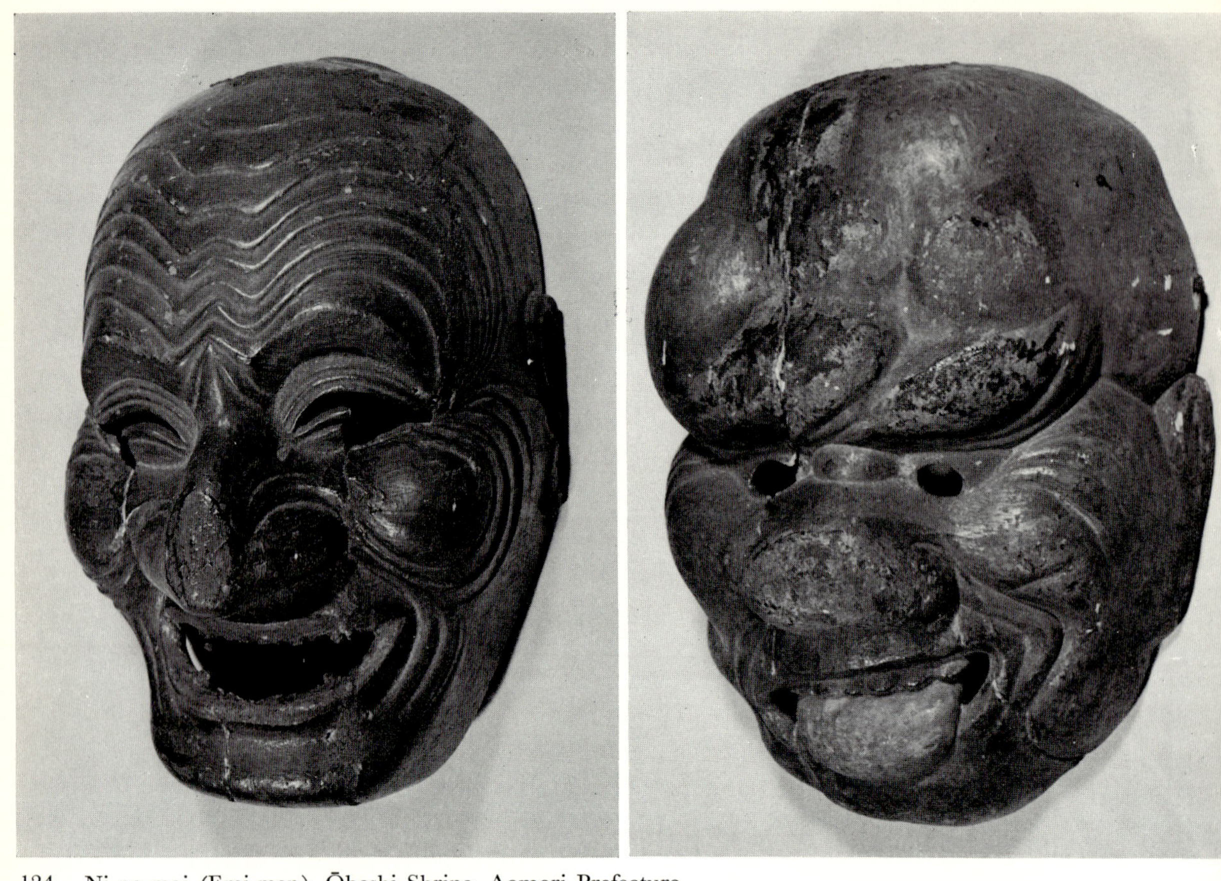

124. Ni-no-mai (Emi-men). Ōboshi Shrine, Aomori Prefecture.
125. Ni-no-mai (Hare-men). Ōboshi Shrine, Aomori Prefecture.

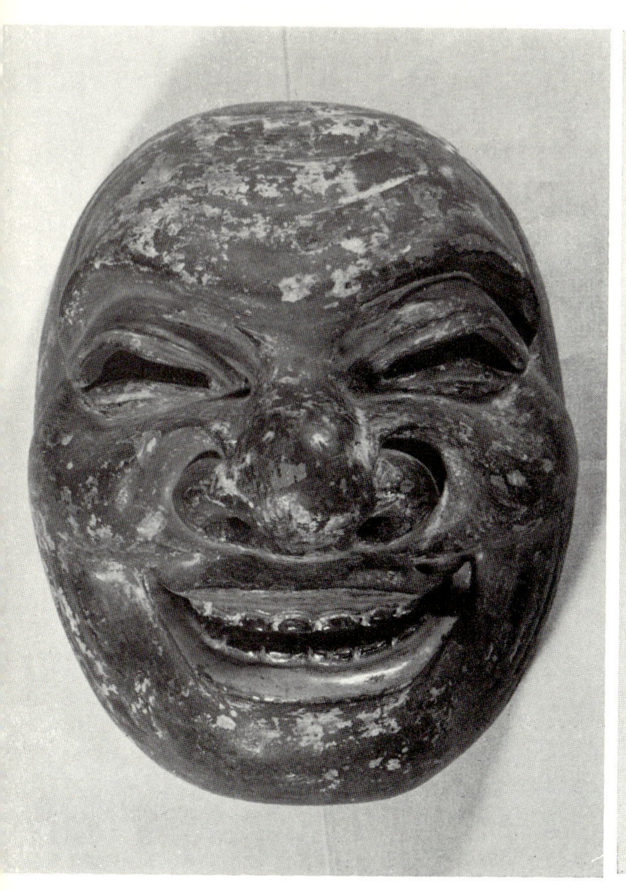

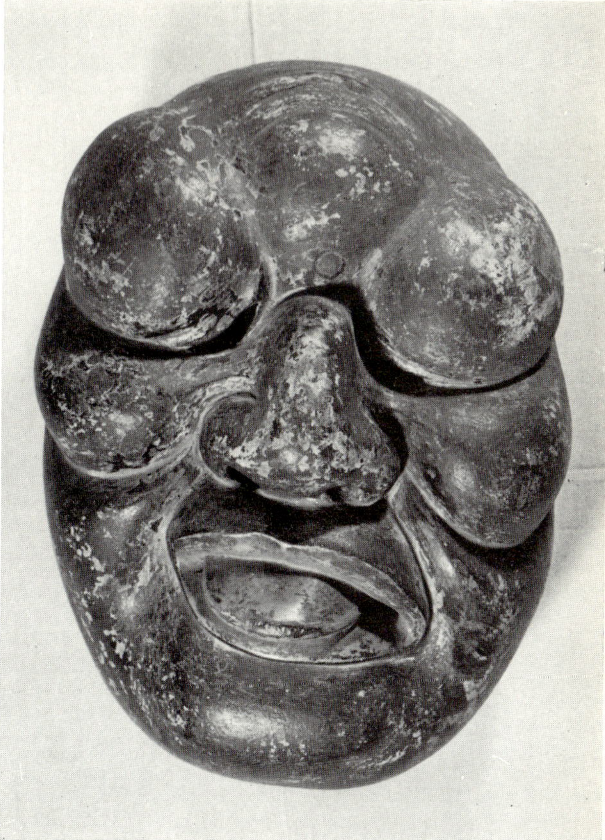

126. Ni-no-mai (Emi-men). Kushibiki Hachiman Shrine, Aomori Prefecture.
127. Ni-no-mai (Hare-men). Kushibiki Hachiman Shrine, Aomori Prefecture.

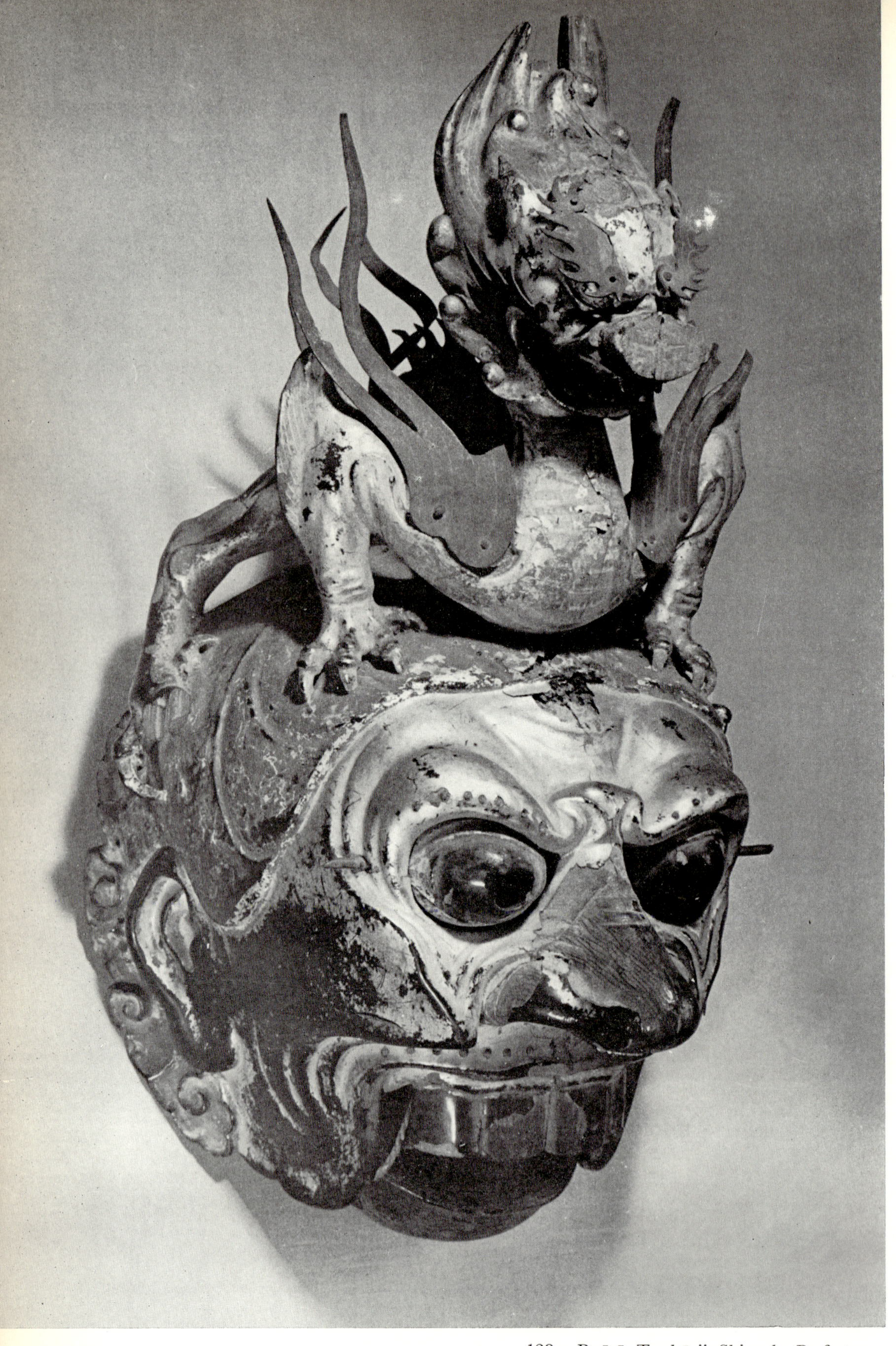

128. Ryō-ō. Tesshū-ji, Shizuoka Prefecture.

129. Ryō-ō. 1328. Ōto Shrine, Chiba Prefecture.

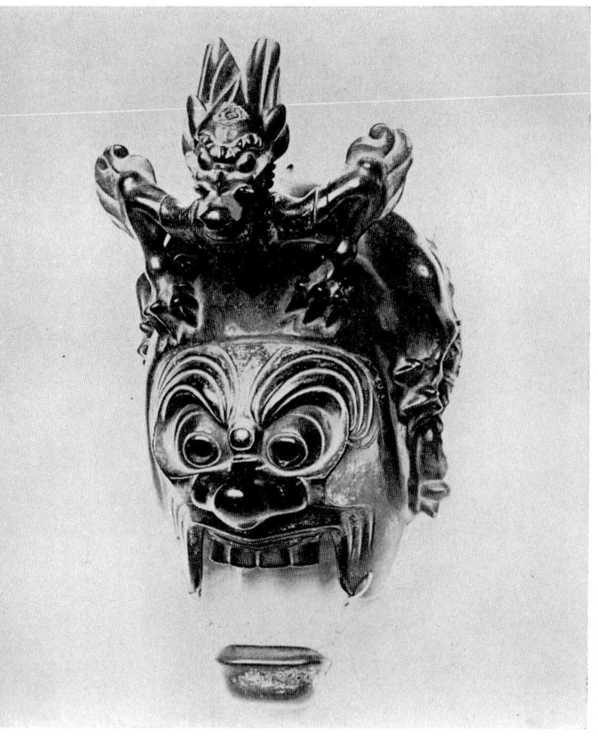

130. Ryō-ō. Tendai-ji, Iwate Prefecture.

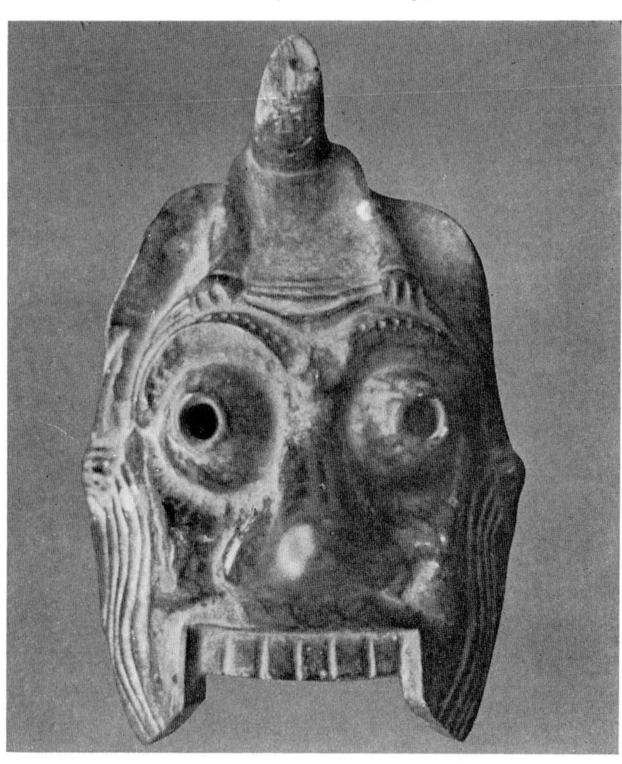

131. Ryō-ō. Tendai-ji, Iwate Prefecture.

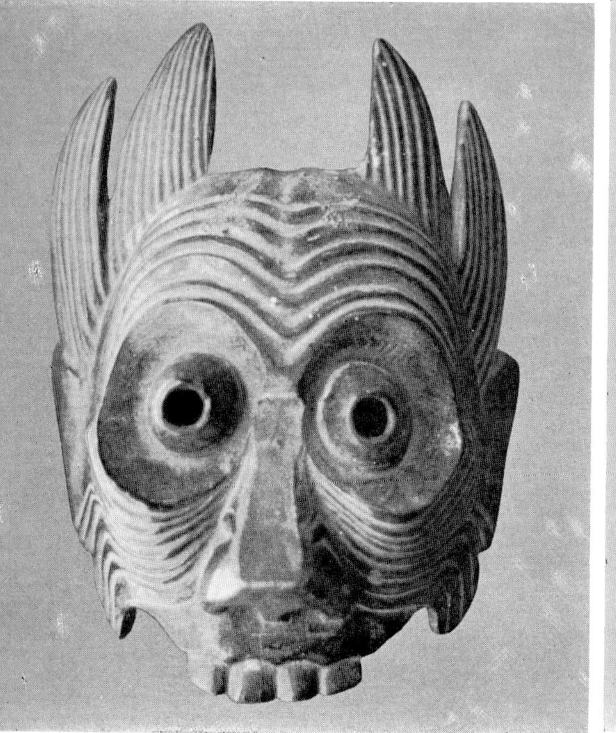

132. Ryō-ō. Hakusan Shrine, Nishi Kubiki County, Niigata Prefecture.

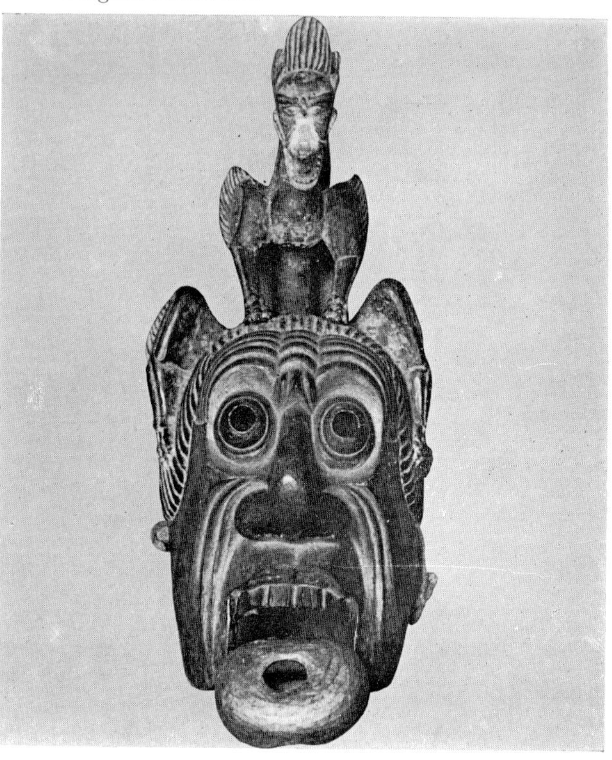

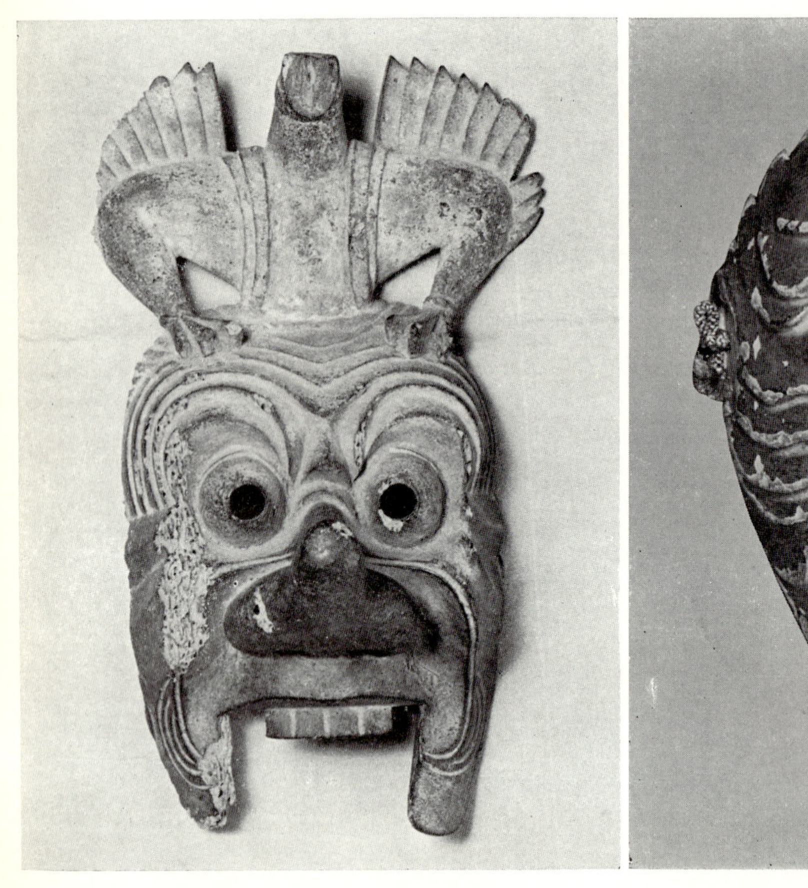

133. Ryō-ō. Nagahama Hachiman Shrine, Ishikawa Prefecture.

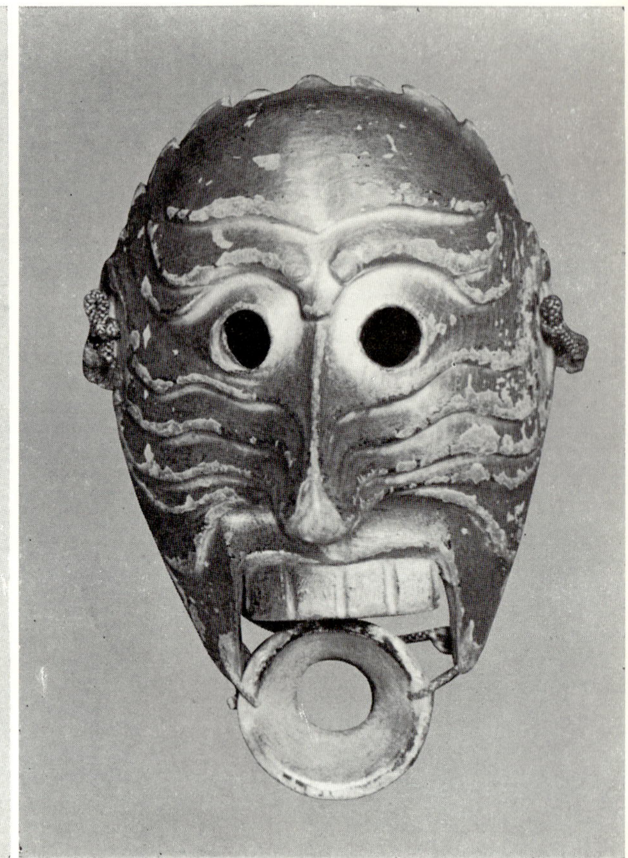

134. Ryō-ō. Amanomiya Shrine, Shizuoka Prefecture.

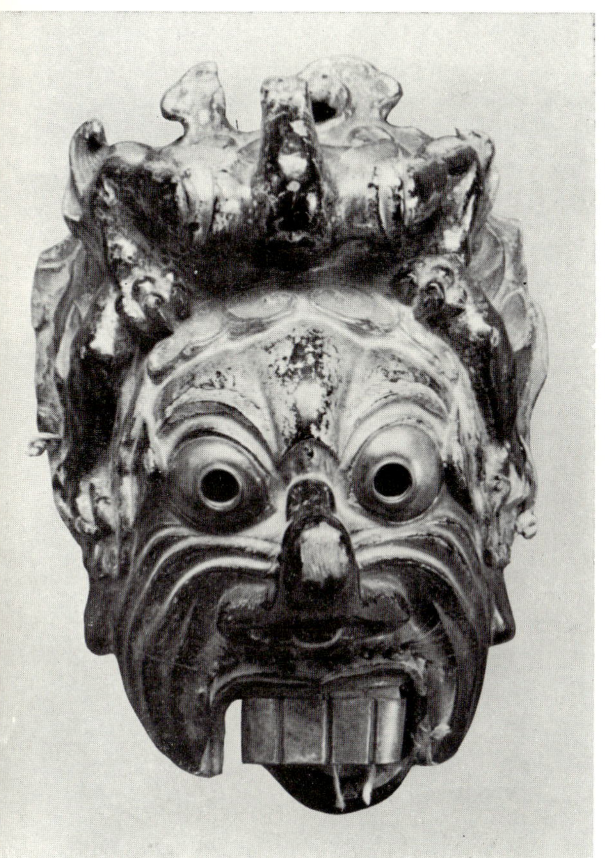

135. Ryō-ō. Sumiyoshi Shrine, Katō County, Hyōgo Prefecture.

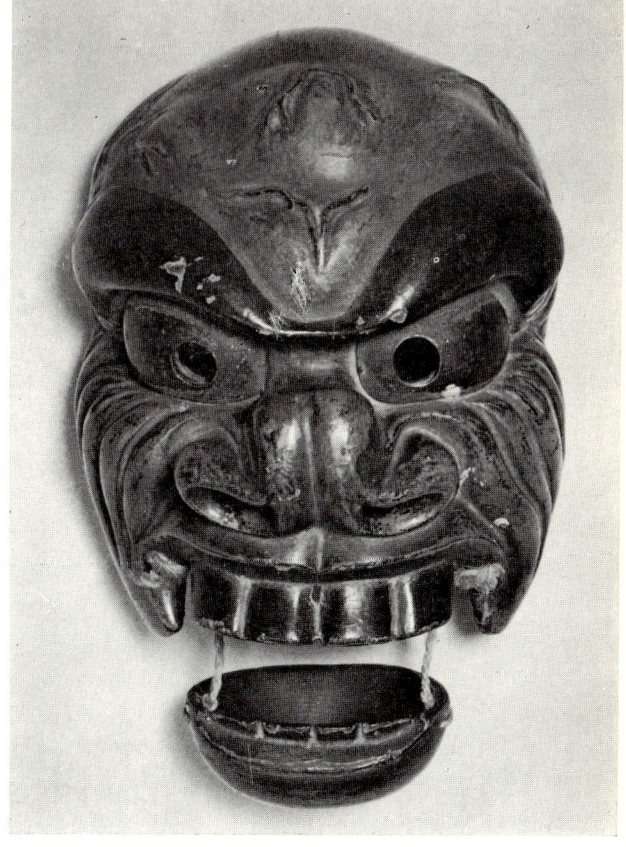

136. Genjōraku. Gokuraku-ji, Kamakura.

137. Genjōraku. Kushibiki Hachiman Shrine, Aomori Prefecture.

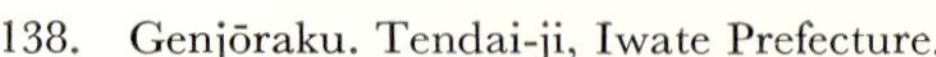

138. Genjōraku. Tendai-ji, Iwate Prefecture.

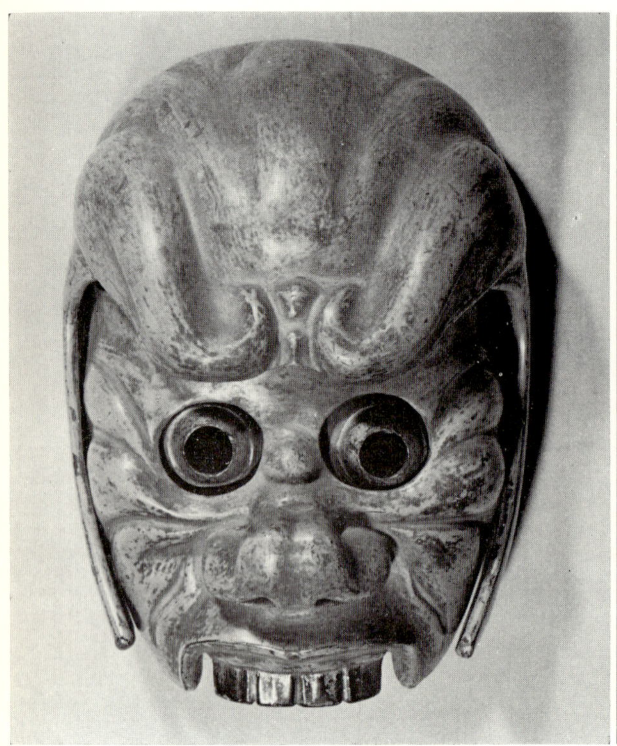

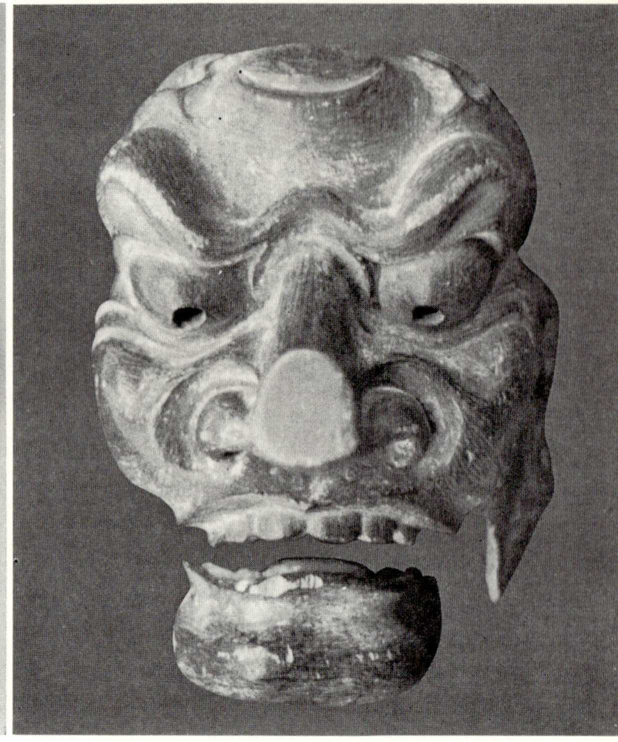

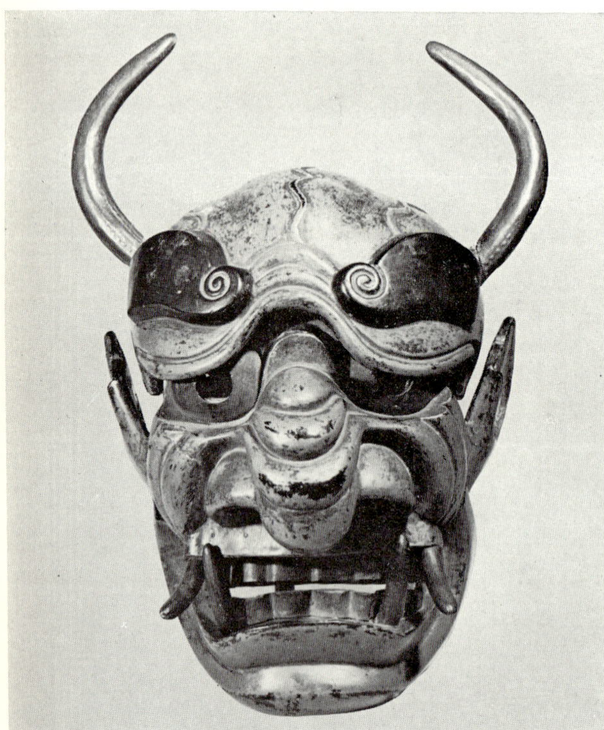

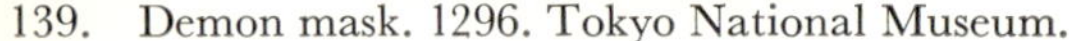

139. Demon mask. 1296. Tokyo National Museum.

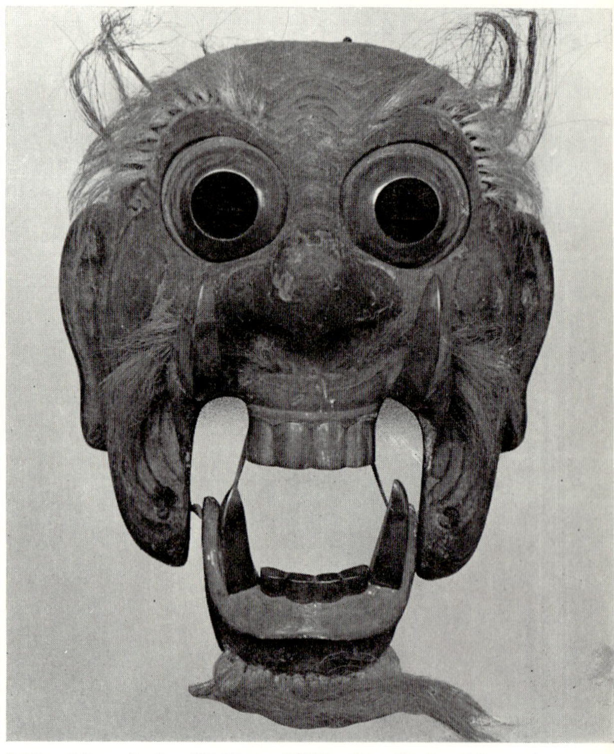

140. Nasori, by Shōjun. 1259. Ise Shrine Repository, Mie Prefecture.

141. Nasori. Tendai-ji, Iwate Prefecture.

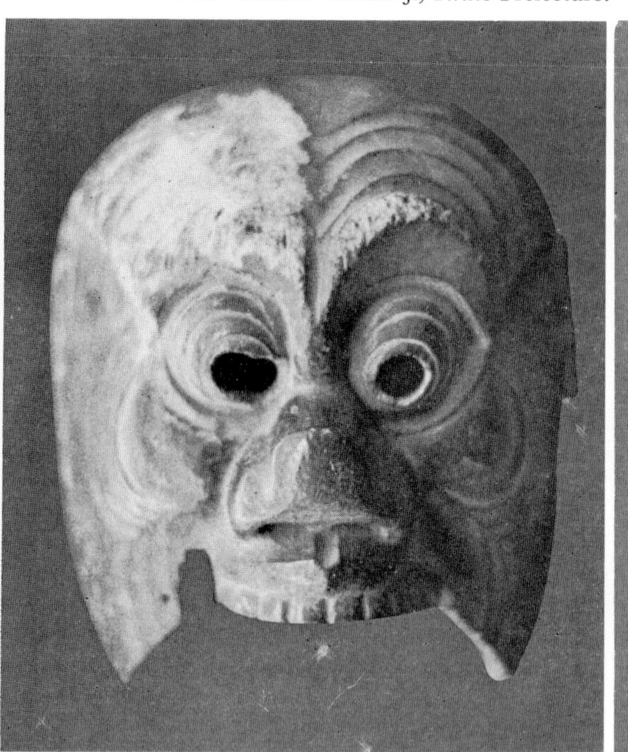

142. Nasori. Amanomiya Shrine, Shizuoka Prefecture.

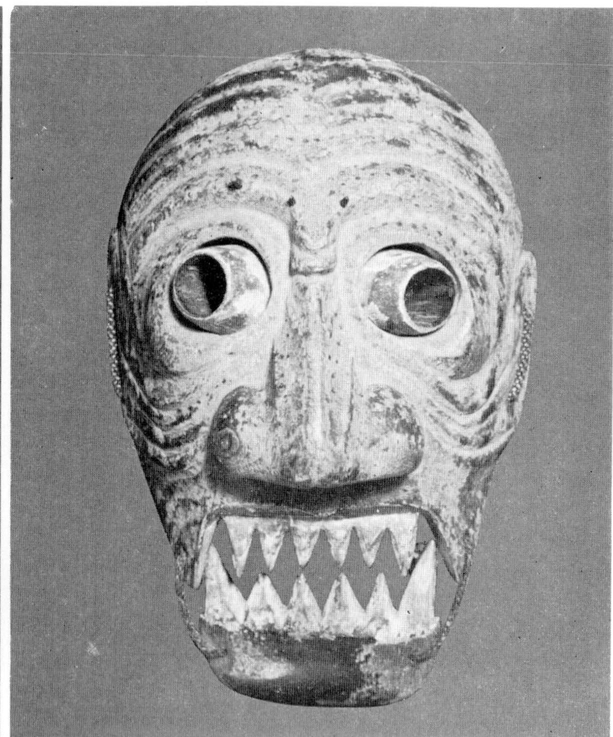

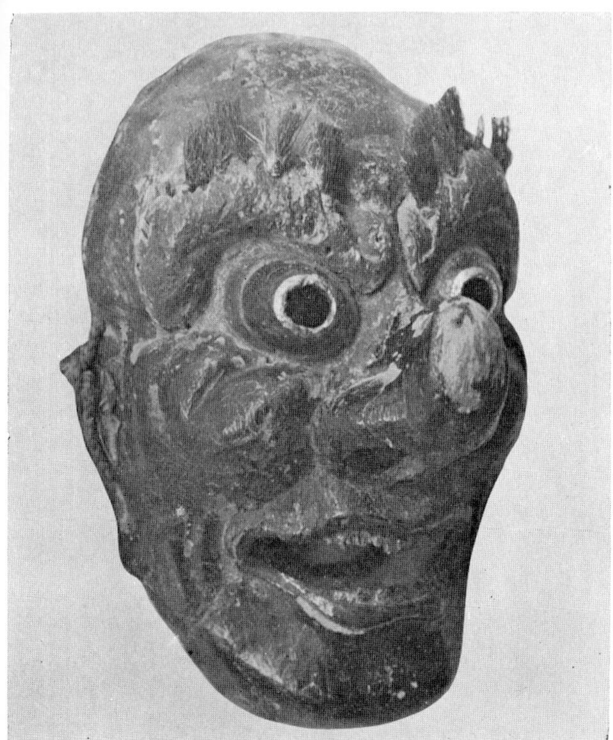

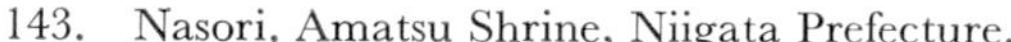

143. Nasori. Amatsu Shrine, Niigata Prefecture.

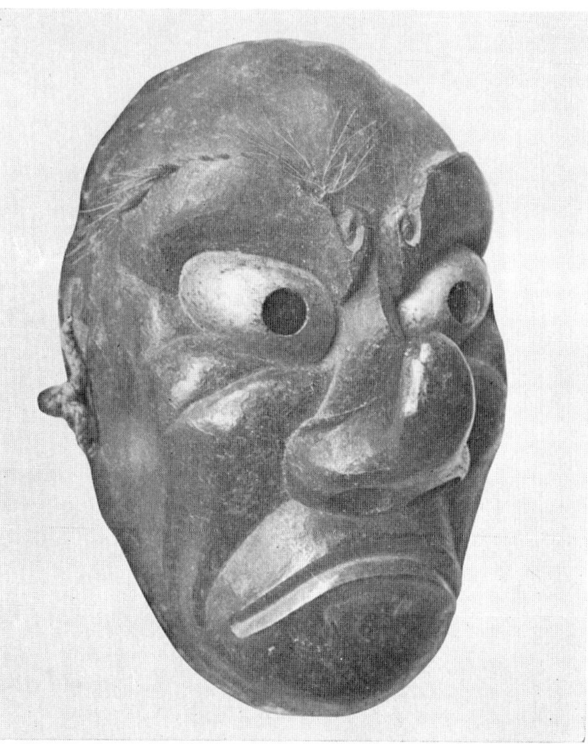

144. Nasori. Amatsu Shrine, Niigata Prefecture.

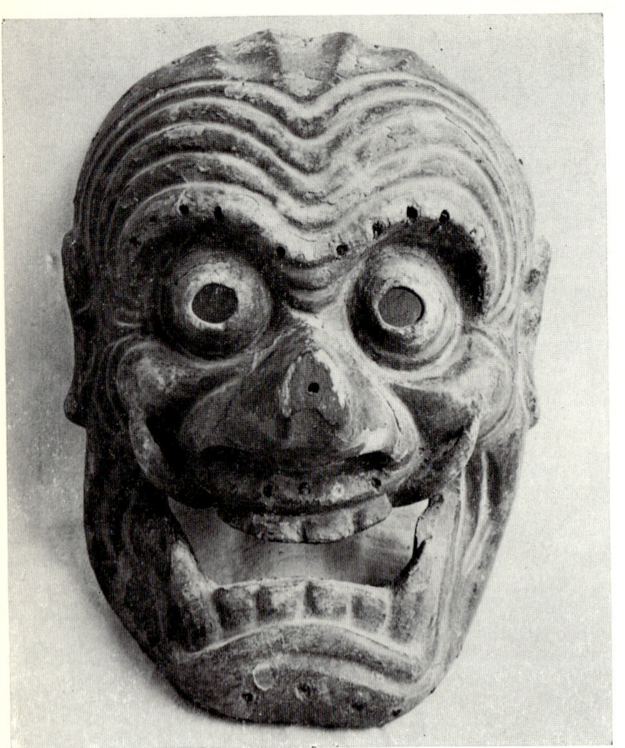

145. Nasori. Futsukamachi Hachiman Shrine, Gifu Prefecture.

146. Batō. Kamitani Shrine, Kagawa Prefecture.

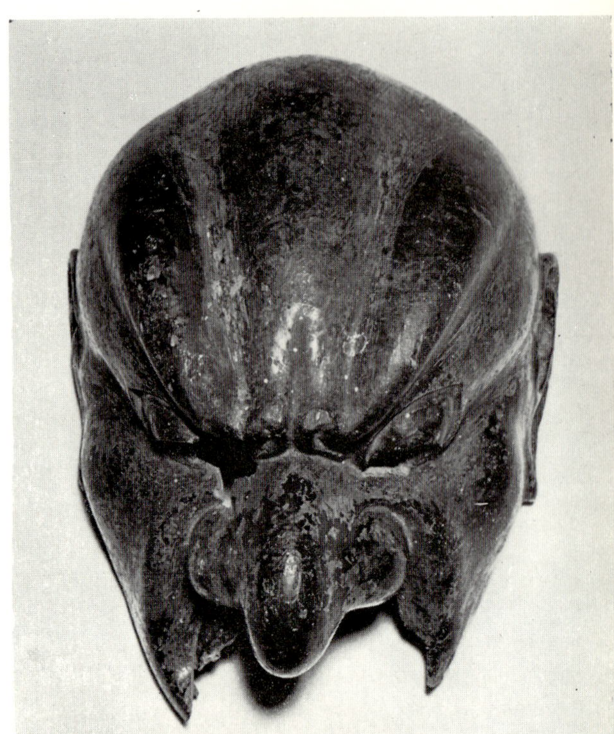

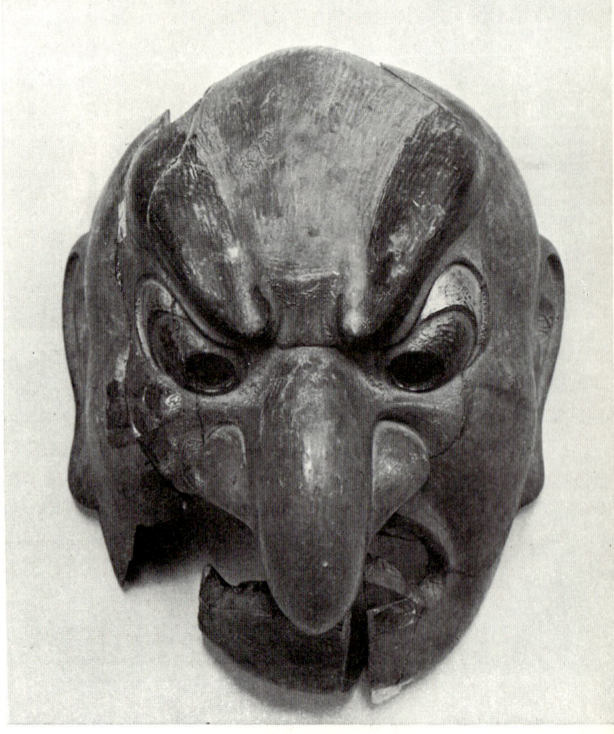



147. Batō. Chiryū Shrine, Aichi Prefecture.

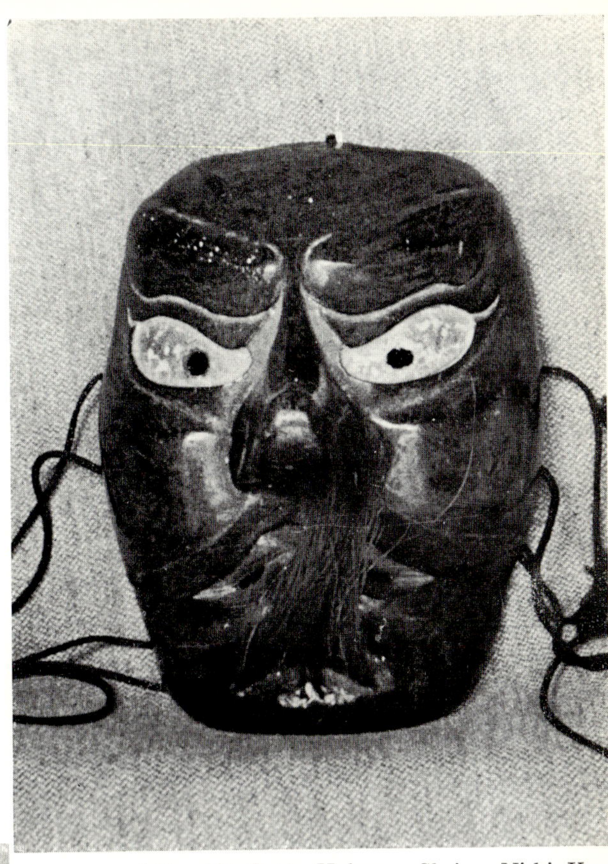

149. Nō Batō. Hakusan Shrine, Nishi Kubiki County, Niigata Prefecture.

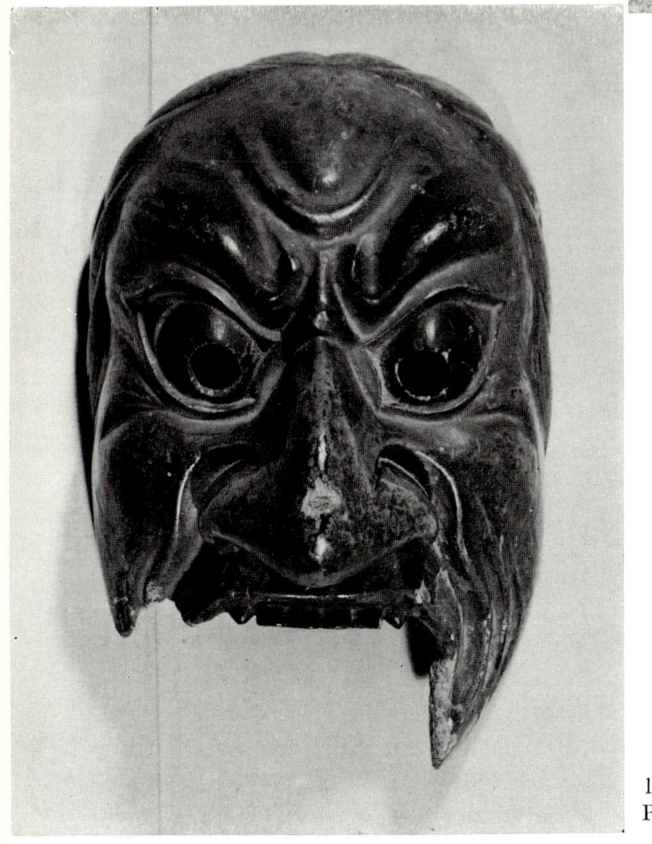

148. Batō. Iwakisan Shrine, Aomori Prefecture.

# 4

# TECHNICAL ASPECTS

As sculpture, Bugaku masks share many carving and painting techniques with Buddhist, Shintō, and secular portrait sculpture of the Heian and Kamakura periods. In fact, most of the Bugaku mask carvers whose names have come down to us were *busshi,* sculptors of Buddhist images, who seem to have carved masks as a sideline. Masks differ from statues in that they are not permanently fixed to be viewed from a determined angle and distance, but are worn in dramatic performance and intended to be seen in motion. As such, masks are fated to be damaged by handling. To keep them fit for use, cracked or broken areas have to be repaired and flaked coloring repainted. When an important inscription is erased from the back by sweat, it is sometimes rewritten. Occasionally a dancer will even recarve the back of the mask around the chin or cheeks to make it fit the contours of his face more comfortably. The poor condition of some masks, however, makes it possible to study their materials and techniques, thus providing valuable insights regarding their construction.

## Types of Wood and Construction

All Bugaku masks are carved from wood, with the single exception of the dry-lacquer Ryō-ō (pl. 114) already discussed in chapter two. Masks made in the Heian period around the cultural centers of Kyoto and Nara are made of lightweight *hinoki* (Japanese cypress; pls. 152–53) or *kiri* (paulownia; pls. 150–51). (The four Shintoriso masks at Kasuga Shrine, pls. 14, 172–73, carved from an unidentified hardwood, are exceptions.) Varieties of Japanese cypress were the standard material not only for masks, but for all wood sculpture made after the Nara period. This preference contrasts with the predominant use of camphor *(kusu)* during the Asuka and Nara periods; accordingly, those Nara-period Gigaku masks that were not made of dry lacquer were generally carved from camphor or less frequently from paulownia. The extremely light weight of paulownia recommended it for masks, but not for Buddhist statues, for which it was too soft and easily damaged.

A far greater variety of woods appear in the provincial masks, which were chiefly made during the Kamakura period and later, and which did not adhere so closely to traditional materials as did the more orthodox masks of the cultural centers. Woods

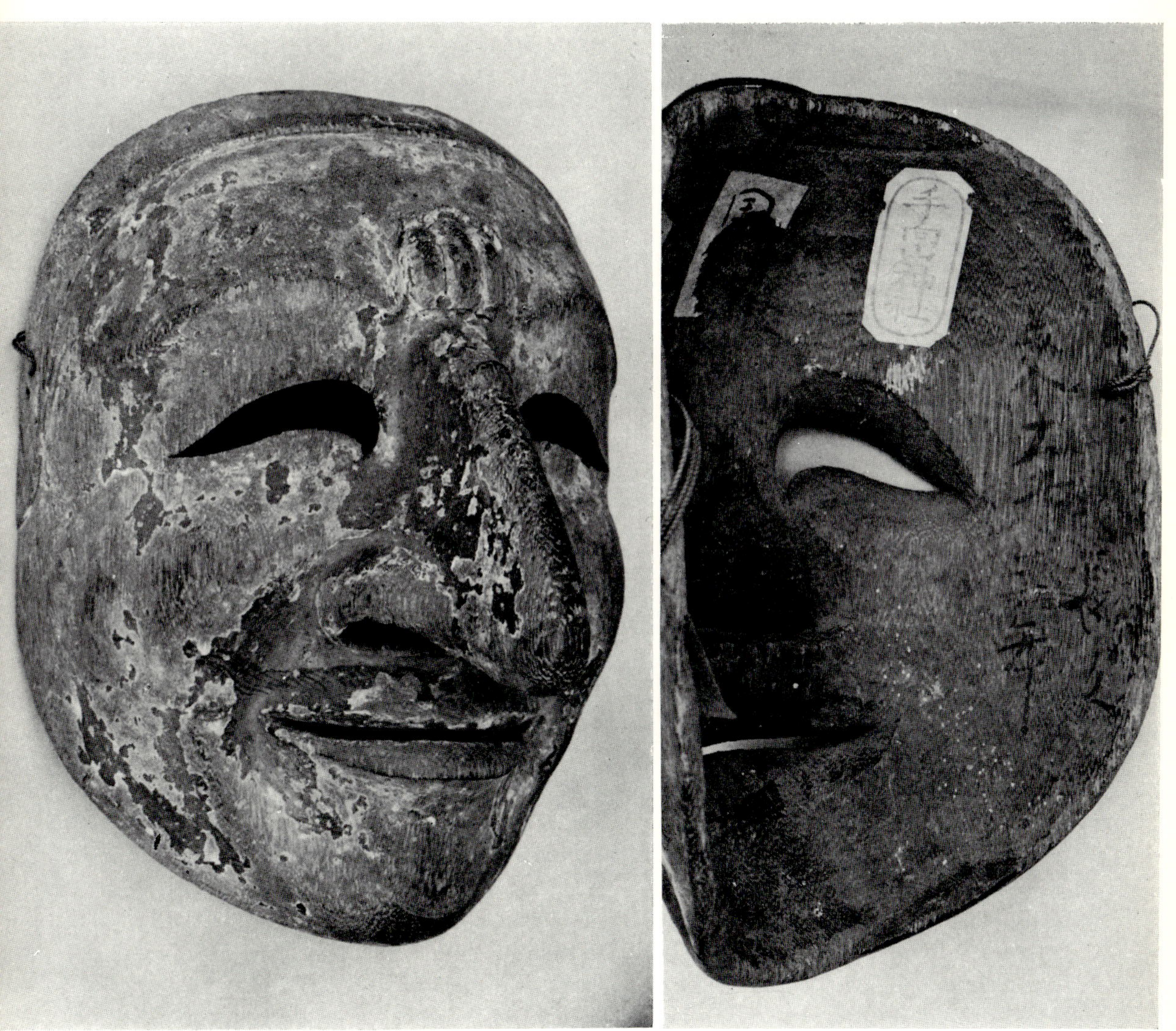

150–51. Chikyū. Paulownia. 1042. Tamukeyama Shrine, Nara.

used include such broad-leafed hardwoods as *hō (Magnolia hypoleuca)* and *katsura (Cercidiphyllum japonicum)* as well as the soft *kaya (Torreya nucifera)* and all kinds of soft Japanese cypresses including *sawara (Chamaecyparis pisifer)*, *asunaro* (hatchet-leaved arborvitae), and *hiba (Thujopsis dolobrata)*.

The majority of Bugaku masks are carved from a single block of wood *(ichiboku)*. Exceptions made by piecing together sections *(warihagi)* arise for two reasons: the largeness of the mask may make it impractical to carve the entire piece from one block, or the thinness of the mask may invite cracking or warping. In the first instance, when the mask is particularly large, extending back to cover the actor's ears and hairline, it can be carved in two sections joined by a horizontal seam down the center (pls. 52, 57). Alternatively, extra slabs of wood can be added at the edges to make up for the insufficient depth of the main block (pl. 53), or the protruding nose can be added separately (pl. 93).

When a mask is carved very thinly, it can be reinforced to minimize the risks of damage by attaching small bracing pieces whose grain lies at right angles to the grain of the main block of wood. Usually such attachments are placed under the chin, or at times around the edges.

In an instance of particular complexity, the dragon on the Ryō-ō mask is made separately and attached to the top of the head. The dragon itself is assembled from two or three pieces fitted together, and occasionally the body is hollowed out to lighten its weight. All movable sections of the masks, such as eyes and chin, are carved separately and then fixed into the mask proper.

When the mask is being carved, both the back and the front are shaped simultaneously, the back being gouged out with curved chisels to form a deep hollow whose concavities correspond to the convex contours of the exterior (pls. 152–53). Holes are opened at the eyes, nostrils, and mouth. Slightly rounded carving knives are used to thin the mask still more and give it a smooth surface.

Although the expression of the face of the mask is of utmost importance, the back of the mask also reveals the quality of the carving. Much can be surmised from the traces left by the knives; even when the chisel work is covered by a layer of cloth and lacquer, one can still recognize the work of a master by the roundness of the hollowed-out contours and by the thinness of the mask. Most twelfth-century masks made around Kyoto are deeply hollowed out, while masks of a later date or of provincial origin are usually more shallowly carved and less precise. In the Edo period, however, when carvers tried to recreate the expression and form of the classic masks, they frequently made faithful copies. Among them are examples hollowed out as deeply as the old models. These late, but sophisticated, copies make carving technique alone an insufficient criterion for judging the age of a mask.

### Priming, Base, and Coloring


The standard method of finishing and painting Bugaku masks consists of three stages:

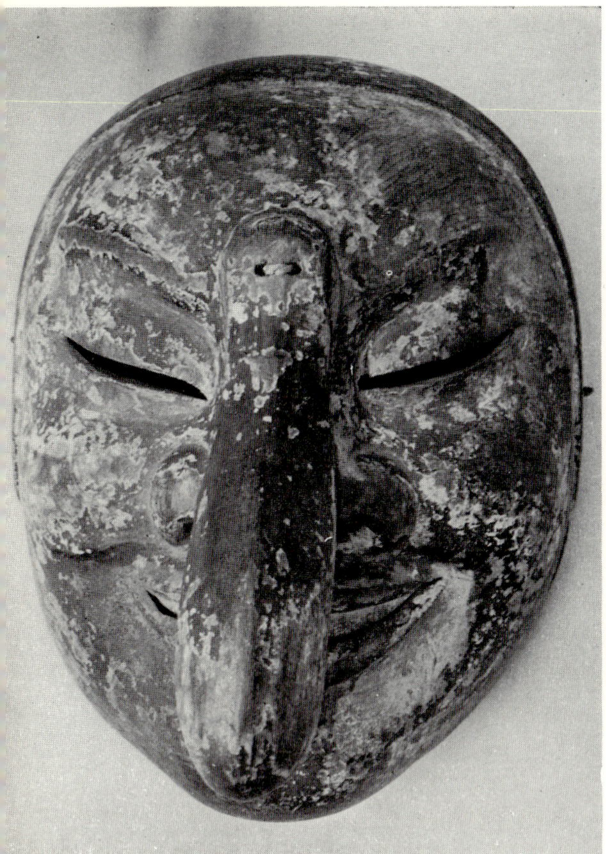

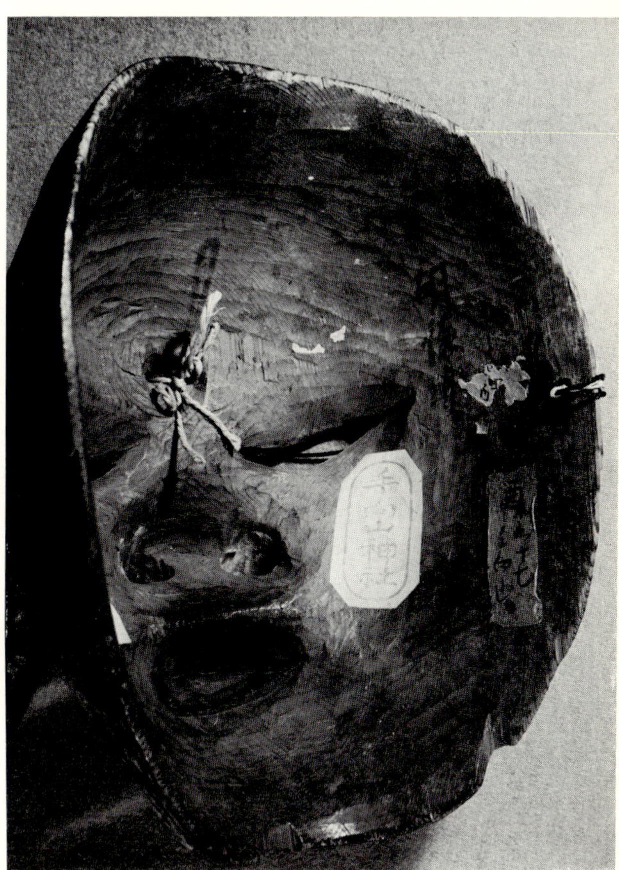

152–53. Kotokuraku. Japanese cypress. 1160. Tamukeyama Shrine, Nara.

1) priming the bare wood to harden the surface and preserve the wood; 2) applying a white kaolin base, which is sanded down; 3) and painting a final application of colored pigments. The hard prime *(kataji)* can be of many kinds, although it is usually made of *sabi urushi,* which is obtained by mixing fine wheat flour with lacquer and then adding *tonoko* (a powder made from impure clay). In some cases, in order to strengthen the surface further, the mask is pasted over with hemp cloth, using lacquer as a binding agent, before the *sabi urushi* is painted on. Such primings are applied to both the front and the back surfaces of the mask, though at times the cloth layer is applied only to the back to protect it from abrasion by the dancer's face.

Once the ground is formed, the back is finished with a layer of black or brown lacquer, while the front is coated with preparatory layers of kaolin. Finally, over the smooth white layer of kaolin, the mask is colored with earth pigments, and in some cases the hair or eyebrows are painted with black lacquer. Some old masks have worn away irregularly to disclose the raw wood, the lacquer ground, or the kaolin base.

Masks such as Batō and Genjōraku, which are finished in red lacquer, have no kaolin coating; the red lacquer is painted directly on the *kataji* priming. For the face of Ryō-ō and for the eyes, teeth, and tusks of Nasori, gold leaf is laid over a coat of special lacquer used as a binding agent.

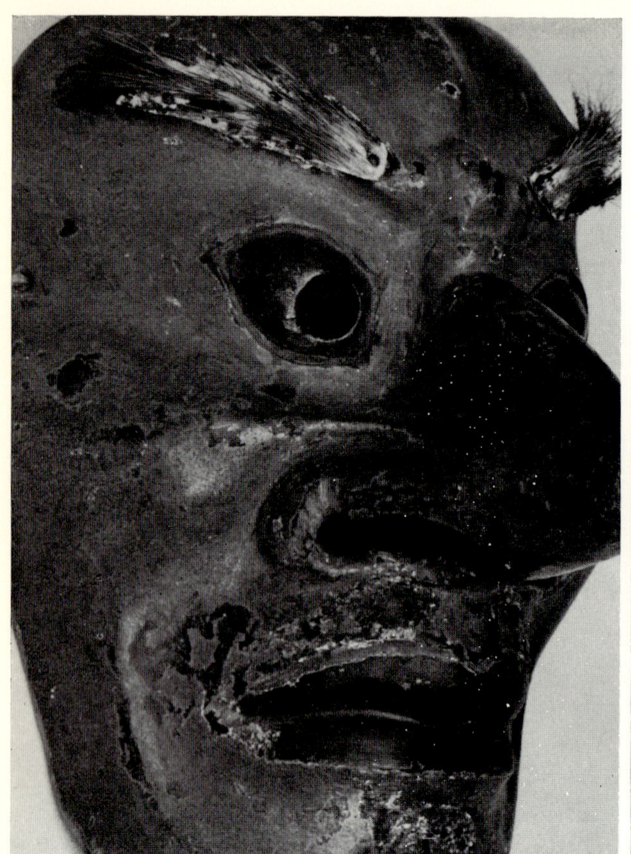

154. Sanju, by Inken. Fur pasted and tacked on for eyebrows and lost mustache. 1207. Tamukeyama Shrine, Nara.

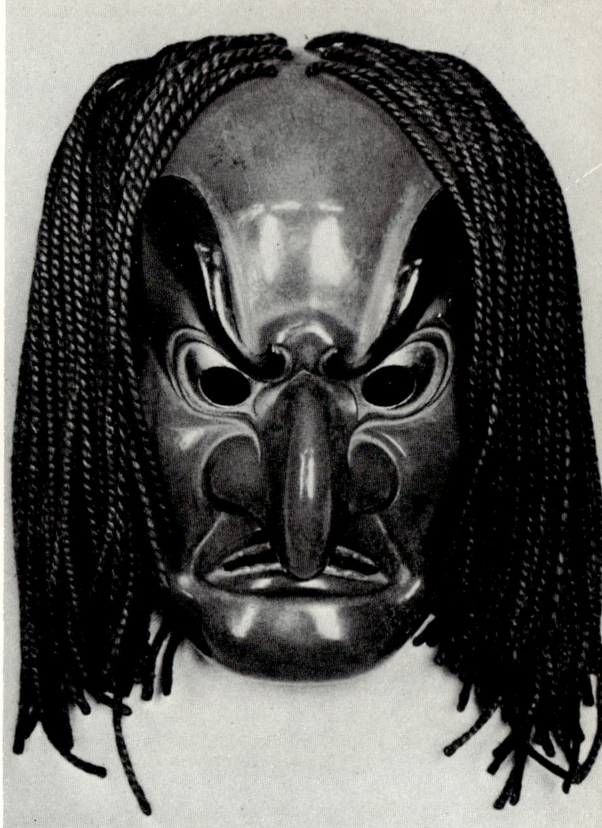

155. Batō. Hair made from tightly twisted navy-blue cords. 1906. Atsuta Shrine, Nagoya.

Most of the masks of the twelfth century (late Heian period) and many of the Kamakura period are made with the standard techniques outlined above, which were borrowed from methods used since the Nara period to finish and paint Buddhist statues. Some masks, however, have been made without the elaborate *kataji* priming, the kaolin base being applied directly to the untreated wood and the back being left untouched. Many Buddhist statues of the ninth and tenth centuries employ this technique. Examples among Bugaku masks include the seven Heian-period Kotokuraku at Hōryū-ji (pls. 35, 38–39), the masks dated 1042 at Tamukeyama Shrine and Tōdai-ji (pls. 16, 21, 25, 42, 45, 150–51, 163), and all masks dated 1160 at Tamukeyama Shrine (pls. 31–32, 36, 152–53).

Comparatively inferior masks of a later date, especially those of provincial origin, simplify the painting in a variety of ways. Some received an initial layer of black lacquer, followed by a coat of *gofun* (which is used also on later sculpture and Nō masks) and then by a final coating of pigments. Some masks have substituted a weak "mud ground" *(doroji)*, made of *tonoko* mixed with animal glue *(nikawa)*, in place of the black lacquer ground. Some even have the colored pigments applied directly to the untreated wood.

### Animal Hair and Fur


The hair, eyebrows, and mustache of a few Bugaku masks are represented natural-

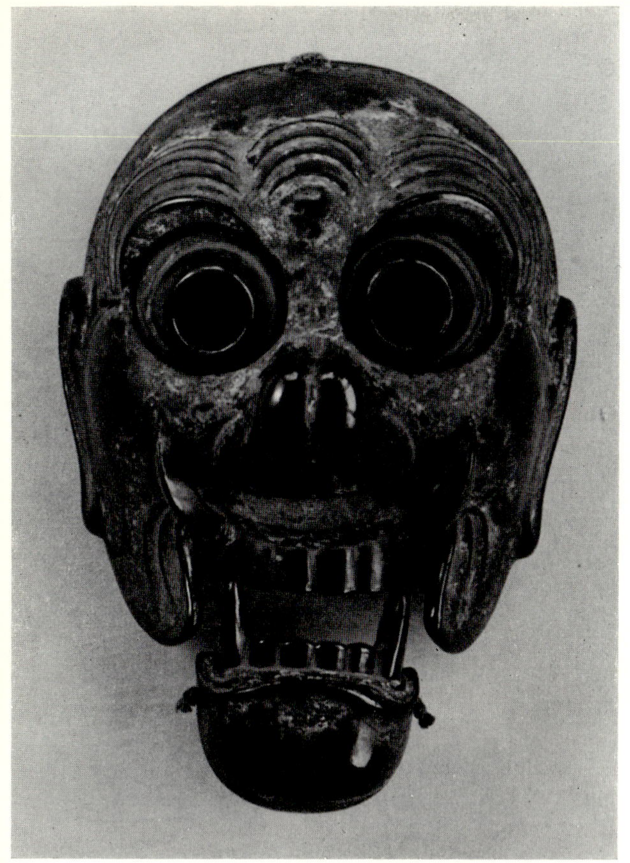

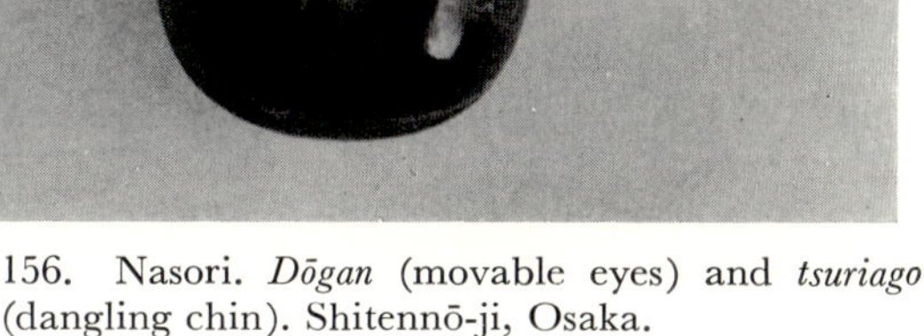

156. Nasori. *Dōgan* (movable eyes) and *tsuriago* (dangling chin). Shitennō-ji, Osaka.

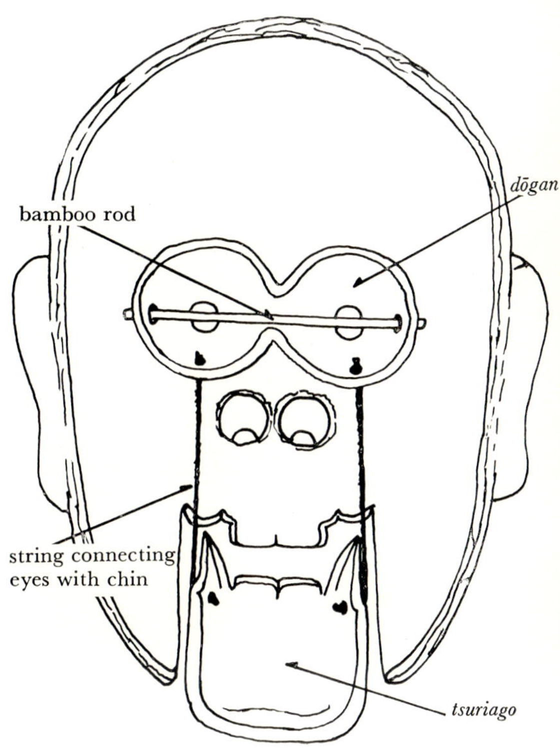



157. Drawing of *dōgan* (movable eyes) and *tsuriago* (dangling chin) in Nasori and how they are attached to each other; by the author.

istically by inserting into prepared holes clusters of animal hair, held fast by small bamboo or wooden pegs. The eyebrows of Sanju (pl. 154), Korobase, and some Genjōraku (pl. 106; fur now lost) are made of fur pasted on with lacquer and held down with small wooden pegs. Although the use of such naturalistic devices appears at first to stem from a desire for realism, they actually heighten the supernatural appearance of the mask, setting off its exaggerated and stylized qualities. In a like manner, Batō, with tightly twisted blue cords in place of glossy hair, aims at an otherwordly effect in the sound of the thick cords rapping against the red-lacquered face (pl. 155).

The hair found on Bugaku masks is generally soft and profuse. In contrast, hair implanted in Nara-period Gigaku masks is usually short, thick, and strong, radiating perpendicularly from the surface of the mask, and sometimes made of vegetable fiber held down by round copper sheets. Muromachi-period Nō masks almost invariably had horse hairs neatly bunched together.

## Movable Parts of the Mask

### *Dōgan (Movable Eyes)*

The eyes of Ryō-ō, Nasori, and Saisōrō are built so as to rotate up and down. The two eyes are carved from a single piece of wood and held in the eye sockets from the back by means of a bamboo or copper rod attached to the temples (pl. 157). This method allows the eyes to move up and down in unison. The eyes of Saisōrō are

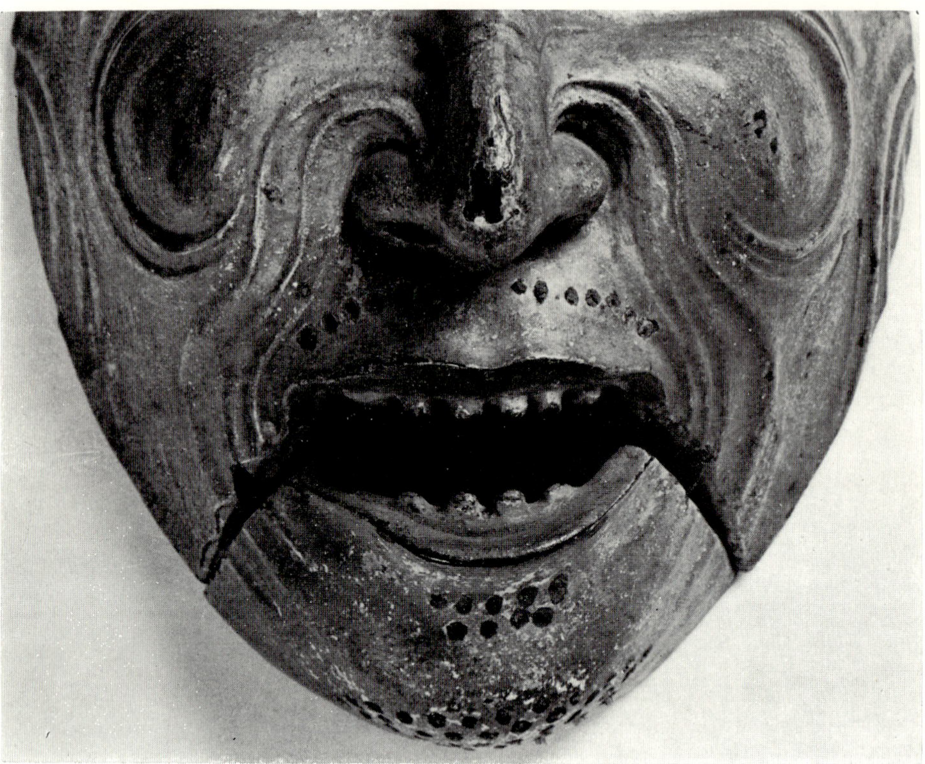

fixed by strings attached to the outer edges of the eye sockets because their lenselike flatness makes it difficult to skewer them with a rod.

*Tsuriago (Dangling Chin)*

The dangling chin of such masks as Ryō-ō, Nasori, and Genjōraku is also made from a separate piece of wood and hung by cords so that it can move freely. In Ryō-ō and Nasori masks the dangling chin is attached to the upper edge of the movable eyes (pls. 156–57). As the chin oscillates with the rhythm of the dance, it induces movement in the eyes. This interacting construction is peculiar to Bugaku masks.

*Kiriago (Detached Chin)*

The detached chin of Saisōrō is also carved from a separate piece of wood and joined to the mask by strings (pls. 158–59). As the joint fits neatly like a seam, the chin appears to have been cut off from the mask, only to be refit in place: hence the name *kiriago,* "cut-off chin." Saisōrō is the only Bugaku mask using this device, but it appears also in the Okina mask (pl. 8) used in the Nō play *Okina.* As the movements of *Okina* bear some resemblance to those of *Saisōrō,* the detached chin of Okina may have been borrowed from Saisōrō. While the strings that join the chin to the mask

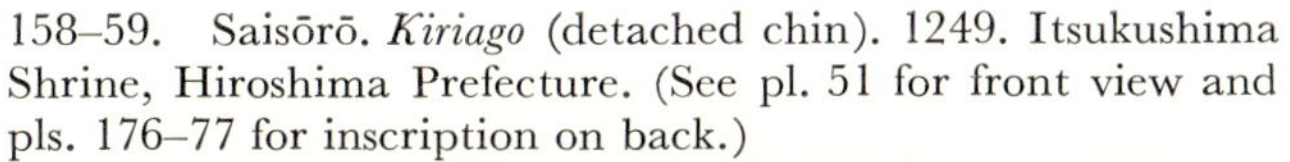

158–59. Saisōrō. *Kiriago* (detached chin). 1249. Itsukushima Shrine, Hiroshima Prefecture. (See pl. 51 for front view and pls. 176–77 for inscription on back.)

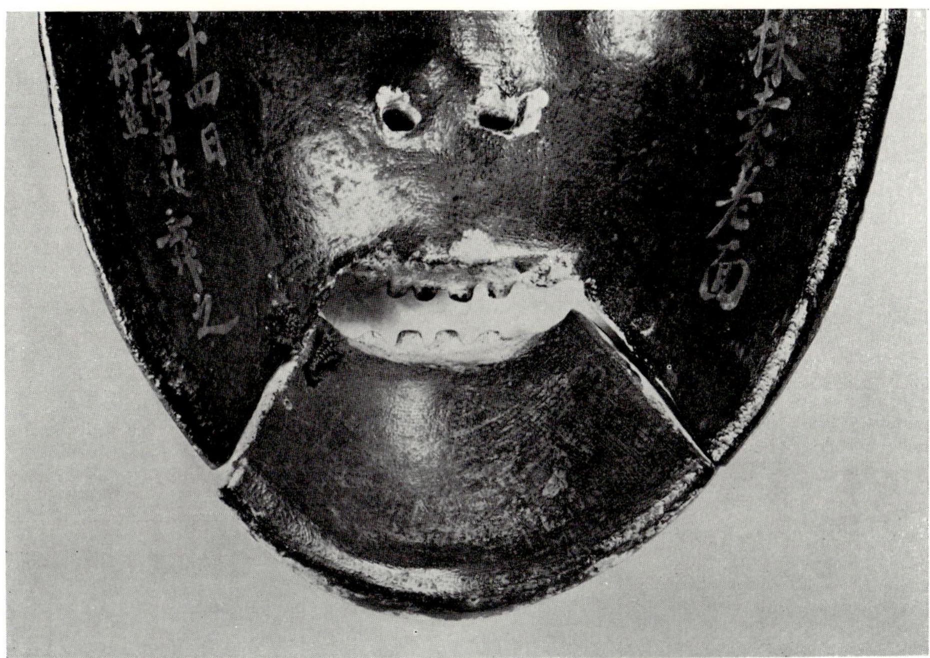

of Saisōrō are threaded through small holes bored through the cross section of the fissure so that the strings are invisible, the heavy cord that connects the chin of Okina is decoratively tied at the corners of the mouth. In both cases the chin cannot actually move with much freedom. Perhaps the detached chin is merely a formal vestige of an earlier movable structure. Or perhaps, as another explanation suggests, the chin once accidentally broke off and, after being hastily reattached with strings, was found to be effective, particularly as it contrasted to the dangling chin. There may be some ancient connection between the detached chin of Saisōrō and similarly constructed chins of certain Indonesian folk masks. Though the extant Indonesian masks go back only to the nineteenth century, they may preserve devices from earlier masks. Their chins are connected to the masks at the back by thin bands made of soft, flexible deerskin. The mouth can open and close freely, and it makes a clicking sound as the mask moves.

*Dōbi (Movable Nose)*

The long nose of Kotokuraku is carved from a separate piece of wood and tied to the mask by means of a string passing through a small hole in the bridge of the nose (pls. 152–53). As mentioned previously, this movable nose is made so that it can sway

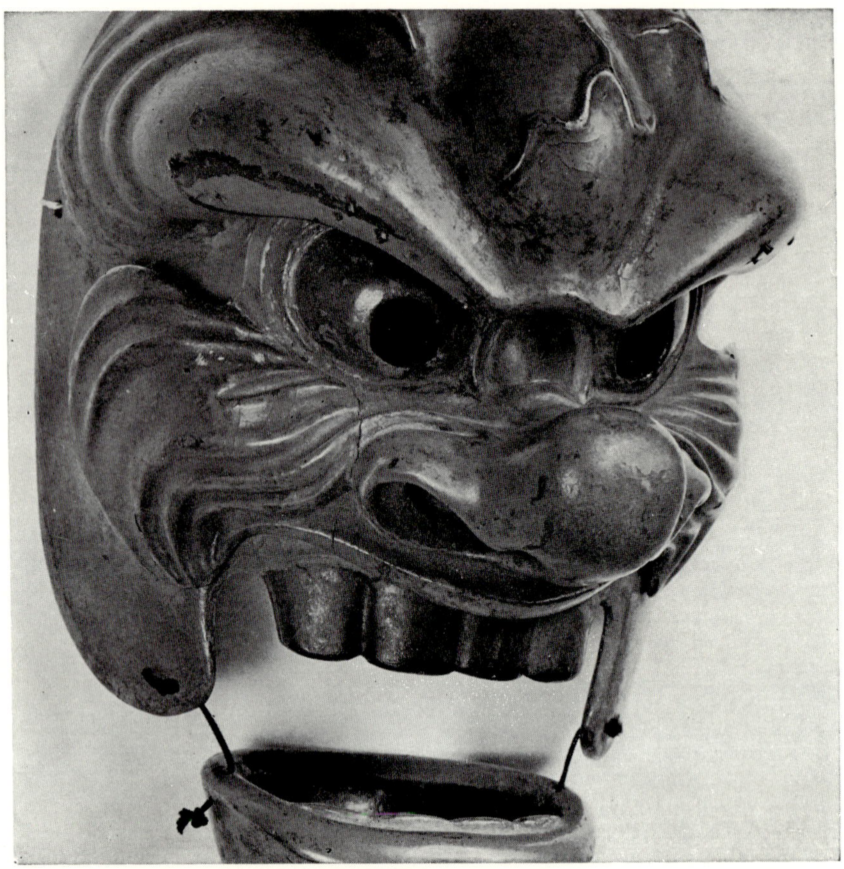

160–61 (above and opposite). Genjōraku, by Gyōmyō. *Dōbō* (movable visage plate). 1173. Itsukushima Shrine, Hiroshima Prefecture. (See also pl. 106.)

from left to right with the drunken movements of the inebriated young barbarians. This construction occurs in no other Japanese mask.

*Dōbō (Movable Visage Plate)*

Genjōraku has a unique construction called the *dōbō*. The entire facial area, including eyes, nose, cheeks, and upper lip, is carved out of a separate block of wood, inserted underneath the eyebrows, and so fixed to the mask that it shakes gently with the dancer's movements (pls. 160–62).

Masks using the devices discussed here are designed to move in response to the rhythms of the dances. The controlled movement of a part of the mask serves to heighten the impact of the exaggerated and staccato gestures of the dancer.

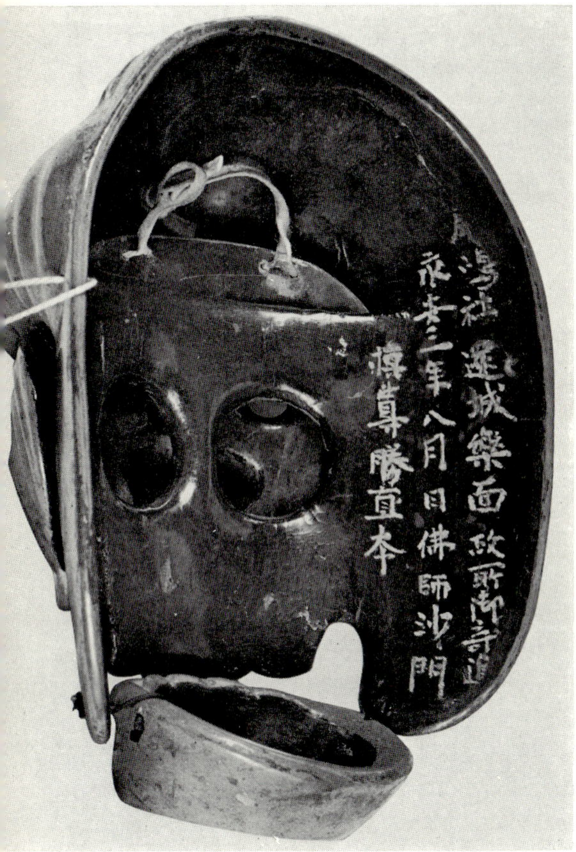

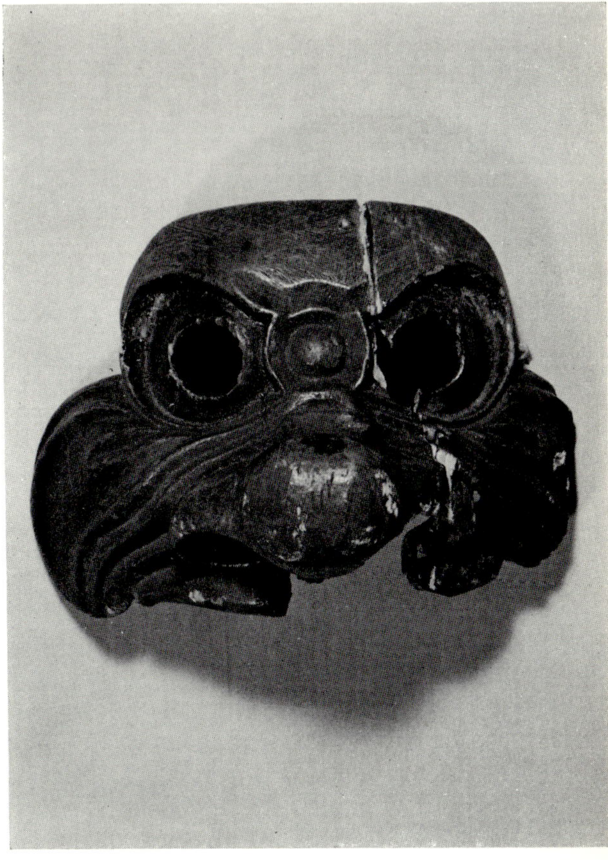

162. Genjōraku (fragment). *Dōbō* (movable visage plate), consisting of eyes, nose, cheeks, and upper lip. Ōboshi Shrine, Aomori Prefecture.

# 5

# INSCRIPTIONS AND MASK CARVERS

## Inscriptions

Bugaku masks frequently bear inscriptions corresponding to the dedications on Buddhist statues. They usually include the date, the name of the sculptor, the name of the client, the name of the mask, the number of dancers in the piece, and the date of repair. These inscriptions provide important clues to the historical study and dating of all Bugaku masks.

For the most part inscriptions are written on the back of the mask, on the right or left side, or sometimes in the bowl of the forehead. When the back of the mask is unlacquered, black *sumi* ink is used for writing the inscription (pls. 163–64). When the back has a lacquer *kataji* priming, the inscription is written with red lacquer or, in a few cases, with red paint (pls. 165–73, 176–79). A few inscriptions are incised and then painted over (pls. 174–75). Since inscriptions are often placed on that portion of the mask that rubs against the dancer's cheeks, they are apt to wear off. Many have been rewritten exactly over the original text. When the entire back is relacquered, the whole inscription may be newly written.

The inscription on the Chikyū mask at Tamukeyama Shrine (pl. 163; right side only) exemplifies the oldest and simplest kind. It reads from right to left:

(right) Tōdai-ji. Chōkyū 3.
(left) Ōtoku 3, 3rd month, 14th day. Repaired.
Chikyū mask.

The inscription indicates that this mask was made for Tōdai-ji in the third year of the Chōkyū era (1042), and was repaired in the third year of the Ōtoku era (1086). The name of the mask, Chikyū, was added later. This is one of a set of sixteen masks dated 1042 and housed in Tōdai-ji, Tamukeyama Shrine, and elsewhere.

The names of the temples or shrines appearing in the inscriptions serve to identify the original owners of the mask. For example, inscriptions prove that those masks now kept in Kasuga Shrine originally belonged to, or were dedicated to, Kōfuku-ji (pls. 172–73; see p. 162). Until the end of the Edo period Kasuga Shrine and Kōfuku-ji were considered one entity, the shrine serving as the guardian of the temple; however,

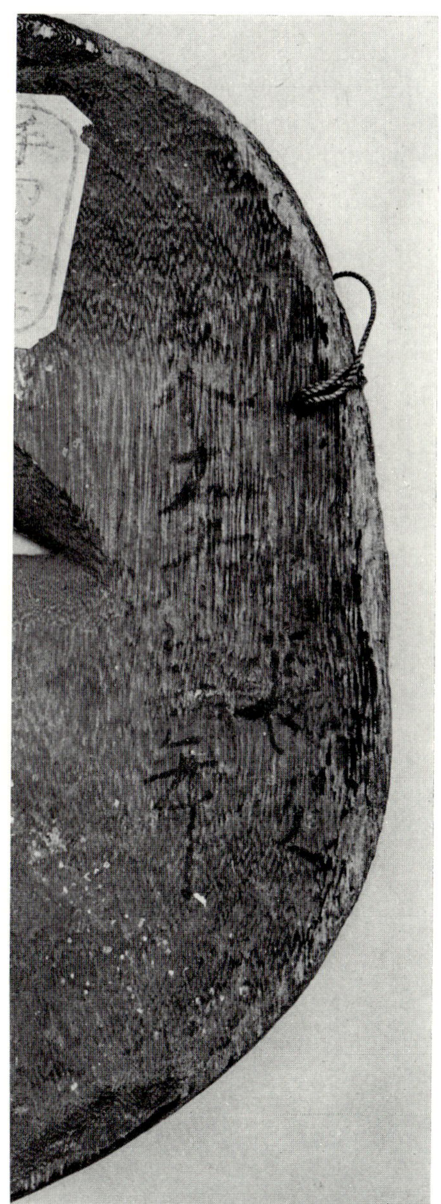

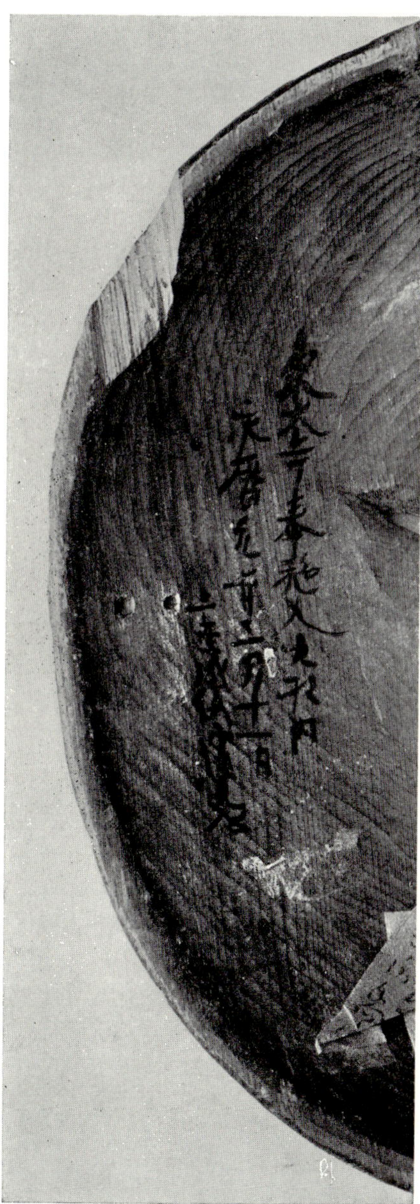

163. Chikyū. Inscription in black *sumi* ink. 1042. Tamukeyama Shrine, Nara.

164. Kotokuraku. Inscription in black *sumi* ink. 1160. Tamukeyama Shrine, Nara. (See pl. 36 for front view.)

with the official separation of Shintōism and Buddhism at the beginning of the Meiji era (1868–1912), all the masks were removed to Kasuga Shrine. A similar relationship between Tōdai-ji and Tamukeyama Shrine would suggest that the masks now housed in both institutions were all kept originally in Tōdai-ji. To judge from the inscriptions on the seven Kotokuraku masks (one a Kotokuraku Kempai) in Tamukeyama Shrine and Himuro Shrine, these masks are what remain of a set of nine dedicated to Tōdai-ji in 1160. The following is an example of one of these inscriptions (all basically the same), the left side of which is shown in plate 164:

(right) Kotokuraku.
(left) One of nine masks presented to Tōdai-ji.
Eiryaku 1 [1160], 3rd month, 11th day.
Abbot Kakunin.

Kakunin's signature indicates either that he wrote the inscription himself or that he commissioned the mask.

Verified by historical data, inscriptions bring out many interesting points. Their few lines can illuminate facts concerning the conditions of Bugaku in a given era. The Kamakura period abounds with records indicating that several shrines would assist each other on major festival days by lending dancers and properties, since most shrines could not support enough musicians for large Bugaku performances. Thus performers from Shitennō-ji in Osaka participated in the Bugaku at Nara's Hōryū-ji during the thirteenth and fourteenth centuries because of the lack of musicians in the Nara district. Inscriptions such as "This mask should not be removed from this shrine except for sacred ceremonies" were meant, it can therefore be deduced, to avoid confusion of masks and costumes when one shrine assisted another. The following inscription suggests that Atsuta Shrine joined forces with the neighboring Masumida Shrine for major festivals (pl. 170–71):

(right) Jishō 2 [1178], the year of the dog. Blue sunny sky. Repaired.
Kōan 2 [1279], the year of the monkey. Red bright sky. Repaired.
(left) Should . . . not . . . be . . . away except for sacred ceremonies of the shrine.

Interpolating from similar inscriptions on other masks at Atsuta Shrine, the writing on the left probably read: "Should not be removed except for sacred ceremonies of the shrine."

The indication of the date of repair in the above inscription is rather intriguing. Since the calligraphy is in a uniform hand, we can assume that the entire inscription was written in 1279. The inscription mentions that the mask was repaired for the first time in 1178, but as the mask itself seems to have been made about that time, it is possible that the word "repair" was first written in the wrong place and then rewritten in its proper place.

165. Sanju, by Inken. Inscription in red lacquer. 1207. Tōdai-ji, Nara. (See pl. 69 for front view.)

166. Ni-no-mai (Emi-men), by Gyōmyō. Inscription in red lacquer. 1173. Itsukushima Shrine, Hiroshima Prefecture. (See pl. 59 for front view.)

167. Batō, by Gyōmyō. Inscription in red lacquer. 1173. Itsukushima Shrine, Hiroshima Prefecture. (See pl. 96 for front view.)

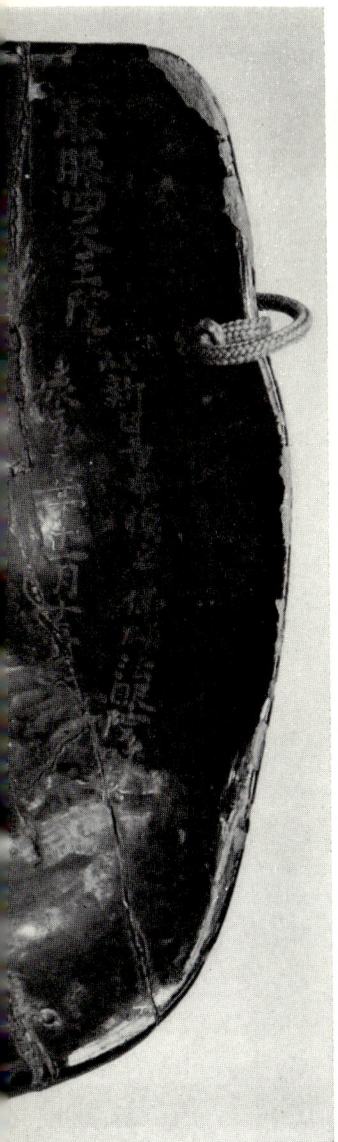

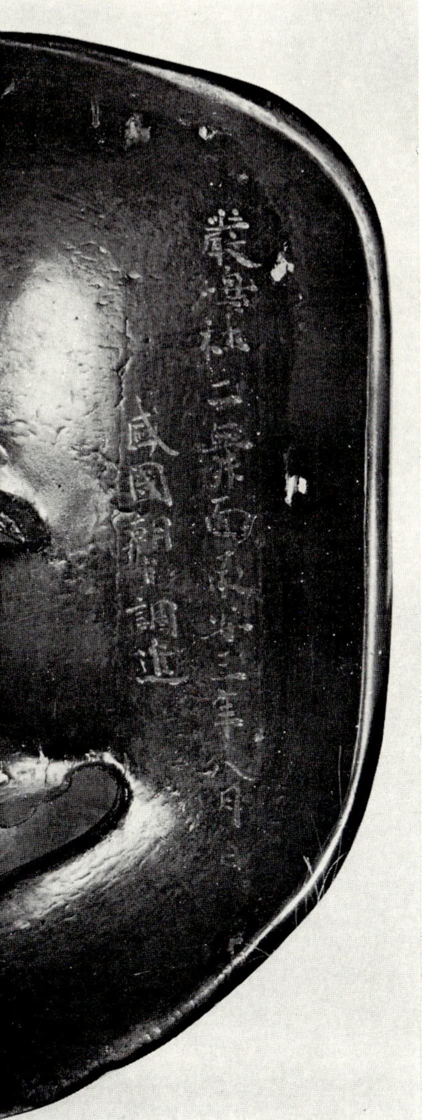

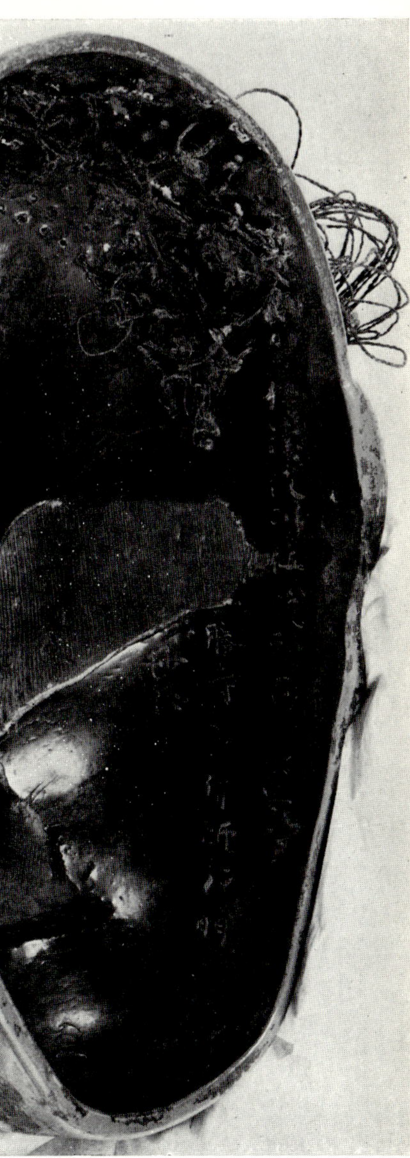

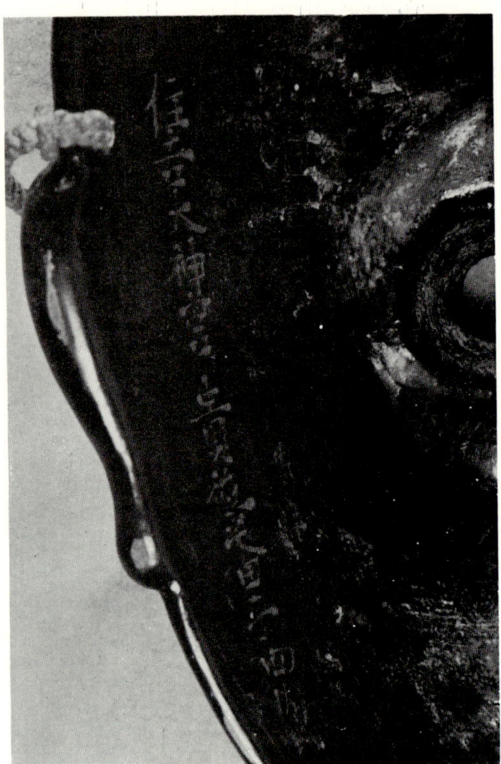

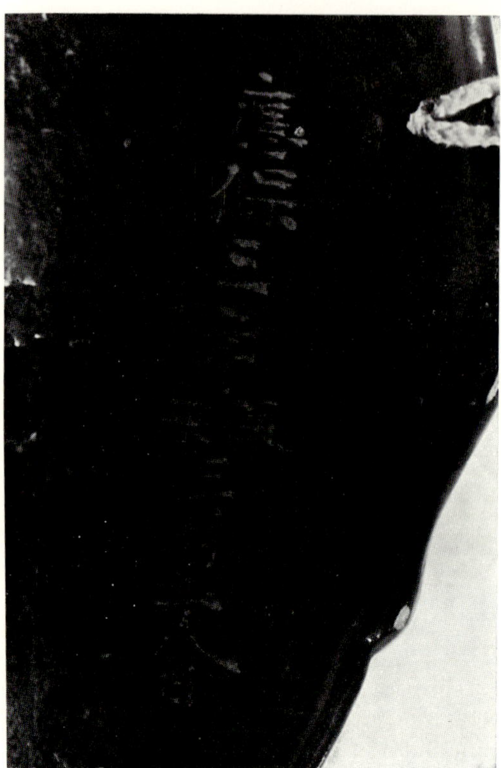

Of note also is the zodiac indication of the year and month. The Japanese adopted from the Chinese a sexagesimal cycle for indicating dates, which was composed of repeating cycles of the five elements and the twelve animal signs. "The year of the dog" in the inscription therefore was an indication of the date 1178. "Blue sunny sky" was an early way of referring to spring, while "red bright sky" indicated summer.

Other inscriptions give us clues as to the number of masks that originally formed one set, or to the names of famous dancers.

Plates 168–69

(left) Ōhō 3 [1163], the year of the goat, 3rd month, 18th day.

(right) Sumiyoshi Shrine. One of four Kitoku Banko masks.

Plates 176–77

(right) Itsukushima Shrine. Saisōrō mask.

(left) Kenchō 1 [1249], 9th month, 14th day.

. . . Hisashige [or Hisasuke], present *ukon-no-shōgen,* dancer.

This inscription on the back of Saisōrō records the name of the dancer, his title, and the date he wore the mask. Considering the workmanship, the year 1249 can be interpreted to be the date of carving as well.

168–69. Kitoku Banko. Inscription in red lacquer. 1163. Sumiyoshi Shrine, Osaka. (See pl. 91 for front view.)

170–71. Genjōraku. Restoration inscriptions in red lacquer. 1178. Atsuta Shrine, Nagoya. (See pl. 105 for front view.)

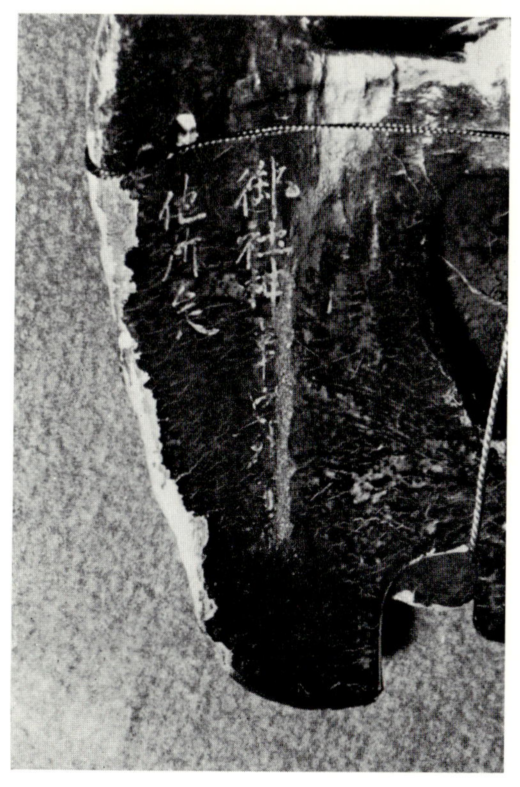

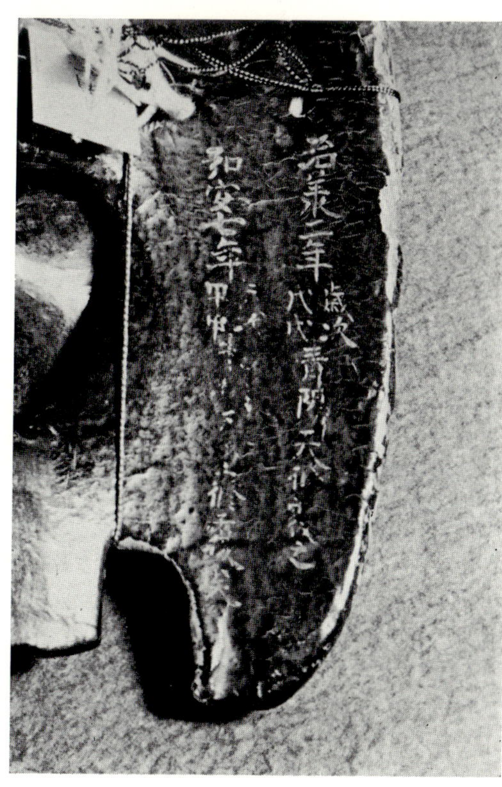

172–73. Shintoriso, by Inshō. Inscription in red lacquer. 1185. Kasuga Shrine, Nara.

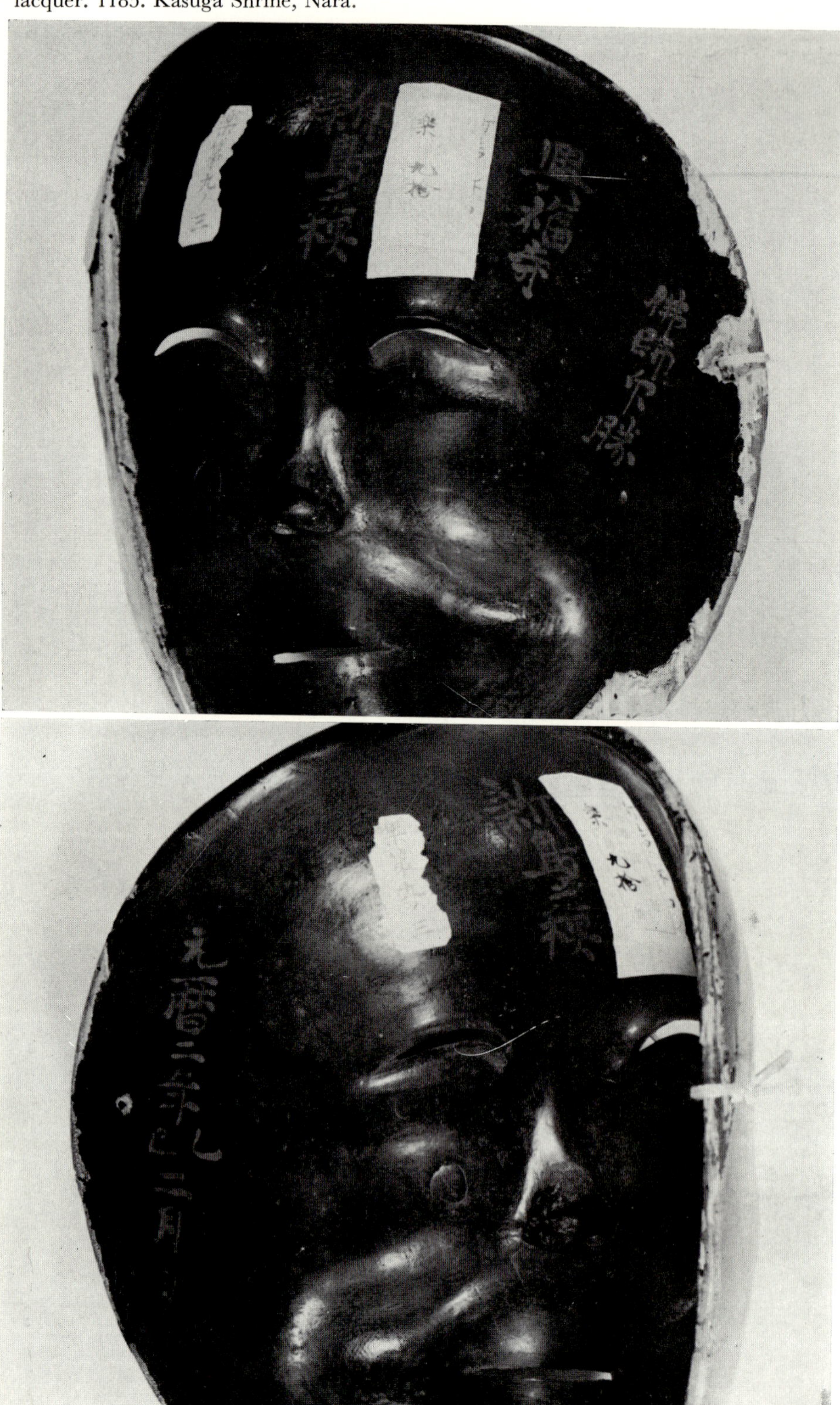

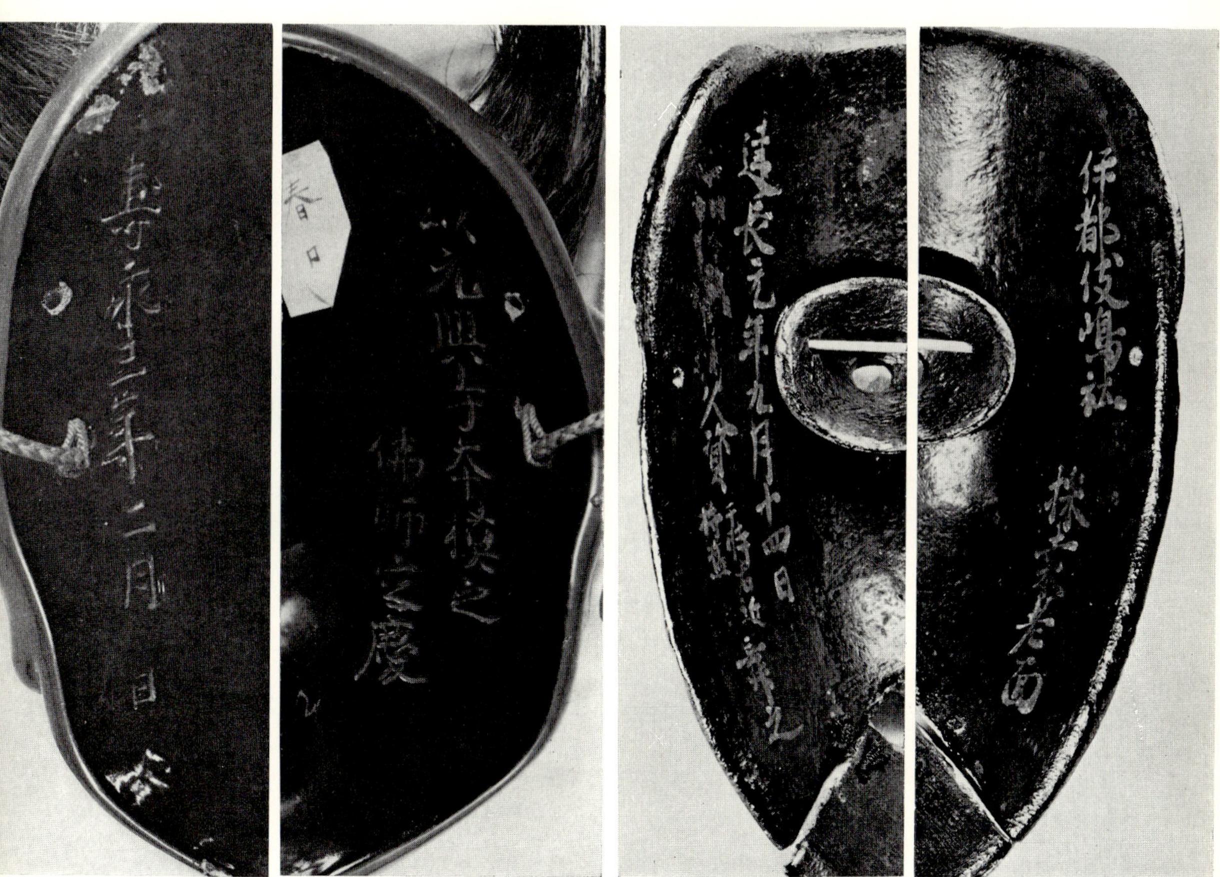

174–75. Sanju, by Jōkei. Incised inscription. 1184. Kasuga Shrine, Nara. (See pl. 61 for front view.)

176–77. Saisōrō. Inscription in red lacquer. 1249. Itsukushima Shrine, Hiroshima Prefecture. (See pl. 51 for front view and pls. 158–59 for details.)

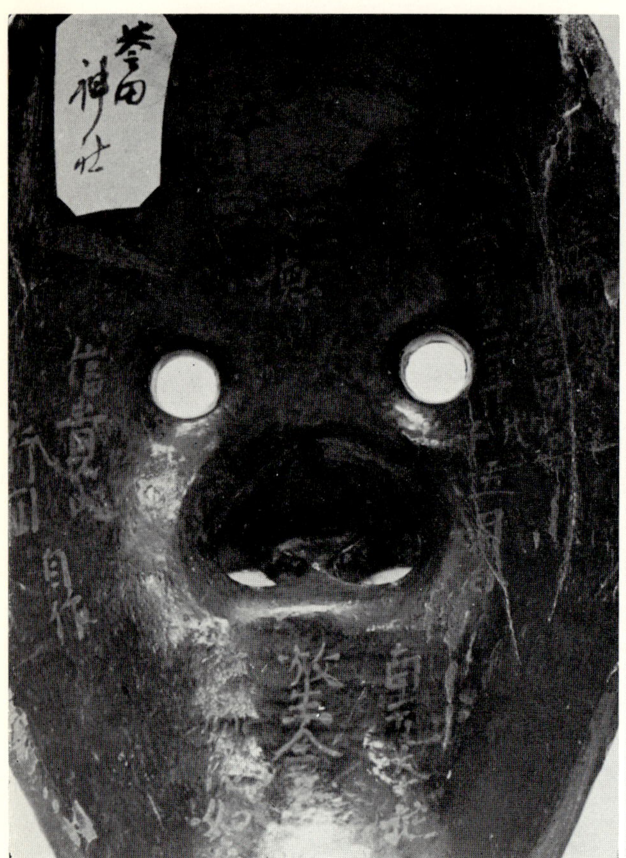

178. Kitoku, by Gyōen. Inscription in red lacquer. 1228. Konda Hachiman Shrine, Osaka Prefecture. (See pl. 74 for front view.)

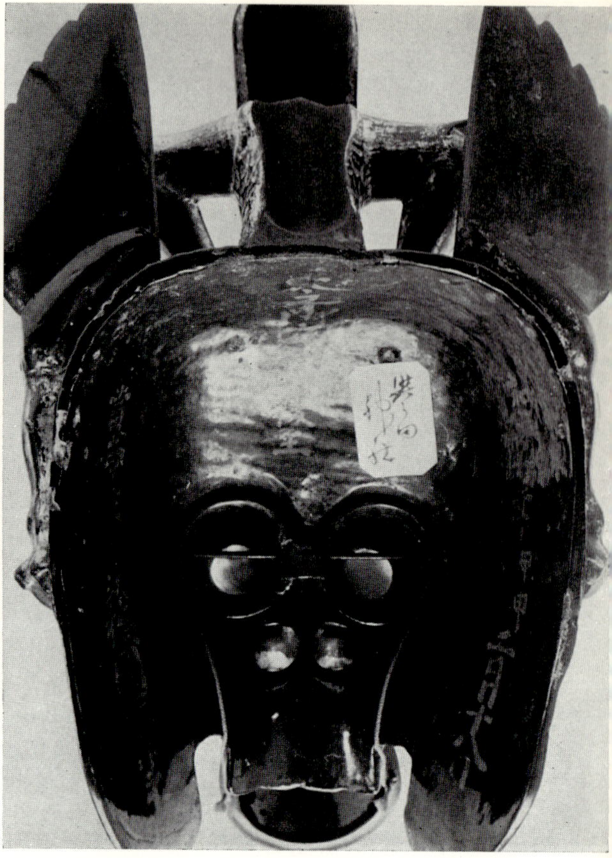

179. Ryō-ō, by Enshin. Inscription in red lacquer. 1284. Konda Hachiman Shrine, Osaka Prefecture.

## Mask Carvers

Inscriptions are our main source of information about mask carvers, but not until the late twelfth century did carvers sign their own names. This could mean that until then no mask carver was of sufficient stature to sign his name, but it is more likely that the signing of masks, like the signing of Buddhist statues, was linked to the growing sense of individualism that became prevalent only in the Kamakura period.

Since the great majority of Heian-period masks are unsigned, we have no absolute proof of who made them. But we are not entirely without evidence, for Bugaku masks and Buddhist sculpture exhibit strong similarities and parallels in carving and painting techniques that suggest a close connection between, if not an identity of, mask carvers and *busshi* (the official sculptors of Buddhist images). Indeed, an episode in the *Kojidan* (a collection of historical stories, sayings, and legends written in the years 1212 to 1215) indicates that it was not unusual for *busshi* to carve masks. According to this story, the *busshi* Jōchō, master sculptor in the latter half of the Heian period, finished a Ryō-ō mask commissioned by the Imperial Bodyguard of the Right and hung it on his wall. Jōchō's disinherited son (or possibly apprentice), the *busshi* Kakujo, thinking the mask unpresentable in that form, took out his knife and recarved it. Although incensed at first, Jōchō was so taken with the excellence of the carving that he forgave Kakujo and revoked the disinheritance.

Almost all those Bugaku mask carvers whose names we know from inscriptions were *busshi*. Their multiple role as carvers of both masks and statues contrasts with the Muromachi- and Edo-period Nō mask carvers, who usually specialized in mask carving.

*Gyōmyō*

The *busshi* Gyōmyō, who was active at the end of the Heian period, made six of the seven masks dedicated by the powerful Taira clan to their family shrine at Itsukushima in 1173: Batō (pl. 96), Genjōraku (pl. 106), Kitoku (pl. 73), Nasori (pl. 115), Hare-men (pl. 58), and Emi-men (pl. 59). Although only some of these still bear his signature, they were all inscribed with the same hand and show the same highly refined technique and scrupulous painting on a priming of cloth and *sabi urushi*. The *Sankaiki* diary of Fujiwara no Tadachika (1151–94) records that, at Itsukushima Shrine in 1178, Gyōmyō also carved a life-sized Eleven-headed Kannon (Avalokiteśvara) as a votive offering for the easy delivery of the emperor Takakura's wife, daughter of Taira no Kiyomori. Unfortunately none of Gyōmyō's statues remain today; his extremely thin and sophisticated masks, however, are ample evidence that he ranks among the top sculptors of the twelfth century.

Gyōmyō apparently used models from renowned temples in Kyoto for some of his masks, as indicated in the following inscription (pl. 167):

(right) Itsukushima Shrine. Batō mask. Shōan 3 [1173].
. . . *shō-ji bon*. *Busshi* Gyōmyō.
. . . imperial order.

Although part of the inscription on this Batō mask has flaked off, it compares closely with a rewritten inscription on the Genjōraku mask in the same shrine (pl. 161). The reference to "*. . . shō-ji bon,*" following the inscription on the Genjōraku mask, indicates that the mask was copied from a mask in Sonshō-ji, a temple in Kyoto no longer extant. "Imperial order" can probably be interpreted to mean that the mask was commissioned by Taira no Kiyomori's wife, Tokiko, the mother of Emperor Takakura's wife.

The inscriptions on Emi-men and Hare-men (pls. 58–59) were written in Gyōmyō's typically square calligraphy, though they do not include a personal signature. Plate 166 shows the right side of Emi-men:

(right) Itsukushima Shrine. Ni-no-mai mask. Shōan 3 [1173], 8th month.
Courtier Morikuni, supervisor.

Taira no Morikuni was one of the chief vassals of Taira no Kiyomori and among those who presented the famous *Heike nōkyō* (Taira Dedicatory Sutras) to Itsukushima Shrine in 1164.

The uninscribed Ryō-ō at the same shrine (pl. 111) differs in workmanship from Gyōmyō's pieces, but it seems to be of about the same time and also made by the hands of a first-rate *busshi*.

*Jōkei*

Renowned at the beginning of the Kamakura period, Jōkei was a *busshi* of the orthodox style in the Kei school, a group of sculptors centered in Nara and imbued with the spirit of realism. Jōkei is known to have carved the statue of Yuima (Vimalakīrti) in Kōfuku-ji in 1196 and, with young *busshi* assistants, the Bonten and Taishakuten statues of the same temple in 1201. All these works still exist. His distinctive, elaborate style, which was influenced by Sung aesthetics, is seen both in his statues and in the Sanju mask he made in 1184 for Kasuga Shrine (pl. 61). This well-balanced, integrated mask has a peculiar plasticity, a realism, and a dynamic modeling that strongly contrast with the style of Bugaku masks of the Heian period. It is a shame that the front and back of the mask have been repainted. The inscription on the back (pls. 174–75) indicates that the Sanju was modeled after a mask in Gangō-ji in Nara:

(right) Copy of a mask in Gangō-ji.
*Busshi* Jōkei.
(left) Juei 3 [1184], 2nd month. Day.

The calligraphy of the carved inscription seems early, but the stiffness of the carving makes it improbable that it is the original inscription of 1184. Perhaps when the mask was relacquered, the inscription was carved out with the intent of preserving it.

*Inshō*

In 1185 Inshō sculpted the four Shintoriso masks (pl. 14), the Ōnintei (pl. 46), and the Chikyū (pl. 13) in Kasuga Shrine. Although the inscription has abraded away, the Korobase at the same shrine (pl. 40) can be ascribed to Inshō on the basis of workmanship. The inscription on one of the Shintoriso masks (pls. 172–73; not that of the mask in pl. 14) is of the original date and shows Inshō's round and liquid letters:

(right) *Busshi* Inshō.
(forehead) Kōfuku-ji. Shintoriso.
(left) Genryaku 2 [1185], the year of the snake, 2nd month. Day.

As a maker of Buddhist images, Inshō is known only for his restoration of the Thousand-armed Kannon (Avalokitésvara) in the Tōshōdai-ji *kondō,* a dry-lacquer statue from the Tempyō period. But judging from the fine workmanship of his masks, he can be ranked among the most skillful *busshi* of his day. His well-balanced and tranquil style is characteristic of the refined Fujiwara taste, in contrast to the prevailing realistic style of the Kei school. All of Inshō's masks are made with standard techniques and painted on primings of cloth and *sabi urushi.* The Ōnintei and Korobase are made of paulownia, the Shintoriso masks of oak, and the Chikyū of Japanese cypress.

*Inken*

Inken was the son of the *busshi* Inshō (not the Inshō discussed above) and an authorized sculptor of the In school working at the Shichijō Ōmiya *bussho,* one of the two major sculpture workshops in Kyoto. He received commissions chiefly from the imperial court and the Fujiwara household. The two masks we know him by were made for a Kyoto temple. Plate 165 shows the inscription on the Sanju now housed as Tōdai-ji (pl. 69):

(right) Saishō Shitennō-in. Copied from a model in the Shin Hiyoshi Shrine by *busshi hōgen* Inken.
Jōgen 1 [1207], 11th month, 15th day.

This original inscription indicates that Inken, who held the Buddhist title of *hōgen,* copied the mask from a Sanju in Hiyoshi Shrine as an offering to the Shimmi-dō, also known as Saishō Shitennō-in, a temple formerly in the Shirakawa district of Kyoto. After the Saishō Shitennō-in was abolished in 1221, the mask was removed to Tōdai-ji. A Sanju with exactly the same inscription exists in Tamukeyama Shrine (pl. 62).

Only these two Sanju masks remain of Inken's work, but records recount that he also made a statue of Amida Nyorai (Amitābha) for the Hosshō-ji in 1200, two Benevolent Kings *(ni-ō)* figures for the south main gate of the same temple in 1212, and a small statue of Jizō (Kṣitigarbha) for the retired emperor Gotoba in 1215.

*Gyōen*

Gyōen is also known as Shigisan Gyōen, after a mountain between Kyoto and Nara on which the temple Chōgo Sonshi-ji is located. He made the two Ni-no-mai, the Sanju (pl. 68), and the Kitoku (pl. 74) at the Konda Hachiman Shrine near Osaka, all dated 1228. These masks are made of Japanese cypress with standard cloth and *sabi urushi* primings. Gyōen's four masks were offered on the occasion of a ceremony called the *hōshō-e* at Konda Hachiman Shine. The inscriptions on all of these masks, as exemplified by that on the Kitoku in plate 178, contain an offering prayer to the "true form" of Amida (Amitābha):

(right) Offering. Konda Shrine. Antei 2 [1228], the year of the rat, 5th month. Day.
(forehead) Kitoku.
(chin) *Namu honji, Amidabutsu.* Dedicated to *hōshō-e.*
(left) Shigisan Gyōen, carver.

Gyōen's profession seems to have been that of making musical instruments, particularly for Gagaku, such as the mouth organ *(shō)* and flute *(yokobue).* A *shō* called *Hatōmaru,* with Gyōen's signature, is still treasured by the imperial family and kept in the Tokyo National Museum along with three other *shō* made by Gyōen.

*Enshin and Shōjun*

Nothing is known about the two carvers Shōjun and Enshin except their masks. Shōjun made a Ryō-ō (pl. 113) and two Nasori (pl. 117) dated 1259. Enshin carved the Ryō-ō, Genjōraku, and Taishōtoku dated 1284 at Konda Hachiman Shrine.

In the inscription on the Ryō-ō, Enshin identified himself with the temple to which the mask is dedicated, Taishi Gobyō (Mausoleum of Shōtoku Taishi), or Eifuku-ji in Osaka Prefecture. Presumably the mask was kept at Eifuku-ji before it passed into the hands of the nearby Konda Hachiman Shrine. The inscription (pl. 179) is as follows:

(right) Kōan 7 [1284], the year of the monkey, 2nd month, 18th day.
(forehead) Taishi Gobyō. Ryō-ō.
(left) Sculpted by Enshin of this temple.

*Unkei*

Unkei (?–1223) is respected as the most distinguished sculptor of the Kamakura period and the leader of the Kei school, and much of his work is still extant. Records indicate that he was active around the city of Kamakura between 1215 and 1219 making Buddhist images, although his school was based in Nara. Thus it is not surprising to find a Batō mask inscribed with his name and the date 1219 in Seto Shrine, Yokohama (pl. 100). Though part of the inscription has rubbed off, this Batō must have been made, if not by Unkei himself, at least by someone of the Kei school. As described earlier, the thick sculpturing and large scale of this mask lend it a masculine appearance.

# BUGAKU MASKS

# APPENDIX 1

## PLACES TO SEE PERFORMANCES AND MASKS

Beautiful as Bugaku masks are as works of art, they are meant to be appreciated in performance. Complemented by brilliant costumes, encompassing hoods, and elaborate headgear, the masks appear to be a part of the dancer. A roll or twist of the head brings alive hidden expressions.

Unfortunately, opportunities to see actual performances are rare, for Bugaku has none of the popularity of Kabuki, Japanese dance *(Nihon buyō)*, or even Nō. From the outset a court entertainment, Bugaku today is performed chiefly by the Imperial Household musicians and small troupes at various shrines. The Imperial Gagaku troupe gives open performances in the palace twice a year, in spring and fall, and at the National Theater in Tokyo on other occasions. It has also toured Europe and America. The Garyō-kai in Osaka and the Heian Gagaku-kai in Kyoto, both composed extensively of amateurs, also give performances several times a year. Most satisfying in atmosphere and setting are the performances given in temples and shrines in conjunction with festivals. The following is a list of the most important Bugaku performances held as a part of such religious festivals (an asterisk precedes dates following the lunar calendar).

Kasuga Shrine, Nara

| | |
|---|---|
| January 5 | *Bugaku hajime* (performance marking the New Year) |
| February 3–4 | *Setsubun* (ceremonies marking the end of winter and the beginning of spring) |
| May 5 | *Kōkai bugaku ensō-kai* (Bugaku performances for the general public) |
| August 15 | *Chūgen mandōrō* (midsummer festival of stone lanterns) |
| November 3 | *Kōkai bugaku ensō-kai* (Bugaku performances for the general public) |
| December 17 | *Wakamiya on-matsuri* (annual festival in honor of Kasuga Wakamiya Shrine) |

Shitennō-ji, Osaka

| | |
|---|---|
| April 22 | *Shōryō-e bugaku daihōyō* (Bugaku performed at annual memorial services for Shōtoku Taishi, 574–622) |
| August 9–10 | *Sennichi mairi, kagari no bugaku* (Bugaku performed by torchlight as part of an annual ceremony) |
| November 4 | *Gaen* (a special performance of Bugaku) |

Itsukushima Shrine, Hiroshima Prefecture

| | |
|---|---|
| January 1–5 | *Shōgatsu bugaku* (daily performances marking the New Year) |

April 15 — *Tōka matsuri* (performances at night during the Peach Blossom Festival)
April 29 — *Tenchōsetsu* (emperor's birthday)
May 18 — *Suiko tennō yōhaishiki* (memorial services for Empress Suiko, r. 592–628)
*5th day of the 5th month (falls within June) — *Jigozen no matsuri* (annual festival at the Jigozen Shrine)
*5th day of the 6th month (falls with July) — *Bugaku-kai* (Bugaku performances)
October 15 — *Kikka matsuri* (performances at night during the Chrysanthemum Festival)
October 23 — *Sannōsha no matsuri* (annual festival at the Sannōsha Shrine)

Atsuta Shrine, Aichi Prefecture

February 11 — *Kigensetsu* (National Foundation Day)

The very oldest masks are too precious and fragile to be used in such annual performances. Generally they are replaced by masks made in the Edo period. Typical examples of Heian-period masks, however, are now stored in the national museums in Tokyo, Nara, and Kyoto and are displayed from time to time. The Tokyo National Museum has a special room for masks, and in the Hōryū-ji Hōmotsukan gallery in the museum (open Thursdays) thirty-one Gigaku masks are on permanent display.

Although the author has not seen them and cannot comment on their quality, small collections of Bugaku masks exist in a number of museums in the West. In the United States the Boston Museum of Fine Arts has a selection of interesting masks in good repair. For a discussion of masks in European museums, refer to Gabbert's *Die Masken des Bugaku* (see Bibliography).

# APPENDIX 2

## DATABLE MASKS

| Date | Original Owner | Masks (present owner in parentheses) | Comments |
|---|---|---|---|
| 1042 | Tōdai-ji, Nara | Shintoriso (Tamukeyama Shrine)<br>Taishōtoku (Ise Shrine Repository)<br>5 Ōnintei (1 at Tamukeyama Shrine)<br>4 Korobase (2 at Fujita Art Museum, 1 at Tamukeyama Shrine, 1 in private collection in Kanagawa Pref.)<br>5 Chikyū (4 at Tamukeyama Shrine, 1 in private collection in Tokyo) | 3 with restoration dates of 1086 |
| 1134 | Hōryū-ji, Nara Pref. | Kitoku (Fujita Art Museum) | |
| 1144 | Hōryū-ji, Nara Pref. | Batō<br>Genjōraku<br>Chikyū (private collection in Tokyo) | |
| 1160 | Tōdai-ji, Nara | 6 Kotokuraku (5 at Tamukeyama Shrine, 1 at Himuro Shrine)<br>Kotokuraku Kempai (Tamukeyama Shrine) | |
| 1161 | Sumiyoshi Shrine, Osaka | Batō<br>4 Ayakiri | |
| 1163 | Sumiyoshi Shrine, Osaka | Kitoku Banko | |
| 1173 | Itsukushima Shrine, Hiroshima Pref. | 2 Ni-no-mai<br>Sanju<br>Batō<br>Genjōraku<br>Kitoku<br>Nasori | all but Sanju carved by Gyōmyō |
| 1178 | Atsuta Shrine, Nagoya | 2 Ni-no-mai<br>Batō<br>Genjōraku<br>4 Korobase<br>Kitoku<br>2 Nasori | 8 with restoration dates of 1279, 1 of 1284, 1 of 1420 |
| 1184 | Kasuga Shrine, Nara | Sanju | signed by Jōkei |
| 1185 | Kasuga Shrine, Nara | 4 Shintoriso<br>Ōnintei<br>Korobase<br>Chikyū | all signed by Inshō |
| 1207 | Saishō Shitennō-in, Kyoto (no longer extant) | 2 Sanju (1 at Tōdai-ji, 1 at Tamukeyama Shrine) | signed by Inken |

| (Date) | (Original Owner) | (Masks) | (Comments) |
|---|---|---|---|
| 1211 | Masumida Shrine, Aichi Pref. | Ryō-ō<br>2 Ni-no-mai<br>Sanju<br>Batō<br>Genjōraku<br>4 Korobase<br>Kitoku<br>2 Warabemai<br>2 Nasori | 3 with restoration dates of 1360 |
| 1219 | Seto Shrine, Yokohama | Batō | perhaps by Unkei |
| 1228 | Konda Hachiman Shrine, Osaka Pref. | 2 Ni-no-mai<br>Sanju<br>Kitoku | all signed by Gyō-en |
| 1249 | Itsukushima Shrine, Hiroshima Pref. | Saisōrō | |
| 1256 | Chiryū Shrine, Aichi Pref. | Nasori | |
| 1259 | Tōdai-ji, Nara | Ryō-ō<br>2 Nasori (1 at Tamukeyama Shrine, 1 at Ise Shrine Repository) | all signed by Shō-jun; 1 restored in 1713 |
| 1279 | Konda Hachiman Shrine, Osaka Pref. | Tendō | |
| 1284 | Eifuku-ji, Osaka Pref. | Ryō-ō (Konda Hachiman Shrine)<br>Genjōraku (Konda Hachiman Shrine)<br>Taishōtoku (Konda Hachiman Shrine) | all signed by En-shin |
| 1288 | Sumiyoshi Shrine, Osaka | Shinnō | |
| 1305 | Ibuki Hachiman Shrine, Aichi Pref. | Sanju | |
| 1307 | Takiyama-dera, Akita Pref. | Ni-no-mai (Hare-men; private collection in Akita Pref.) | |
| 1308 | Masumida Shrine, Aichi Pref. | Ōnintei | |
| 1328 | Ōto Shrine, Chiba Pref. | Ryō-ō | |
| 1343 | Konda Hachiman Shrine, Osaka Pref. | 3 Taishōtoku | |
| 1403 | Kanzeon-ji, Fukuoka Pref. | Ryō-ō<br>2 Nasori | date is that of restoration |
| 1430 | Hōryū-ji, Nara Pref. | Sanju | |
| 1452 | Hōryū-ji, Nara Pref. | Korobase | signed by Jōchō Jōshumbō |
| 1465 | Hakusan Shrine, Nishi Kubiki County, Niigata Pref. | Ryō-ō | |
| 1498 | Konda Hachiman Shrine, Osaka Pref. | Taishōtoku | signed by Shōni |

| (Date) | (Original Owner) | (Masks) | (Comments) |
|---|---|---|---|
| 1537 | Kasuga Shrine, Nara | Kitoku Koikuchi<br>3 Korobase | |
| 1636 | Tōshōgū Shrine, Nikko | 2 Ni-no-mai<br>6 Chikyū | |
| 1637 | Shitennō-ji, Osaka | 5 Kotokuraku | |
| 1656 | Tōshōgū, Nikko | Ryō-ō<br>Sanju<br>6 Kotokuraku<br>Saisōrō<br>6 Korobase<br>Kitoku<br>2 Nasori | |
| 1669 | Kasuga Shrine, Nara | Ryō-ō<br>Ni-no-mai (Emi-men)<br>Saisōrō<br>Genjōraku<br>6 Kotokuraku | stamped *Tenka-ichi Echizen*<br>date appears on masks' presentation boxes |
| 1691 | Amatsu Shrine, Niigata Pref. | Nasori | |
| 1713 | Tōdai-ji, Nara | Ryō-ō (Ise Shrine Repository) | date is that of restoration |
| 1740 | Sumiyoshi Shrine, Osaka | Ryō-ō | date appears on mask's presentation box |
| 1783 | Sumiyoshi Shrine, Osaka | Kitoku | date appears on mask's presentation box |
| 1784 | Sumiyoshi Shrine, Osaka | Sanju | date appears on mask's presentation box |
| 1795 | Itsukushima Shrine, Hiroshima Pref. | Batō<br>Genjōraku | |
| 1796 | Itsukushima Shrine, Hiroshima Pref. | Sanju | |
| 1822 | Atsuta Shrine, Nagoya | Sanju<br>Kitoku | |
| 1843 | Tokyo National Museum | Kitoku Koikuchi<br>Kitoku Banko<br>Chikyū | |
| 1845 | Amanomiya Shrine, Shizuoka Pref. | 2 Kitoku | |

# APPENDIX 3

## BUGAKU MASKS IN JAPAN

| Type and Total Number | Location | Collection | Number in Collection | Inscribed Dates |
|---|---|---|---|---|
| Ayakiri (15) | Osaka | Shitennō-ji | 4 | |
| | | Sumiyoshi Shrine | 4 | 1161 |
| | Nara Pref. | Hōryū-ji | 3 | |
| | Hiroshima Pref. | Itsukushima Shrine (male face) | 4 | |
| Batō (20) | Aomori Pref. | Ōboshi Shrine | 1 | |
| | | Iwakisan Shrine | 1 | |
| | Nikko | Tōshōgū Shrine | 1 | |
| | Kanagawa Pref. | Gokuraku-ji | 1 | |
| | | Seto Shrine | 1 | 1219 |
| | Niigata Pref. (Nishi Kubiki Co.) | Hakusan Shrine (Nō Batō) | 1 | |
| | Aichi Pref. | Atsuta Shrine | 2 | 1906 (1) restored 1178 (1) |
| | | Masumida Shrine | 2 | 1211 (1) |
| | | Chiryū Shrine | 1 | |
| | Osaka | Shitennō-ji | 1 | |
| | | Sumiyoshi Shrine | 1 | 1161 |
| | Nara Pref. | Kasuga Shrine | 2 | |
| | | Hōryū-ji | 1 | 1144 |
| | Hiroshima Pref. | Itsukushima Shrine | 3 | 1173 (1) 1795 (1) |
| | Kagawa Pref. | Kamitani Shrine | 1 | |
| Chikyū (39) | Nikko | Tōshōgū Shrine | 6 | 1636 |
| | Tokyo | Tokyo National Museum (3 originally Amanosha Shrine) | 4 | 1843 (1) |
| | | private collection (originally Tōdai-ji) | 1 | 1042 |
| | | private collection (originally Hōryū-ji) | 1 | 1144 |
| | Yamanashi Pref. | Kuon-ji | 1 | |
| | Osaka | Shitennō-ji | 4 | |
| | Nara Pref. | Tamukeyama Shrine (originally Tōdai-ji) | 4 | 1042 |
| | | Kasuga Shrine | 11 | 1185 (1) |
| | | Hōryū-ji | 7 | |
| Genjōraku (23) | Aomori Pref. | Ōboshi Shrine (fragment) | 1 | |
| | | Kushibiki Hachiman Shrine | 1 | |
| | | Iwakisan Shrine (fragment) | 1 | |

| (Type and Total Number) | (Location) | (Collection) | (Number in Collection) | (Inscribed Dates) |
|---|---|---|---|---|
| | Iwate Pref. | Tendai-ji | 1 | |
| | Kanagawa Pref. | Gokuraku-ji | 1 | |
| | | Takabeya Shrine (fragment) | 1 | |
| | Yamanashi Pref. | Kuon-ji | 1 | |
| | Aichi Pref. | Atsuta Shrine | 2 | restored 1178 & 1284 (1) 1906 (1) |
| | | Masumida Shrine | 1 | 1211 |
| | | Chiryū Shrine | 1 | |
| | Kyoto | Hiyoshi Shrine | 1 | |
| | Osaka Pref. | Shitennō-ji | 1 | |
| | | Sumiyoshi Shrine | 1 | |
| | | Konda Hachiman Shrine (originally Eifuku-ji) | 1 | 1284 |
| | Nara Pref. | Kasuga Shrine | 2 | 1669 (1) |
| | | Yakushi-ji | 1 | |
| | | Hōryū-ji | 1 | 1144 |
| | Hiroshima Pref. | Itsukushima Shrine | 3 | 1183 (1) 1795 (1) |
| | Kagawa Pref. | Kamitani Shrine | 1 | |
| Kitoku (22) | Aomori Pref. | Kushibiki Hachiman Shrine | 1 | |
| | Yamagata Pref. | private collection (originally Yachi Shrine) | 1 | |
| | Nikko | Tōshōgū Shrine | 1 | 1656 |
| | Tokyo | Tokyo National Museum (1 originally Amanosha Shrine) | 2 | |
| | Shizuoka Pref. | Amanomiya Shrine | 2 | 1845 |
| | Aichi Pref. | Atsuta Shrine | 2 | restored 1178 (1) 1822 (1) |
| | | Masumida Shrine | 1 | 1211 |
| | | Chiryū Shrine | 1 | |
| | Osaka Pref. | Shitennō-ji | 2 | |
| | | Sumiyoshi Shrine | 1 | 1783 |
| | | Fujita Art Museum (originally Hōryū-ji) | 1 | 1134 |
| | | Konda Hachiman Shrine | 1 | 1228 |
| | Nara | Tōdai-ji | 1 | |
| | | Tamukeyama Shrine (originally Tōdai-ji) | 1 | |
| | | Kasuga Shrine | 1 | |
| | Shimane Pref. | Oki Kokubun-ji | 1 | |
| | Hiroshima Pref. | Itsukushima Shrine | 2 | 1173 (1) |
| Kitoku Banko (3) | Tokyo | Tokyo National Museum | 1 | 1843 |
| | Kanagawa Pref. | Tsurugaoka Hachiman Shrine (child's face) | 1 | |
| | Osaka | Sumiyoshi Shrine | 1 | 1163 |

| (TYPE AND TOTAL NUMBER) | (LOCATION) | (COLLECTION) | (NUMBER IN COLLECTION) | (INSCRIBED DATES) |
|---|---|---|---|---|
| Kitoku Koikuchi (5) | Iwate Pref. | Tendai-ji | 1 | |
| | Tokyo | Tokyo National Museum | 1 | 1843 |
| | Kanagawa Pref. | Tsurugaoka Hachiman Shrine | 1 | |
| | Nara Pref. | Kasuga Shrine | 1 | 1537 |
| | | Hōryū-ji | 1 | |
| Konju (2) | Aichi Pref. | Masumida Shrine | 1 | 1912 |
| | Nara | Tamukeyama Shrine | 1 | |
| Korobase (37) | Nikko | Tōshōgū Shrine | 4 | 1656 |
| | Kanagawa Pref. | private collection (originally Tōdai-ji) | 1 | 1042 |
| | Aichi Pref. | Atsuta Shrine | 4 | restored 1178 |
| | | Masumida Shrine | 4 | 1211 (1) restored 1360 (3) |
| | Osaka | Shitennō-ji | 4 | |
| | | Fujita Art Museum (originally Tōdai-ji) | 2 | 1042 |
| | Nara | Tamukeyama Shrine | 1 | 1042 |
| | | Kasuga Shrine | 8 | 1537 (3) 1185 (1) |
| | | Hōryū-ji | 5 | 1452 (1) |
| | Hiroshima Pref. | Itsukushima Shrine | 4 | |
| Kotokuraku (41) | Nikko | Tōshōgū Shrine | 6 | 1656 |
| | Osaka | Shitennō-ji | 10 | 1637 (5) |
| | Nara Pref. | Tamukeyama Shrine (originally Tōdai-ji) | 5 | 1160 |
| | | Himuro Shrine (originally Tōdai-ji) | 1 | 1160 |
| | | Kasuga Shrine | 6 | 1669 |
| | | Hōryū-ji | 9 | |
| | Hiroshima Pref. | Itsukushima Shrine | 4 | |
| Kotokuraku Heishitori (3) | Yamanashi Pref. | Kuon-ji (Emi-men?) | 1 | |
| | Osaka | Shitennō-ji | 1 | |
| | Nara | Kasuga Shrine (originally Tōdai-ji) | 1 | |
| Kotokuraku Kempai (1) | Nara | Tamukeyama Shrine (originally Tōdai-ji) | 1 | 1160 |
| Nasori (63) | Aomori Pref. | Ōboshi Shrine | 1 | |
| | | Kushibiki Hachiman Shrine | 1 | |
| | Iwate Pref. | Tendai-ji | 2 | |
| | | Chūson-ji | 1 | |
| | Yamagata Pref. | Honzanjion-ji | 1 | |
| | | Risshaku-ji | 1 | |
| | Nikko | Tōshōgū Shrine | 2 | 1656 |
| | Chiba Pref. | Ōto Shrine | 2 | |

| (Type and Total Number) | (Location) | (Collection) | (Number in Collection) | (Inscribed Dates) |
|---|---|---|---|---|
| | Tokyo | Tokyo National Museum | 5 | |
| | Niigata Pref. | Amatsu Shrine | 4 | 1691 (1) |
| | | Hakusan Shrine (Nishi Kubiki County) | 2 | |
| | Nagano | Chikuma Shrine | 1 | |
| | Gifu Pref. | Futsukamachi Hachiman Shrine | 1 | |
| | Shizuoka Pref. | Amanomiya Shrine | 1 | |
| | Aichi Pref. | Atsuta Shrine | 2 | restored 1178 |
| | | Masumida Shrine | 4 | 1211 (2) |
| | | Chiryū Shrine | 1 | 1256 |
| | Mie Pref. | Ise Shrine Repository (originally Tōdai-ji) | 1 | 1259 |
| | Osaka Pref. | Shitennō-ji | 4 | |
| | | Sumiyoshi Shrine | 1 | |
| | | Konda Hachiman Shrine | 2 | |
| | Nara Pref. | Tōdai-ji | 2 | |
| | | Tamukeyama Shrine (originally Tōdai-ji) | 1 | 1259 |
| | | Kasuga Shrine | 6 | |
| | | Hōryū-ji | 4 | |
| | Shimane Pref. | Susa Shrine | 1 | |
| | Hiroshima Pref. | Kibitsu Shrine | 2 | |
| | | Itsukushima Shrine | 3 | 1173 (1) |
| | Kagawa Pref. | Kotohira Shrine | 1 | |
| | Fukuoka Pref. | Kanzeon-ji | 2 | restored 1403 |
| | Ōita Pref. | Usa Shrine | 1 | |
| Ni-no-mai (50) | Aomori Pref. | Ōboshi Shrine | 2 | |
| | | Kushibiki Hachiman Shrine | 2 | |
| | | Iwakisan Shrine (Hare-men) | 1 | |
| | Iwate Pref. | Tendai-ji | 2 | |
| | Akita Pref. | private collection (Hare-men; originally Takiyama-dera) | 1 | 1307 |
| | | private collection (Emi-men; originally Takiyama-dera) | 1 | |
| | | Emman-ji | 2 | |
| | Yamagata Pref. | Honzanjion-ji | 2 | |
| | | Risshaku-ji | 2 | |
| | Nikko | Tōshōgū Shrine | 2 | 1636 |
| | Tokyo | Tokyo National Museum | 2 | |
| | | Shinagawa Shrine (Hare-men) | 1 | |
| | | private collection (Hare-men) | 1 | |
| | Kanagawa Pref. | Tsurugaoka Hachiman Shrine (Emi-men) | 1 | |
| | Niigata Pref. | Yahiko Shrine | 2 | |
| | Yamanashi Pref. | Kuon-ji | 2 | |
| | Shizuoka Pref. | Amanomiya Shrine | 2 | |
| | | Kōshō-ji (Hare-men) | 1 | |

| (Type and Total Number) | (Location) | (Collection) | (Number in Collection) | (Inscribed Dates) |
|---|---|---|---|---|
| | Aichi Pref. | Atsuta Shrine | 4 | restored 1178 (2) |
| | | Masumida Shrine | 2 | 1211 |
| | Osaka Pref. | Konda Hachiman Shrine | 2 | 1228 |
| | Nara Pref. | Tamukeyama Shrine (Hare-men; originally Tōdai-ji) | 1 | |
| | | Kasuga Shrine (Emi-men) | 1 | 1669 |
| | | Hōryū-ji (2 Hare-men) | 3 | |
| | Hiroshima Pref. | Itsukushima Shrine | 4 | 1173 (2) |
| | Yamaguchi Pref. | Kōryū-ji | 2 | |
| | Kagawa Pref. | private collection (originally Shiramine Shrine) | 2 | |
| Ōnintei (17) | Tokyo | Tokyo National Museum (originally Amanosha Shrine) | 3 | |
| | Aichi Pref. | Masumida Shrine | 1 | 1308 |
| | Osaka | Shitennō-ji | 4 | |
| | | Sumiyoshi Shrine | 1 | |
| | Nara Pref. | Tōdai-ji | 4 | 1042 |
| | | Tamukeyama Shrine (originally Tōdai-ji) | 1 | 1042 |
| | | Kasuga Shrine | 1 | 1185 |
| | | Hōryū-ji | 2 | |
| Ryō-ō (64) | Aomori Pref. | Ōboshi Shrine | 1 | |
| | | Kushibiki Hachiman Shrine | 1 | |
| | | Iwakisan Shrine | 1 | |
| | Iwate Pref. | Tendai-ji | 2 | |
| | Yamagata Pref. | private collection (originally Narushima Hachiman Shrine) | 1 | |
| | | Kumano Shrine | 1 | |
| | | Honzanjion-ji | 1 | |
| | | Risshaku-ji | 1 | |
| | Fukushima Pref. | Kumano Shrine | 1 | |
| | Nikko | Tōshōgū Shrine | 1 | 1656 |
| | Chiba Pref. | Ōto Shrine | 1 | 1328 |
| | Tokyo | Tokyo National Museum (originally Kongōbu-ji) | 1 | |
| | Kanagawa Pref. | Tsurugaoka Hachiman Shrine | 1 | |
| | | Seto Shrine | 1 | |
| | | Takabeya Shrine | 1 | |
| | Niigata Pref. | Hakusan Shrine (Nishi Kubiki County) | 2 | 1465 (1) |
| | | Yahiko Shrine | 1 | |
| | | Amatsu Shrine | 1 | |
| | Ishikawa Pref. | Nagahama Hachiman Shrine | 1 | |
| | Fukui Pref. | Yasaka Shrine | 1 | |
| | Nagano | Chikuma Shrine | 1 | |
| | | Kōzen-ji | 1 | |
| | Shizuoka Pref. | Tesshū-ji | 1 | |
| | | Amanomiya Shrine | 1 | |

| (Type and Total Number) | (Location) | (Collection) | (Number in Collection) | (Inscribed Dates) |
|---|---|---|---|---|
| | Aichi Pref. | Atsuta Shrine | 2 | restored 1284 (1) |
| | | Masumida Shrine | 1 | 1211 |
| | | Chiryū Shrine | 1 | |
| | Mie Pref. | Ise Shrine Repository (originally Tōdai-ji) | 1 | restored 1173 |
| | Kyoto | Komori Shrine | 1 | |
| | Osaka Pref. | Shitennō-ji | 2 | |
| | | Sumiyoshi Shrine | 3 | 1740 (1) |
| | | Fujita Art Museum (originally Ryōsen-ji) | 1 | |
| | | Konda Hachiman Shrine | 2 | 1284 (1) |
| | Hyōgo Pref. | Ōsake Shrine | 1 | |
| | | Sumiyoshi Shrine (Katō County) | 1 | |
| | Nara Pref. | Tōdai-ji | 1 | 1259 |
| | | Himuro Shrine | 1 | |
| | | Kasuga Shrine | 4 | 1669 (1) |
| | | Hōryū-ji | 1 | |
| | Shimane Pref. | Sada Shrine | 1 | |
| | | Susa Shrine | 1 | |
| | | Oki Kokubun-ji | 1 | |
| | Hiroshima Pref. | Kibitsu Shrine | 6 | |
| | | Itsukushima Shrine | 2 | |
| | Kagawa Pref. | private collection (originally Shiramine Shrine) | 1 | |
| | Fukuoka Pref. | Kanzeon-ji | 1 | 1403 |
| | Ōita Pref. | Usa Shrine | 1 | |
| | Miyazaki Pref. | Shinnatsume Hachiman Shrine | 1 | |
| Saisōrō (10) | Nikko | Tōshōgū Shrine | 1 | 1656 |
| | Tokyo | Tokyo National Museum | 1 | |
| | Osaka | Shitennō-ji | 1 | |
| | Hyōgo Pref. | Ōsake Shrine | 1 | |
| | Nara | Tamukeyama Shrine | 1 | |
| | | Kasuga Shrine | 2 | 1669 (1) |
| | Shimane Pref. | Oki Kokubun-ji | 1 | |
| | Hiroshima Pref. | Itsukushima Shrine | 1 | 1249 |
| | Kagawa Pref. | Kotohira Shrine | 1 | |
| Sanju (28) | Aomori Pref. | Ōboshi Shrine | 3 | |
| | | Kushibiki Hachiman Shrine | 2 | |
| | | Iwakisan Shrine | 1 | |
| | Iwate Pref. | Tendai-ji | 1 | |
| | Yamagata Pref. | Honzanjion-ji | 1 | |
| | Nikko | Tōshōgū Shrine | 1 | 1656 |
| | Kanagawa Pref. | Tsurugaoka Hachiman Shrine | 1 | |
| | Shizuoka Pref. | Tsumori Shrine | 1 | |
| | Aichi Pref. | Atsuta Shrine | 1 | 1822 |
| | | Masumida Shrine | 1 | 1211 |
| | | Chiryū Shrine (Kitoku?) | 1 | |

| (Type and Total Number) | (Location) | (Collection) | (Number in Collection) | (Inscribed Dates) |
|---|---|---|---|---|
| | Osaka Pref. | Shitennō-ji | 2 | |
| | | Sumiyoshi Shrine | 1 | 1784 |
| | | Konda Hachiman Shrine | 1 | 1228 |
| | Nara Pref. | Tōdai-ji (originally Saishō Shitennō-in) | 1 | 1207 |
| | | Tamukeyama Shrine (originally Saishō Shitennō-in) | 1 | 1207 |
| | | Kasuga Shrine | 3 | 1184 (1) |
| | | Hōryū-ji | 1 | 1430 |
| | Hiroshima Pref. | Itsukushima Shrine | 2 | 1173, 1796 |
| | Kagawa Pref. | private collection (originally Shiramine Shrine) | 1 | |
| | Ehime Pref. | Ibuki Hachiman Shrine | 1 | 1305 |
| Sessen (2) | Nara Pref. | Hōryū-ji | 1 | |
| | | Chōgo Sonshi-ji | 1 | |
| Shinnō (1) | Osaka | Sumiyoshi Shrine | 1 | 1288 |
| Shintoriso (10) | Nara Pref. | Tamukeyama Shrine (originally Tōdai-ji) | 1 | |
| | | Kasuga Shrine | 4 | 1185 |
| | | Hōryū-ji | 5 | |
| Somakusha (3) | Nara | Shōsō-in | 1 | |
| | Osaka | Shitennō-ji | 1 | |
| | Hiroshima Pref. | Itsukushima Shrine | 1 | |
| Taishōtoku (32) | Nikko | Tōshōgū Shrine | 6 | |
| | Tokyo | Tokyo National Museum (2 originally Amanosha Shrine) | 3 | |
| | Mie Pref. | Ise Shrine Repository (originally Tōdai-ji) | 2 | 1042 (1) |
| | Osaka Pref. | Shitennō-ji | 4 | |
| | | Konda Hachiman Shrine (1 originally Eifuku-ji) | 5 | 1284 (1)<br>1343 (3)<br>1498 (1) |
| | Nara Pref. | Tamukeyama Shrine (originally Tōdai-ji) | 1 | |
| | | Kasuga Shrine | 6 | |
| | | Hōryū-ji | 4 | |
| | | Chōgo Sonshi-ji | 1 | |
| Warabemai, Tendō (3) | Aichi Pref. | Masumida Shrine | 2 | 1211 |
| | Osaka Pref. | Konda Hachiman Shrine | 1 | 1279 |
| | | | Total 494 | |

# LIST OF ILLUSTRATIONS IN JAPANESE

1. 雅楽に使われる楽器 (『信西古楽図』より 京都市 陽明文庫)
2. 酔胡従 伎楽面 (東京国立博物館)
3. 崑崙 伎楽面 (奈良市 東大寺)
4. 迦楼羅 伎楽面 (東京国立博物館)
5. 大孤父 伎楽面 (奈良市 東大寺)
6. 梵天 行道面 (京都国立博物館)
7. 多聞天 行道面 (京都国立博物館)
8. 翁 能面
9. 小面 能面
10. 小牛尉 能面
11. 天神 能面
12. 舞楽図屛風 宗達筆 (十七世紀前半 京都市 醍醐寺)
13. 地久 印勝作 (寿永四年銘 奈良市 春日大社)
14. 新鳥蘇 印勝作 (寿永四年銘 奈良市 春日大社)
15. 地久 (宮内庁書陵部)
16. 皇仁庭 (長久三年銘 奈良市 手向山神社)
17. 綾切 (宮内庁書陵部)
18. 胡徳楽 (『信西古楽図』より 東京芸術大学)
19. 胡徳楽と勧杯 (『舞楽稿本』より 東京国立博物館)
20. 案摩と二ノ舞 (『舞楽図屛風』より 桃翁筆)
21. 新鳥蘇 (長久三年頃 奈良市 手向山神社)
22. 新鳥蘇 (奈良県 法隆寺)
23. 地久 (長久三年銘)
24. 地久 (奈良県 法隆寺)
25. 地久 (長久三年銘 奈良市 手向山神社)
26. 地久 (奈良県 法隆寺)
27. 退宿徳 (長久三年銘 三重県 神宮徴古館)
28. 退宿徳 (奈良市 手向山神社)
29. 退宿徳 (興国四年銘 大阪府 誉田八幡宮)
30. 綾切 (永暦二年銘 大阪市 住吉大社)
31. 胡徳楽 (永暦元年銘 奈良市 手向山神社)
32. 胡徳楽勧杯 (永暦元年銘 奈良市 手向山神社)
33. 胡徳楽瓶子取の瓶子 (鎌倉時代 奈良市 手向山神社)
34. 胡徳楽瓶子取 (十三世紀初 奈良市 手向山神社)
35. 胡徳楽 (十世紀末～十一世紀初 奈良県 法隆寺)
36. 胡徳楽 (永暦元年銘 奈良市 手向山神社)
37. 胡徳楽 (十世紀末～十一世紀初 奈良県 法隆寺)
38. 胡徳楽 (奈良県 法隆寺)
39. 胡徳楽 (奈良県 法隆寺)
40. 崑崙八仙 印勝作? (元暦二年頃 奈良市 春日大社)
41. 崑崙八仙 (建暦元年銘 愛知県 真清田神社)
42. 崑崙八仙 (長久三年銘 奈良市 手向山神社)
43. 崑崙八仙 (治承二年修理銘 名古屋市 熱田神宮)
44. 崑崙八仙 (『舞楽図屛風』より 桃翁筆)
45. 皇仁庭 (長久三年銘 奈良市 東大寺)
46. 皇仁庭 印勝作 (元暦二年銘 奈良市 春日大社)
47. 案摩 (『信西古楽図』より 京都市 陽明文庫)
48. 蘇利古 (蔵面 大阪市 四天王寺)
49. 案摩 (蔵面 大阪市 四天王寺)
50. 採桑老 (『信西古楽図』より 東京芸術大学)
51. 採桑老 (建長元年銘 広島県 厳島神社)
52. 採桑老 (十二世紀後半 奈良市 手向山神社)
53. 二ノ舞 咲面 (治承二年修理銘 名古屋市 熱田神宮)
54. 二ノ舞 腫面 (治承二年修理銘 名古屋市 熱田神宮)
55. 二ノ舞 咲面 (承元五年銘 愛知県 真清神社)
56. 二ノ舞 腫面 (承元五年銘 愛知県 真清神社)
57. 二ノ舞 腫面 (奈良市 手向山神社)
58. 二ノ舞 腫面 行明作 (承安三年銘 広島県 厳島神社)
59. 二ノ舞 咲面 行明作 (承安三年銘 広島県 厳島神社)
60. 秦王 (『信西古楽図』より 東京芸術大学)
61. 散手 定慶作 (寿永三年銘 奈良市 春日大社)

62. 散手　院賢作　(承元元年銘　奈良市　手向山神社)
63. 貴徳　(『応永古楽図』より　東京国立博物館)
64. 肩喰　(太平楽用　大阪市　四天王寺)
65. 帯喰　(秦王用　正応元年銘　大阪市　住吉大社)
66. 秦王　(正応元年銘　大阪市　住吉大社)
67. 散手　(承安三年銘　広島県　厳島神社)
68. 散手　行円作　(安貞二年銘　大阪府　誉田八幡宮)
69. 散手　院賢作　(承元元年銘　奈良市　東大寺)
70. 散手　(鎌倉市　鶴岡八幡宮)
71. 散手　(青森県　櫛引八幡宮)
72. 貴徳　(長承三年銘　大阪市　藤田美術館)
73. 貴徳　行明作　(承安三年銘　広島県　厳島神社)
74. 貴徳　行円作　(安貞二年銘　大阪府　誉田八幡宮)
75. 貴徳鯉口　(天文六年銘　奈良市　春日大社)
76. 貴徳番子　(東京国立博物館)
77. 貴徳番子　(鎌倉市　鶴岡八幡宮)
78. 童舞　(承元五年銘　愛知県　真清田神社)
79. 天童　(弘安二年銘　大阪府　誉田八幡宮)
80. 師子　(『信西古楽図』より　京都市　陽明文庫)
81. 蘇芳菲　(『信西古楽図』より　京都市　陽明文庫)
82. 蘇莫者　(『信西古楽図』より　東京芸術大学)
83. 蘇莫者　(昭和　大阪市　四天王寺)
84. 古仮面　(推定蘇莫者　奈良市　正倉院)
85. 石川　(奈良県　朝護孫子寺)
86. 菩薩　行道面　(兵庫県　浄土寺)
87. 胡飲酒　(『信西古楽図』より　東京芸術大学)
88. 胡飲酒　(奈良市　手向山神社)
89. 胡飲酒　(明治四十五年銘　名古屋市　熱田神宮)
90. 秦王　(正応元年銘　大阪市　住吉大社)
91. 貴徳番子　(応保三年銘　大阪市　住吉大社)
92. 貴徳　(十三世紀初　奈良市　東大寺)
93. 貴徳鯉口　(十三世紀　鎌倉市　鶴岡八幡宮)
94. 抜頭　(『信西古楽図』より　東京芸術大学)
95. 石川　(十世紀末～十一世紀初　奈良県　法隆寺)
96. 抜頭　行明作　(承安三年銘　広島県　厳島神社)
97. 抜頭　(天養元年銘　奈良県　法隆寺)
98. 抜頭　(永暦二年銘　大阪市　住吉大社)
99. 抜頭　(治承二年修理銘　名古屋市　熱田神宮)
100. 抜頭　運慶作？　(建保七年銘　横浜市　瀬戸神社)
101. 還城楽　(『信西古楽図』より　東京芸術大学)
102. 還城楽　(三重県　伊勢神宮)
103. 還城楽　(天養元年銘　奈良県　法隆寺)
104. 還城楽　残片　(青森県　岩木山神社)
105. 還城楽　(治承二年　名古屋市　熱田神宮)
105. 還城楽　行明作　(承安三年銘　広島市　厳島神社)
107. 陵王　(『信西古楽図』より　東京芸術大学)
108. 陵王　(弘安七年修理銘　名古屋市　熱田神宮)
109. 陵王　(奈良市　水室神社)
110. 陵王　(大阪市　四天王寺)
111. 陵王　(十二世紀後半　広島県　厳島神社)
112. 陵王　(十三世紀　鎌倉市　鶴岡八幡宮)
113. 陵王　承順作　(正元元年銘　奈良市　東大寺)
114. 陵王　乾漆　(大阪市　藤田美術館)
115. 納曾利　行明作　(承安三年銘　広島県　厳島神社)
116. 納曾利　(治承二年修理銘　名古屋市　熱田神宮)
117. 納曾利　承順作　(正元元年銘　奈良市　手向山神社)
118. 納曾利　(十二世紀後半　奈良市　春日大社)
119. 納曾利　(『舞楽図屏風』より　桃翁筆)
120. 陵王　(青森県　大星神社)
121. 陵王　(青森県　岩木山神社)
122. 納曾利　(青森県　櫛引八幡宮)
123. 散手　(青森県　大星神社)
124. 二ノ舞　咲面　(青森県　大星神社)
125. 二ノ舞　腫面　(青森県　大星神社)
126. 二ノ舞　咲面　(青森県　櫛引八幡宮)
127. 二ノ舞　腫面　(青森県　櫛引八幡宮)
128. 陵王　(静岡県　鉄舟寺)
129. 陵王　(嘉暦三年銘　千葉県　大戸神社)
130. 陵王　(岩手県　天台寺)
131. 陵王　(岩手県　天台寺)
132. 陵王　(新潟県　西頸城郡　白山神社)
133. 陵王　(石川県　長浜八幡神社)
134. 陵王　(静岡県　天宮神社)
135. 陵王　(兵庫県　加東郡　住吉神社)
136. 還城楽　(鎌倉市　極楽寺)
137. 還城楽　(青森県　櫛引八幡宮)
138. 還城楽　(岩手県　天台寺)
139. 鬼面　(永仁四年銘　東京国立博物館)
140. 納曾利　承順作　(正元元年銘　三重県　神宮徴古館)

141. 納曾利 (岩手県　天台寺)
142. 納曾利 (静岡県　天宮神社)
143. 納曾利 (新潟県　天津神社)
144. 納曾利 (新潟県　天津神社)
145. 納曾利 (岐阜県　二日町八幡宮)
146. 抜頭 (香川県　神谷神社)
147. 抜頭 (愛知県　知立神社)
148. 抜頭 (青森県　岩木山神社)
149. 能抜頭 (新潟県　西頸城郡　白山神社)
150–51. 地久　桐材(きりざい)の例 (奈良市　手向山神社)
152–53. 胡徳楽　檜材(ひのきざい)の例 (永暦元年銘　奈良市　手向山神社)
154. 散手　院賢作　眉(まゆ)・髭(くちひげ)に毛革(けがわ)を貼る例 (承元元年銘　奈良市　手向山神社)
155. 抜頭　紺紐(こんひも)の頭髪(とうはつ) (明治三十九年銘　名古屋市　熱田神宮)
156. 納曾利　動眼と吊顎 (大阪市　四天王寺)
157. 納曾利に見られる動眼と吊顎
158–59. 採桑老　切顎 (建長元年銘　広島県　厳島神社)
160–61. 還城楽　行明作　動貌 (承安三年銘　広島県　厳島神社)
162. 還城楽　残片　動貌部 (青森県　大星神社)
163. 地久　長久三年の墨書銘 (奈良市　手向山神社)
164. 胡徳楽　永暦元年の墨書銘(ぼくしよめい) (奈良市　手向山神社)
165. 散手　院賢作　承元元年の朱漆銘(しゆうるしめい) (奈良市　東大寺)
166. 二ノ舞 (咲面)　行明作　承安三年の朱漆銘 (広島県　厳島神社)
167. 抜頭　行明作　承安三年の朱漆銘 (広島県　厳島神社)
168–69. 貴徳番子　応保三年の朱漆銘 (大阪市　住吉大社)
170–71. 還城楽　治承二年及び弘安七年の朱漆修理銘 (名古屋市　熱田神宮)
172–73. 新鳥蘇　印勝作　元暦二年の朱漆銘 (奈良市　春日大社)
174–75. 散手　定慶作　寿永三年の刻銘(こくめい) (奈良市　春日大社)
176–77. 採桑老　建長元年の朱漆銘 (広島県　厳島神社)
178. 貴徳　行円作　安貞二年の朱漆銘 (大阪府　誉田八幡宮)
178. 陵王　円信作　弘安七年の朱漆銘 (大阪府　誉田八幡宮)

# GLOSSARY

*Ama* 案摩: Bugaku dance. Bugaku type: *tōgaku,* Left; dance type: *hiramai;* number of dancers: 2.

Asuka period 飛鳥時代 (538–644): The introduction of Buddhism marks the first historic period of Japan. The first steps to convert the loosely bound clan system into a centralized kingdom were taken by the Soga family. Shōtoku Taishi, in particular, started the massive borrowing of ideas, institutions, craftsmen, and specialists from the continent. In accordance with his attempt to emulate China and its Confucian principles, music was given a place of great importance and integrated into court ceremonies. Musicians, instruments, and dancers were among the earliest imports.

*Ayakiri* 綾切: Bugaku dance. Bugaku type: *komagaku,* Right; dance type: *hiramai;* number of dancers: 4 (with special costume, 6); alternate name: *Aikirijo.*

*Batō* 抜頭: Bugaku dance. Bugaku type: *tōgaku,* Left; dance type: *hashirimai;* number of dancers: 1.

*Bosatsu* 菩薩: Bugaku dance. Bugaku type: *tōgaku.* No longer extant.

*bun-no-mai* 文の舞: "Literary dances." Slow, graceful pieces. Essentially synonymous with *hiramai.*

*bu-no-mai* 武の舞: "Military dances." Active, heroic pieces performed in military costume with sword and halberd.

*Bushō Taiheiraku* 武将太平楽: Bugaku dance. Bugaku type: *tōgaku,* Left; dance type: *bu-no-mai;* number of dancers: 4; alternate names: *Bushōraku, Taiheiraku.*

*busshi* 仏師: A term for sculptors of Buddhist images, but also applied to painters, who were specifically called *e-busshi* ("picture *busshi*"). Almost all Bugaku masks bearing inscriptions were made by *busshi.* The term is first mentioned in the Nara period, when *busshi* were part of the court office in charge of the construction of temples. This system was abolished in the eighth century, after which *busshi* attached themselves to powerful temples. Jōchō (?–1057), a master sculptor of the mid-Heian period, is regarded as the founder of the *busshi* system as it was to develop in the succeeding decades. Famous *busshi* coming after Jōchō organized separate groups of sculptors, such as the In, En, and Kei schools. From the mid-eleventh into the twelfth centuries these schools solidified and established workshops, *bussho,* where work was carried out by the head *busshi* (大仏師 *daibusshi*) and numerous assistants (小仏師 *shōbusshi*). In the Muromachi period, *busshi* lost their special status and came to be classed as general artisans, and their work gradually declined in quality. This system continued until the first years of the Meiji period (1868–1912), when it was abandoned.

*Chikyū* 地久: Bugaku dance. Bugaku type: *komagaku,* Right; dance type: *hiramai;* number of dancers: 4 or 6; alternate name: *Enjiraku.*

*dōbi* 動鼻: The swinging nose peculiar to Kotokuraku masks. It is made separately and attached to the mask at the bridge. See plates 152–53.

*dōbō* 動貌: The movable central plate of Genjōraku masks. The portion of the face including the eyes, cheeks, nose, and upper lip is carved separately and attached to the mask so that it hangs loosely under the jutting eyebrows. See plates 160–62.

*dōgan* 動眼: Movable eyes. Both eyeballs are carved from a single separate piece of wood and then fixed into the mask by means of a bamboo skewer. This allows the eyes to rotate freely. Often their movement is induced by the swaying of the dangling chin, to which the eyes are attached by a string. See plates 156–57.

*doroji* 泥地: "Mud base" used in provincial masks of the Muromachi period in place of the more permanent *kataji. Doroji* is made from *tonoko* mixed with *nikawa*.

Edo period 江戸時代 (1600–1867): The Tokugawa family that ruled in Edo (modern Tokyo) during this period established peace in the country and instituted an isolationist policy that shut Japan off from most outside influences. The Tokugawa extended their patronage to many artisans and performers, spurring a renaissance of several art forms. Conservatism led them back to Confucian precepts and the reestablishment of the central importance of music. They again put Bugaku under official protection, calling forth musicians and dancers from the temples and shrines to which they had retired four hundred years earlier. Again Bugaku, along with Nō, held a place in court functions, and masks were made with meticulous care and craftsmanship.

Enshin 円信: The thirteenth-century carver who made the Ryō-ō, Genjōraku, and Taishōtoku dated 1284 at Konda Hachiman Shrine.

Gagaku 雅楽: "Elegant Music." "Gagaku" referred to a variety of imported musical styles in the Nara period, but since the ninth century it designates the official court music played by a large orchestra of string, wind, and percussion instruments. A reduced orchestra accompanies Bugaku dances, while the full orchestra plays instrumental pieces called *kangen*. The term "Gagaku" can refer to both music and dance, and is often used interchangeably with "Bugaku."

*Gakkaroku* 楽家録 (The Records of a Musician): A fifty-volume (plus index) compendium of information on Bugaku and Gagaku written in 1690 by Abe Suenao. In an effort to collect all the expertise on Bugaku and to aid the reestablishment of its orthodox form after several centuries of neglect, the *Gakkaroku* details technical information on instruments, including sketches and measurements; on the music, giving background, commentary, and scores of notation; on music theory; on the dances, their choreography and costumes; and on masks, including sketches. There is also a list of dancers and musicians.

*Genjōraku* 還城楽: Bugaku dance. Bugaku type: *tōgaku,* Right; dance type: *hashirimai;* number of dancers: 1; alternate name: *Kenjaraku*.

Gigaku 伎楽: Masked theatrical performances given at temples, particularly in the Nara period. Gigaku is said to have originated in the Chinese country of Wu, but it is quite likely that it originated in West or Southeast Asia. Little is known today of its actual contents, but a number of excellent masks remain in the Shōsō-in in Nara.

*gofun* 胡粉: Calcium carbonate (powdered shell); a common base on statues and masks after the Kamakura period.

Gyōdō 行道: Temple processions related to three distinct Buddhist ceremonies: the circumambulation of the main image to the chant of sutras; the masked processions around the temple precincts as a part of memorial services; and, most importantly, the enactment of the *raigō*—Amida's (Amitābha's) descent to meet the dying faithful and escort them to the Pure Land.

Gyōmyō 行明: The twelfth-century *busshi,* also known as Shamon Gyōmyō (沙門行明), who made the Genjōraku (pl. 106), Kitoku (pl. 73), Nasori (pl. 115), Hare-men (pl. 58), Eme-men (pl. 59), and Batō (pl. 96) dated 1173 at Itsukushima Shrine.

*hashirimai* 走舞: "Running dances." Quick-tempoed dances, usually coming at the end of the program, featuring one person wearing a dynamic mask and dancing with large expressive movements.

Heian period 平安時代 (782–1184): Following the decline of the T'ang dynasty (618–c. 907) in China, and owing to internal pressures in Japan, the international spirit of the Nara period gradually gave way to isolationism in the Heian period. The country turned increasingly inward and toward Japanization. During the first half of the period, the many divergent styles of music were amalgamated into one system and the training of musicians and dancers was put under government protection, producing Bugaku as we know it today. Performances began to grace informal court functions as well as government ceremonies, and Bugaku became an essential part of the education of young courtiers.

The second half of the Heian period is characterized by the political domination of the Fujiwara family. The emperor was relegated to leading the ornate ceremonies that set the elegant mood of life at court. Ample evidence of the importance of Bugaku at this time appears in numerous novels and diaries. Along with other arts, the making of Bugaku masks flourished. While the earliest extant masks, dating from the eleventh century, are carved freely, those from the end of the Heian period display unsurpassed sophistication of modeling and proportion.

*hiramai* 平舞: "Peaceful dances." Slow, sedate dances usually performed in symetrical unison by groups of four or six. Now essentially synonymous with *bun-no-mai.*

Inken 院賢: A *busshi* of the In school in Kyoto who was active at the end of the twelfth and beginning of the thirteenth centuries. He made the Sanju masks dated 1207 now at Tōdai-ji and Tamukeyama Shrine (pls. 62, 69).

Inshō 印勝: The twelfth-century *busshi* who made the Shintoriso (pl. 14), Ōnintei (pl. 46), Korobase (pl. 40), and Chikyū (pl. 13) dated 1185 at Kasuga Shrine.

*jo-ha-kyū* 序破急: The underlying aesthetic theory of Bugaku: "introduction, development, and finale," involving a slow beginning, a quickening of pace, and a fast finish. It applies to each individual step as well as to the progression of the dance as a whole. A dance is made up of three basic movements, labeled *jo,* for the opening steps to a free rhythm; *ha,* for the lengthy middle section often in eight- or four-measure units; and *kyū,* for the last movement, often danced to a two-measure unit. *Jo-ha-kyū* has been borrowed and developed by most Japanese performing arts.

Jōkei 定慶: The thirteenth-century *busshi* of the Kei school who carved the Sanju mask dated 1184 at Kasuga Shrine (pl. 61).

Kamakura period 鎌倉時代 (1185–1332): The wars between the Heike (Taira) and Genji (Minamoto) clans ended the Heian period, and the shift of political power from the court to the military government in Kamakura foreshadowed the decline of Bugaku. While the Heike had mingled with the court and supported its ceremonial activities, the Genji rigorously abstained from court pleasures. The feudal system erected by the Genji limited the court to nominal functions. Reduced funds necessitated the dispersion of musicians and dancers to protective shrines and temples, bringing about the spread of Bugaku to the provinces. As long as the memory of Heian court life lingered, good masks continued to be produced with standard methods. Gradually, however, forms and techniques were drastically altered by time and distance.

kaolin (J. 白土 *hakudo*): A fine white clay produced by the decomposition of feldspar and used as a base for finishing Bugaku masks and colored statues of the Nara to Kamakura periods. It is also an element in porcelain. In the Muromachi period it was often replaced by *gofun.*

*kataji* 硬地: A preliminary layer of lacquer applied to the mask to reinforce and preserve the wood.

*kiriago* 切顎: "Detached chin," referring to the chin of Saisōrō, which is carved out of a separate piece of wood and attached snugly to the mask with strings through small holes. See plates 158–59.

*Kitoku* 貴徳: Bugaku dance. Bugaku type: *komagaku,* Right; dance type: *bu-no-mai;* number of dancers: 1.

*komagaku* 高麗楽: "Dances from Koryō." By the tenth century *komagaku* came to refer to all dances originally introduced by way of the Korean peninsula. Now synonymous with *u-no-mai.*

*Konju* 胡飲酒: Bugaku dance. Bugaku type: *tōgaku,* Left; dance type: *bun-no-mai;* number of dancers: 1; alternate names: *Suikoraku, En'onraku.*

*Korobase* 崑崙八仙: Bugaku dance. Bugaku type: *komagaku,* Right; dance type: *hiramai;* number of dancers: 4; alternate names: *Hassen, Tsurumai.*

*Kotokuraku* 胡徳楽: Bugaku dance. Bugaku type: *komagaku,* Right; dance type: *hiramai;* number of dancers: 6; alternate names: *Kodōraku, Hembikotoku.*

*Kotoriso* 古鳥蘇: Bugaku dance. Bugaku type: *komagaku,* Right; dance type: *hiramai;* number of dancers: 4 or 6.

*Kyōkunshō* 教訓抄: Written in 1233 by the dancer of the Left Koma Chikazane (1177–1242), the *Kyōkunshō* (in ten volumes) is the oldest extant work on the technical aspects of Bugaku. After describing the Bugaku traditions maintained by the Koma family, Chikazane goes on to discuss Bugaku and Gigaku performed by other houses, as well as *komagaku* and instrumental pieces without dances. A discussion of general instructions is followed by a recounting of oral traditions concerning Gagaku instruments and other matters.

*mai* 舞: "Dance." This term designates dances (such as Bugaku and Nō) that are based on abstract rather than realistic movements, on sliding footwork, and on a broad correlation with the rhythm. In contrast, *odori* ("dance"; Kabuki, folk dances, *Nihon buyō*) uses high-stepping, large movements correlated to the beat of the music and acts out a story.

Momoyama period: *See* Nambokuchō period.

Muromachi period: *See* Nambokuchō period.

Nambokuchō 南北朝時代 (1333–91), Muromachi 室町時代 (1392–1572), and Momoyama 桃山時代 (1573–99) periods: The ruling military aristocracy were attracted to new forms of artistic expression during these periods. Frequent wars and local disturbances caused many samurai to turn to Zen Buddhism. These disciplined warriors preferred the monotonal chanting of Nō and *kōwaka* to the harmonies of Gagaku. Bugaku was left to blend with other performing arts, and very few Bugaku masks were made.

Nara period 奈良時代 (645–781): Continuing the process of centralization and Sinification begun in the Asuka period, the Nakatomi family instituted the Taika reforms, which revamped the agricultural and administrative bases of Japan. The Taihō Code of 701 established the Chinese system of court ranks and ministries, including a Bureau of Music. Eager to absorb the new and superior culture, the court at the new capital at Nara sent missions to Korea and China to bring back knowledge and artifacts, including many dances and instruments. All manner of performing arts flourished in and out of court. The dramatic dances of Gigaku, performed mostly at temples, were at their height of popularity, and such occasions as the consecration of the Great Buddha of Tōdai-ji in 752 featured magnificent performances of dances from Korea, China, Manchuria, Southeast Asia, and India, as well as native Japanese dances.

*Nasori* 納曾利: Bugaku dance. Bugaku type: *komagaku,* Right; dance type: *hashirimai;* alternate name: *Rakuson* (when danced by one person).

*nikawa* 膠: Glue made out of animal skin or animal bones. It is mixed, as an adhesive, with *gofun, tonoko,* or earth pigments.

*Ni-no-mai* 二ノ舞: Bugaku dance. Bugaku type: *tōgaku,* Left; dance type: *hiramai;* number of dancers: 2.

*Ōnintei* 皇仁庭: Bugaku dance. Bugaku type:

*komagaku,* Right; dance type: *hiramai;* number of dancers: 4; alternate name: *Ōnin.*

*ritsu-ryō* 律呂: A system of musical modes imported from T'ang China (618–c. 907) forming the basis of Gagaku music. Roughly equivalent to the *kyu* and *u* scales used in China, these two scales are basically pentatonic, including two extra exchange tones of ½ step intervals. The position of these in the *ryō* scale is on the fourth and seventh, in the *ritsu* on the third and seventh, paralleling, in conception at least, the distinction between major and minor scales in the Western system. The types of *ritsu* and *ryō* scales are known by their modal note.

*Ryō-ō* 陵王: Bugaku dance. Bugaku type: *tōgaku,* Left; dance type: *hashirimai;* number of dancers: 1; alternate names: *Raryō-ō, Ranryō-ō.*

*sabi urushi* 錆漆: A mixture of lacquer, fine wheat flour, and *tonoko* used as a priming on many Bugaku masks, particularly in the late Heian period and the Kamakura period.

*Saisōrō* 採桑老: Bugaku dance. Bugaku type: *tōgaku,* Left; dance type: *hiramai;* number of dancers: 1.

*Sanju* 散手: Bugaku dance. Bugaku type: *tōgaku,* Left; dance type: *bu-no-mai;* number of dancers: 1, plus assistants; alternate name: *Sanju Hajinraku.*

*sa-no-mai* 左の舞: "Dances of the Left." Most of them came directly from T'ang China. The costumes are generally red and gold. Now synonymous with *tōgaku.*

*Sessen* 石川: Bugaku dance. Bugaku type: *komagaku,* Right; dance type: *hiramai.* No longer extant.

*Shinnō* 秦王: Bugaku dance. Bugaku type: *tōgaku,* Left; dance type: *bu-no-mai;* number of dancers: 4; alternate names: *Shinnō Hajinraku, Shinkō Hajinraku.*

*Shintoriso* 新鳥蘇: Bugaku dance. Bugaku type: *komagaku,* Right; dance type: *hiramai;* number of dancers: 4 or 6.

*Shinzei kogakuzu* 信西古楽図 (Shinzei's Illustrations of Ancient Music): Also called *Bugaku-zu* 舞楽図 (Illustrations of Bugaku). A monochrome ink handscroll by a contemporary of the Heian period, this work depicts old dances, including many Bugaku pieces, and the musical instruments of the Gagaku orchestra. The lively sketches give a vivid picture of the costumes and movements of the dancers. The scroll gets its name from Fujiwara no Michinori (1106?–59), whose Buddhist name is Shinzei, perhaps the most learned man of his day. It is likely that the handscroll was compiled not by Shinzei himself, though his name is recorded in the scroll, but by artists of his circle. The original has been lost, but later copies (the oldest dated 1449) survive in the Tokyo National Museum, the Tokyo University of Fine Arts, and the Yōmei Bunko in Kyoto.

*Shishi* 師子: Bugaku dance. Bugaku type: *tōgaku,* Left. No longer extant.

*Sohōhi* 蘇芳非: Bugaku dance. Bugaku type: *tōgaku,* Left. No longer extant.

*Somakusha* 蘇莫者: Bugaku dance. Bugaku type: *tōgaku,* Left; number of dancers: 1. No longer extant.

*Taishōtoku* 退宿徳 and *Shinshōtoku* 進宿徳: Bugaku dance. Bugaku type: *komagaku,* Right; dance type: *hiramai;* number of dancers: 4 or 6; alternate names: *(Taishōtoku) Oimai, (Shinshōtoku) Wakamai.*

*tōgaku* 唐楽: Pieces imported directly from T'ang China. The rhythmic patterns are more complex and the dances more syncopated than those of *komagaku.* Now synonymous with *sa-no-mai.*

*tonoko* 砥の粉: A powder made from finely ground impure clay. It is used as a base paint when mixed with *nikawa* to form *doroji,* or as a paste when mixed with other binding agents. It is one ingredient of *sabi urushi.*

*tsugaimai* 番舞: Partner dances of Left and Right.

*tsuriago* 吊顎: A "dangling chin" carved separately and hung by strings from the rod securing the movable eyes. See plates 156–57.

Unkei 運慶 (?–1223): Master *busshi* of the Kei school and one of the greatest of Japanese sculptors. His name is inscribed on the Batō dated 1219 at Seto Shrine (pl. 100).

*u-no-mai* 右の舞: "Dances of the Right." Primarily imported through Korea. The costumes are often green or white. Now synonymous with *komagaku*.

*zōmen* 蔵面: A white paper or cloth mask that is decorated with abstract designs painted in stripes of black. For durability the mask can be made of silk pasted onto stiff paper. *Zōmen* are worn in *Ama, Soriko,* and *Kotokuraku*. A number of Gigaku *zōmen* are kept in the Shōsō-in in Nara, but they are far more realistic than those used in Bugaku. See plates 47–49.

# BIBLIOGRAPHY

## JAPANESE SOURCES
(selected and annotated by the author)

安倍季尚『楽家録』(日本古典全集 第五期) 東京 日本古典全集刊行会 昭和 10 年 [Abe, Suenao. *The Records of a Musician.* Japanese Classics, 5th series. Tokyo: Nihon Koten Zenshū Kankōkai, 1935].

Written in 1690 by a Kyoto musician, this work, the *Gakkaroku,* is an encyclopedic summary of all that was known about Bugaku in the Edo period.

芸能史研究会編『雅楽』(日本の古典芸能 2) 東京 平凡社 昭和 45 年 [Research Center for the History of Performing Arts, ed. *Gagaku.* Classic Performing Arts of Japan, vol. 2. Tokyo: Heibonsha, 1970].

A compilation by the foremost specialists on Gagaku. A complete study of performance, theory, and history, with attention to technical detail.

林屋辰三郎『中世芸能史の研究』東京 岩波書店 昭和 35 年 [Hayashiya, Tatsusaburō. *Studies of Medieval Performing Arts.* Tokyo: Iwanami Shoten, 1960].

Detailed and specialized, this history presents an objective account of the development of Japanese performing arts.

井浦芳信『日本演劇史』東京 至文堂 昭和 38 年 [Iura, Yoshinobu. *A History of Japanese Theater.* Tokyo: Shibundō, 1963].

A good overall history of Japanese drama, including a summary of Bugaku.

狛 近真『教訓抄』(日本古典全集 第二期) 東京 日本古典全集刊行会 昭和 3 年 [Koma, Chikazane. *Books of Instruction.* Japanese Classics, 2nd series. Tokyo: Nihon Koten Zenshū Kankōkai, 1928].

Written in 1233 by a Nara dancer, this work, the *Kyōkunshō,* gives a general description of Bugaku before the Kamakura period. As the only extensive description of Heian-period Bugaku, it is an invaluable source. It also presents a concrete picture of what Gigaku must have been like.

毛利 久『日本の仮面』京都 京都国立博物館 昭和 30 年 [Mōri, Hisashi. *Japanese Masks.* Kyoto: Kyoto National Museum, 1955].

A memorial publication of the magnificent exhibition of masks of all genres held at the Kyoto National Museum in 1955. This work presented for the first time postwar discoveries of fine old masks. The illustrations are mostly in black and white. The text is informative and scholarly, though short.

西川杏太郎「住吉大社の舞楽面」(『Museum』208) 昭和 43 年 [Nishikawa, Kyōtarō. "Bugaku Masks at Sumiyoshi Shrine." *Museum,* no. 208, 1968].

The Sumiyoshi masks presented here are introduced to the public for the first time. Each mask is analyzed for its special characteristics as well as for its historical and artistic importance.

——— 『舞楽面 (東大寺)』(奈良六大寺大観 第十巻) 東京 岩波書店 昭和 43 年 [———. *Bugaku Masks at Tōdai-ji*. The Six Great Temples of Nara, vol. 10. Tokyo: Iwanami Shoten, 1968]. Basic data and descriptions of the masks at Tōdai-ji. The Six Great Temples of Nara *(Nara rokudaiji taikan)* is an important series of fourteen volumes on six major temples in Nara, containing precise, scholarly, thorough information. It is a sequel to the Catalogue of Art Treasures of the Ten Great Temples of Nara (南都十大寺大鏡 *Nanto jūdaiji ōkagami*), a series of twenty-eight volumes published by Ōtsuka Kōgeisha, Tokyo, 1932.

———『舞楽面（法隆寺）』（奈良六大寺大観 第三巻）東京 岩波書店 昭和44年 [———. *Bugaku Masks at Hōryū-ji*. The Six Great Temples of Nara, vol. 3. Tokyo: Iwanami Shoten, 1969].
Part of the same series as the immediately preceding book.

西川新次「伎楽面・舞楽面」（『月刊文化財』11）昭和39年 [Nishikawa, Shinji. "Gigaku and Bugaku Masks." *Gekkan bunkazai,* no. 11, 1964].
A short history of Gigaku and Bugaku masks for the general public.

野間清六『日本仮面史』東京 芸文書院 昭和18年 [Noma, Seiroku. *History of Japanese Masks*. Tokyo: Geibun Shoin, 1943].
The first thorough study of masks from the art-historical point of view. A classic illustrated entirely with hand-drawn sketches, it is unfortunately difficult to obtain.

田辺三郎助「舞楽面の地方分布とその変遷について」（『三浦古文化』8）昭和45年 [Tanabe, Saburōnosuke. "The Dispersion to the Countryside and Diversification of Bugaku Masks." *Miura kobunka,* no. 8, 1970].
The first investigation of the dispersion of Bugaku to the countryside based on the dispersion of the masks. The author points up ways in which orthodox forms influenced and were influenced by provincial traditions.

——— 他『面と肖像』（原色日本の美術 23）東京 小学館 昭和46年 [——— et al. *Masks and Portrait Sculpture*. Japanese Art in Color, vol. 23. Tokyo: Shōgakkan, 1971].
A survey of Japanese masks with many valuable insights based on an original approach. The section on masks is written by Mr. Tanabe. There are full-sized color illustrations with detailed captions, as well as a list of illustrations in English.

帝室博物館編『日本古楽面』東京 聚楽社 昭和10年 [Imperial Museum, ed. *Old Japanese Masks*. Tokyo: Jurakusha, 1935].
First Japanese publication showing masterpieces of Gigaku, Bugaku, Gyōdō, Nō, and Kyōgen in full color.

## FURTHER READING
(selected and annotated by the translator)

Eckhardt, Hans. "Somakusha." *Sinologica* 3 (1966).

Gabbert, Gunhild. *Die Masken des Bugaku*. Wiesbaden: Franz Steiner Verlag, 1972.
A thorough and very academic study of Bugaku masks and problems relating to style.

Garfias, Robert. *Gagaku: The Music and Dances of the Japanese Imperial Household*. New York: Theatre Arts Books, 1957.
A good introduction to Gagaku concentrating on the music, with a short explanation of Bugaku.

———. *Music of a Thousand Autumns: The Tōgaku Style of Japanese Court Music*. Berkeley and Los Angeles: University of California Press, 1975.

An extensive analysis of *tōgaku* music with a detailed description of the historical background of Gagaku.

Harich-Schneider, Eta. *The Rhythmical Patterns in Gagaku and Bugaku.* Leiden: Brill, 1954.
A presentation of the rhythmic systems of Gagaku, their notation and ramifications, based on tablature books and firsthand experience.

———. *A History of Japanese Music.* London: Oxford University Press, 1973.
A clearly written study of Japanese music and the development of Gagaku. Detailed description of the background to the dances culled from visual and written sources.

Kishibe, Shigeo. *The Traditional Music of Japan.* Tokyo: Kokusai Bunka Shinkokai, 1966.
A short introduction to Japanese music including one chapter on Gagaku.

Kleinschmidt, Peter. *Die Masken der Gigaku, der Ältesten Theaterform Japans.* Wiesbaden: As Forsch, 1967.
A German book on the little-known subject of Gigaku.

Kummel, O. "Zwei Bugaku Masken der Fujiwara-Zeit." *Ostasiatische Zeitschrift* (April 1941).

Malm, William P. *Japanese Music and Musical Instruments.* Rutland, Vermont: Tuttle, 1959.
The best survey of Japanese music, with a chapter devoted to Gagaku and its instruments.

Noma, Seiroku. *The Arts of Japan: Ancient and Medieval.* Translated by John Rosenfield. Tokyo and New York: Kodansha International, 1966.
A sociocultural introduction to Japanese art history from prehistorical times to the Muromachi period. Some reference to Bugaku and Gigaku.

Tazawa, Yutaka. *History of Japanese Sculpture: From the Pre-Buddhist Period Through the Edo Period.* Pageant of Japanese Art (6 vols.). Edited by Tokyo National Museum. Tokyo: Tōto Shuppan, 1953.
A short history of Japanese sculpture indicating all the major pieces and the development of styles.

Togi, Masataro. *Gagaku: Court Music and Dance.* Translated by Don Kenny. Tokyo and New York: Weatherhill and Tankosha, 1971.
In an introductory fashion this book explains all aspects of Gagaku—history, instruments, costumes, performances, and theory—from the vantage point of present-day practices.

Wolz, Carl. *Bugaku: Japanese Court Dance.* Seattle: Asian Music Publications, 1971.
An analysis with annotation of the dance movements of Bugaku, particularly of *Nasori.* Limited, but unique.

# INDEX